Cowboy Courage

Cowboy Courage

Westerns and the Portrayal of Bravery

WILLIAM HAMPES

McFarland & Company, Inc., Publishers
Jefferson, North Carolina

Library of Congress and British Library
cataloguing data are available

ISBN (print) 978-1-4766-7606-7
ISBN (ebook) 978-1-4766-3523-1

© 2019 William Hampes. All rights reserved

No part of this book may be reproduced or transmitted in any form or by any means, electronic or mechanical, including photocopying or recording, or by any information storage and retrieval system, without permission in writing from the publisher.

Front cover: background poster art from *The Wild Bunch*, 1969 (Warner Bros./Photofest); insets © 2019 Shutterstock

Printed in the United States of America

McFarland & Company, Inc., Publishers
Box 611, Jefferson, North Carolina 28640
www.mcfarlandpub.com

To the loving memory of
Louis Hampes, Mary Lou Schoenegge, Andrew Hampes
and Bob and Phyllis Martino

Acknowledgments

I want to thank the Black Hawk College librarians for finding the articles and books I used in writing this book. If a lending library or institution has a book or article of interest, they will find it.

I would also like to thank Verity Whitley, still going strong at Black Hawk College after 55 years, for reviewing the manuscript. Her corrections and comments were very helpful. Any errors are strictly mine.

I appreciate the help that my editor at McFarland, Layla Milholen, has given me in the gradual evolution of the book. Her efforts, which were tactful, encouraging, and challenging, kept me enthusiastic about the project and gave me fresh insights about how to develop the themes of the book. She would make a great teacher.

Finally, I want to thank wholeheartedly my wife Anita, who read the manuscript and gave me invaluable advice about how to improve it. Nobody has taught me more about the courage to love than Anita; my mother, Mary Hampes; and my children, Matthew Hampes and Elizabeth Hampes.

Table of Contents

Acknowledgments vi
Preface 1
Introduction 3

1. The Quality of Courage 9
2. Redemption 18
3. Love, Friendship and Bonds to the Community 50
4. Justice 70
5. Temperance 92
6. Growing Up and Growing Old 105
7. Being Authentic 120
8. The Revisionist Western 142
9. *Lonesome Dove* 159

Conclusion 164
Filmography 167
Bibliography 193
Index 195

Preface

One could trace the trajectory of my life through Westerns. When I was a boy, I was primarily interested in anything that involved the drama of a contest: military history, the athletic venues of my beloved Chicago sports teams, or the dusty streets of Hadleyville and the O.K. Corral. As a young man, I looked to Westerns as a guide to facing the challenges in my life and how a person should live life.

However, in late adulthood I view life through a much wider lens afforded by Westerns. According to the psychoanalyst Erik Erikson, the main task of old age is to establish a sense of integrity, or wholeness, an understanding of the meaning or meanings that permeate a person's life from beginning to the end. My understanding of the wider lens through which Westerns illuminate the meanings of life comes from a long journey in and out of my chosen field of psychology. (The connection between Westerns and my area of research, the psychology of humor, is something I will have to work out at a future date.)

There has been a great deal of valuable scholarship about the appeal of Westerns. Some of it is reviewed in this book, particularly in the introduction: Jim Kitses' notion of the opposition of wilderness vs. civilization and the "open horizons" that Westerns present, William Indick's discussion of the importance of Westerns in portraying the "American creation myth," and Blake Lucas' belief that Westerns express "everlasting archetypes," to mention just a few examples.

However, slowly but surely, I have come to understand that the primary appeal of Westerns, for me at least, lies in what they say about courage, and their importance as a "gateway" to the other virtues. If Westerns were only about physical courage, the willingness to risk physical danger to achieve a goal, Westerns would still have a great deal to say, but would not provide as nearly as "wide" a gateway to the other virtues as they do.

Recent scholarship in the area of positive psychology reveals what has been reflected in the best of the Westerns, that courage also involves moral courage, the determination to do or say what one feels is right, despite the social consequences, and psychological courage, struggling with the conflicts within oneself to do what is best for oneself or others. Without all three kinds of courage, it would very difficult, if not impossible, to face not only physical danger, but also to love, to be part of a community, to redeem oneself for past failures, to forgive or have mercy, to restrain oneself, to see that justice is served, to be oneself, and even to grow up and to grow old. By portraying these three types of courage and the virtues to which they lead, they provide a guide to how a person should lead his or her life to its fullest potential.

As individuals in late adulthood, or even at other times in adulthood, look back on their lives, perhaps Westerns can help them develop a sense of integrity or meaning for their lives by making a connection between their acts of courage and the virtues they have demonstrated.

Introduction

There are numerous theories concerning the extraordinary appeal that television and film Westerns have had for the American public, especially during the Golden Age of Westerns during the 1950s and early 1960s. According to Jim Kitses (2004, pp. 12–13), "there should be no mystery about why the Western demanded attention. By the middle of the 1960s it was obvious to any critic not blinded by notions of popular culture's inferiority that the Western was Hollywood's richest tradition, producing a unique, distinctively American body of work that was the envy of other national cinemas." Kitses credits the success of the Western to its "openness," its ability to articulate the "frontier's dialectical play of forces embodied in the master binary opposition of the wilderness and civilization." Kitses broke the opposition of wilderness and civilization down into the individual (wilderness) vs. community (civilization), nature (wilderness) vs. culture (civilization), and the West (wilderness) vs. the East (civilization). These themes all play nicely into the myth of Americans conquering the untamed wilderness. According to John H. Lenihan (1980, p. 20) the theme of wilderness vs. civilization led to numerous interpretations:

> Even more important are the diverse implications drawn from the Western's basic premise that civilization supplants wilderness. This diversity related primarily to how films have defined the values of civilization as well as the roles and motives of both heroes and villains. By emphasizing the good and progressive character of frontier society, Westerns could justify the killing of marauding Indians or demand the lone hero's commitment to society. Other Westerns posited a greedy, corrupt, or self-righteous society that cruelly exploited the noble savage or clashed with the more honorable nonconformist hero. The Western, therefore, became either supportive or

critical (often both in the same film) of the growing American democracy, depending on how the formula's conventional elements were employed. Character traits, similarly, implied values that were either socially desirable or detrimental according to who possessed them and how the story was worked out in relation to them.

William Indick (2008, p.13) explains why the "American creation myth" that is the foundation of the Western is so powerful and open to many different possibilities:

> The Western film provides a type of psychological catharsis that goes beyond temporal societal issues. The Western provides its nation with its own book of Genesis—an American creation myth. Like the book of Genesis in the Bible, the American creation myth offers not only a historical interpretation of its ancestral heritage, but a set of morals and values that provide meaning for its successors, and most importantly, a canon of legends to be told and retold for generations to come. From these legends were born a legion of heroes to be worshipped and revered. The hook of the Western genre is that it often aspires to be a historical recollection of the building of America told in an exciting and meaningful manner. The caveat is that the history is inaccurate, and the message is filtered through the values and ideals within the era in which each film was made.

Blake Lucas (1998, p. 301) explains the potential of the Western to express many different varieties of human experience:

> Some kind of alchemy blesses artistic forms which are especially rich—think of the sonnet or the string quartet—and of narrative forms, the Western movie is one of the most satisfying, its combination of landscape and dramatic motifs endlessly stimulating. Here and in the older forms cited, expressiveness and invention go hand in hand with a respect for the specific limitations of the form. So the best Westerns tend to cleave closely to familiar outlines, the same basic characters and situations steadily recurring but revitalized by individual artists and at times given the force of revelation. This ritual quality is an overriding one which suggests that something very universal is at work: and without doubt, the genre is not just about specific American history, or even the interplay of history and myth, but a *form* which gives a supple choreography and voice to everlasting archetypes and to archetypal human experience.

All of these interpretations of the influence and meaning of Westerns have merit in a genre as rich and as complex as the Western. However, the theme of this book takes a different perspective. The reason why Westerns have been so influential and meaningful is that they are about courage, a concept that leads to very profound and complex implications about how people live and should lead their lives.

The general public often has a rather narrow conception of what constitutes courage in Westerns, i.e., a physical courage largely imbued with masculine stereotypes: "A man has to do what a man has to do," "There's some things a man can't ride around." Certainly, there are many Westerns replete with examples of heroes having the physical courage to reach their objectives despite overwhelming external opposition: Will Kane (Gary

Cooper) in *High Noon* (1952), facing the four criminals who want to kill him; the seven professional gunmen in *The Magnificent Seven* (1960), trying to protect peaceful villagers against an overwhelming number of bandits; and Shane (Alan Ladd), in the 1953 film of the same name, facing the professional gunman Wilson (Jack Palance) and the Rykers (Emile Meyer and John Dierkes). However, as Josh Randall (Steve McQueen), in the *Wanted: Dead or Alive* episode "The Legend" (1959), tells a gentle and cautious son (Michael Landon) whose father (Victor Jory) considers him to be weak and less than a man, "Strength doesn't come just wrapped up one way. A mule can carry 1000 pounds and he's got a lot of muscle, but that's all." In *High Noon*, Amy Kane (Grace Kelly) has to have the courage to wrestle with her deeply held Quaker pacifistic beliefs to come to the conclusion that at least in this one situation, she has to go against those beliefs and risk her life and even kill to save her husband. After Shane has vanquished Wilson and the Rykers, he has to have the courage to ride away from the Starretts, not only because he believes, as he tells Joey, that he has the brand of a killer that he cannot shake, but because if he stays, he would cause tension and even conflict in a family whose son idolizes him, whose wife is likely attracted to him, and whose husband is a friend. In a scene from *The Magnificent Seven*, Bernado O'Reilly (Charles Bronson) chastises the Mexican child who idolizes him and who belittles his own father for not being a gunman like O'Reilly. O'Reilly tells the boy that his *campesino* father is the one with the real courage and he is the coward because the father has assumed the responsibility of battling the elements year after year to provide for his family, and a gunman like him lacks the courage to accept responsibility for anyone else but himself.

Based on the ways in which it is portrayed in film and television Westerns, courage does indeed come wrapped up more than one way. What makes Westerns, at least the best Westerns, so special is their emphasis on other types of bravery besides physical bravery. Whereas physical bravery is characterized by a fear of dying or bodily injury, moral bravery, overcoming the fear of others' reactions, and psychological bravery, overcoming the fear of psychological stability, are more complex (Peterson and Seligman, 2004). Before 1946, there were numerous examples of physical courage, leading to noble ends, such as the defense of the community, but even in this era before the "psychological Westerns" of the period from the late 1940s to early 1960s, there were a few examples of moral or psychological bravery. In the period of the revisionist and post-modern Westerns starting in the late 1960s, courage was largely, although not entirely, replaced by self-interest or deployed in its service or deployed in defense of marginalized groups (Native Americans, Mexicans, women, etc.). However, the Golden Age of Westerns, which lasted roughly from 1946 to 1964, is replete with films and television episodes that explored many different types of courage other than just physical courage in defense of oneself or others.

David Meuel (2015, p. 14) discusses insightfully how the "psychological Westerns" of the Golden Age of Westerns revitalized the genre:

> Rather than corrupting or polluting the western as some purist might have assumed, these changes had a decidedly different impact. Because they were so antithetical to the norms of the traditional western, they gave the genre added dimension, complexity and dramatic tension—an enormous creative spark, if you will. The result was a synthesis of sorts, and, from the late 1940s to the early 1960s, the genre enjoyed a period of popularity and inspired creativity unequaled at any other time in its long, rich history. An enormous number of fine to great westerns were made, and tens of millions of appreciative filmgoers flocked to them.

To give just one example of the complexity of Westerns in this Golden Age, in the little known 1956 film *Tension at Table Rock*, Wes Tancred's physical courage, often deployed in the defense of others, is never in doubt in the mind of the viewer from the beginning of the film to the end. However, Wes (Richard Egan) is a moral coward who changed his name because he is falsely accused of being a back-shooter. By the end of the film, he has found the moral courage to admit that he is Wes Tancred during a public trial, in order to bolster the physical courage of Sheriff Fred Miller (Cameron Mitchell).

Chapter 1 will define courage and bravery in all their varieties and how they were demonstrated in a television episode (*Wagon Train*'s "The Jose Morales Story") and a film (*They Came to Cordura*).

In Chapter 2, the role that redemption plays in courage will be examined. Three different types of redemption will be discussed. The first will be redeeming oneself for failures of physical courage in the past, as is the case of Lee (Robert Vaughn) in *The Magnificent Seven*. The second will be redeeming oneself for other failures, losses or weaknesses, such as alcoholism, as is the case of Dude (Dean Martin) in *Rio Bravo* (1959). The third will be redeeming oneself for hurtful actions towards others in the past, as is the case in numerous films and television programs about reformed gunfighters. To redeem oneself is painful, and it takes courage to face something that painful.

Sometimes it takes courage to overcome fear, particularly the fear of being rejected and hurt, in order to love, be a friend, or be true to a group. In Chapter 3, the role that love, friendship and bonds to the community play in courage will be examined. Love can motivate someone to great physical valor, great moral valor or great psychological valor, as in the case of Amy Kane.

In Chapter 4, the role that justice plays in courage will be examined. The characters in countless films and television programs show abundant courage because their honor, integrity and sense of fairness demand it, as exemplified by Will Kane.

In Chapter 5, the role that temperance plays in courage will be examined. Paradoxically, sometimes a person shows great courage because forgiveness and mercy, humility, prudence and self-control demand that he or she avoid rather than have a physical confrontation at the risk of losing the respect of others, experiencing humiliation or foregoing revenge. As Dan Troop (John Russell) says in the 1959 *Lawman* episode "The Gunman," a lesson a man has to learn is when to back down.

In Chapter 6, the role that courage plays in growing up and growing old is examined. According to Philip French (p. 43),

> In a rather old-fashioned way, the western assumes that young people have a lot to learn from their elders and very little to teach them, and that the process of learning is long and painful, that a man must prove himself in a variety of rituals before he can take his place in adult society. ... Such instruction has a clearly symbolic purpose— to teach judgment, self-restraint, self-sufficiency, a code of conduct and morality that goes with the acquiring of character.

In this respect, the theory of the psychoanalyst Erik Erikson and his psychosocial stage of identity achievement vs. identity diffusion will be useful in analyzing how Westerns portray this very important transition. It also takes courage to grow old gracefully and accept one's fate. Again, Erikson's theory and in particular his psychosocial stage of ego integrity vs. despair will be particularly important in explaining this final transition.

Chapter 7 will examine one particular "strength" of the virtue of courage, authenticity, being able to be true to oneself and others in thought, speech and deed.

Chapter 8 will examine how the revisionist Westerns that came of age beginning in the 1960s changed the concept of courage and its role in the Western.

Chapter 9 will focus on one particular Western, *Lonesome Dove*, and the way it illustrates the different varieties of courage and the virtues that can come from it.

The Conclusion will summarize the ways that courage in all its forms as demonstrated in Westerns is a gateway to the other virtues.

Chapter 1

The Quality of Courage

"What is courage? What is cowardice?"—*They Came to Cordura*

Classified by the positive psychologists Christopher Peterson and Martin Seligman (2004), courage is one of the six virtues, each of which includes various "strengths." Courage involves the emotional strengths (bravery, persistence, integrity and vitality) that underlie the will to accomplish goals in the face of opposition, either external or internal. Bravery is refusing to retreat from threat, challenge, difficulty or pain. Persistence is completing what one starts despite obstacles along the way. Integrity is being honest and authentic. Vitality is approaching life with passion and energy.

Bravery involves three criteria (Peterson and Seligman, 2004, p. 214). The first is that it's an action that must be voluntary and not coerced. Secondly, it involves thoughtfulness, "an understanding of the risk and an acceptance of the consequences of action." That rules out recklessness or unconsidered risks. Thirdly, it "requires the presence of danger, loss, risk or potential injury."

Peterson and Seligman (2004, p. 216) go on to discuss three different types of bravery: physical, moral and psychological. Physical bravery involves acting despite "a fear of bodily injury or death." Moral courage is quite a bit more complex:

> Moral bravery often relates to fear of others' opinions. Looking foolish before peers, for example, is a common fear. But moral bravery compels or allows an individual to do what he or she believes is right, despite fear of social or economic consequences. The fear that can summon moral bravery takes many forms: fear of job loss, fear of poverty, fear of losing friends, fear of criticism, fear of ostracism, fear of embarrassment,

fear of making enemies, or fear of losing status. The consequences of these fears may be of short or long duration. Though physical bravery is often expressed quickly, in fleeting bursts of action, a morally courageous choice to do what is right may extend its impact on the individual over a lifetime, calling forth the bravery of endurance [Peterson and Seligman, p. 216].

Wes Tancred revealing his true identity in front of a crowded courtroom in *Tension at Table Rock* despite the infamy associated with his real name is a good example of this type of moral bravery. Psychological bravery is also quite complex:

The distinction between physical and moral bravery seems obvious. Less obvious, at least initially, is a distinction between moral bravery and what may be a third variation in the complex, psychological bravery. According to Putnam (1997), an individual in need of psychological bravery fears loss of psychic stability. Millions of individuals summon psychological bravery every day to face their fears and anxieties, but their courageous behavior can be invisible to others. For example, few would be aware of the emotional distress of an individual with obsessive-compulsive disorder who shakes hands, despite an intense fear of contamination. Admitting a psychological problem and seeking help may have social costs, such as embarrassment or ostracism ... and a fear of this type of consequence links psychological bravery to moral bravery.... But a major difference lies beyond the similarities. Whereas an individual may fear a loss of ethical integrity if moral bravery fails, psychological bravery confronts a fear of "loss of the psyche"—a destabilizing of the "self" [Putnam, 1997, p. 2].

Dr. Frail in *The Hanging Tree* (see Chapter 3) is an example of psychological bravery. Throughout the film he clearly is brave in both the physical and even the moral sense, facing physical danger and acting in a totally uninhibited way when it comes to the criticism and opinions of others; but it is not until the very end that he is brave enough to face and overcome his fear of being hurt and abandoned to love again after so many years.

Persistence is the "voluntary continuation of a goal-directed action in spite of obstacles, difficulties or discouragement" (Peterson and Seligman, 2004, p. 229). A good example of persistence is Hull Barret in *Pale Rider* (see Chapter 8). A more important virtue, at least when it comes to Westerns, is integrity. Integrity includes "a regular pattern of behavior that is consistent with espoused values," "public justification of moral convictions, even if those convictions are not popular," and "treatment of others with care ... sensitivity to the needs of others" (Peterson and Seligman, 2004, p. 250). Integrity overlaps with authenticity ("emotional genuineness and interpersonal sincerity") and honesty ("facing truthfulness and interpersonal sincerity"). A good example of all three qualities is Steve Judd in *Ride the High Country* (see Chapter 2). Integrity is basically what he means by "All I want is to enter my house justified." Vitality is "a dynamic aspect of well-being marked by the subjective experience of energy and aliveness

(Ryan and Frederick, 1997)" (Peterson and Seligman, 2004, p. 273). Tom Dunson in *Red River* is a prime example of this strength (see Chapter 6).

An interesting and thoughtful example of the virtue of courage is found in "The Jose Morales Story" (1960), an episode of *Wagon Train*. Bill Hawks (Terry Wilson) has separated from the main wagon train to guide three wagons, occupied by a Quaker, Aaron Oliver (Clark Howat), Aaron's son Joseph (Charles Herbert), Aaron's wife Patience (Aline Towne), Dr. Stern (Steve Darrell), Raleigh (Gregg Palmer) and Louis Roque (Lon Chaney, Jr.). Roque, a chronic malcontent and misanthrope anxious to sell his $5000 worth of hardware out west, complains to Hawks that he is leading the wagon train into hostile Indian country. To make sure that it is safe, Hawks scouts ahead and runs into a gang headed by Jose Morales (Lee Marvin with a bad Mexican accent). They capture Hawks and bring him back to the wagon train. When Morales tells the travelers he is going to take their wagons, Roque and Raleigh unsuccessfully resist him, resulting in the death of Raleigh.

Morales recognizes Roque as the only man who decided to leave the Alamo when Colonel Travis gave the men there the choice to leave or stay against impossible odds. After he left the Alamo, Roque, who spoke fluent Spanish, stole a Mexican soldier's uniform and stabbed Morales, who was in the Mexican army at the time, to keep Morales from finding out who he was. Roque defends his decision in front of the bandits and travelers by claiming that others in the Alamo wished that they could speak Spanish as well as he could so they could escape as well. A disgusted Hawks will have none of this excuse and considers Roque a coward.

The wagons with the bandits and the travelers start heading for an abandoned stage/wagon station where Morales plans to take the wagons and leave the travelers stranded. Mescalero Apaches kill a Morales gang member and wound another. The Mescaleros attack the station, forcing Morales—the last of the bandits—to give guns to Roque, Hawks and the doctor. The pacifist Aaron, who plans to build a mission for the Indians, refuses to accept one. Aaron believes, contrary to the others in the station, that he can reason with the Mescaleros. Against the wishes of the others, Aaron leaves the station to reason with the Mescaleros and is promptly killed.

At this point, Hawks tells the doctor that there is very little chance that they will survive. Roque and Morales, who is wounded and is likely to be hanged if he does make it out, decide to stay to confront the Mescaleros. They tell Hawks to escape with the doctor, Patience and Joseph. Roque thinks it's ironic that the judgmental Hawks will be the one escaping this time and he will be the one staying. Roque explains that he is staying because Jose and the Olivers were the only people who treated him well in the 30 years since the Alamo fell and he wanted Patience and Joseph to be able to establish their Quaker mission. He tells Hawks that he left the Alamo because he had been in the country only a month after leaving France (he had previously fought with Napoleon in Russia) and was living in a tent while others were living in houses. Therefore, he felt that although for him the Texan cause was worth fighting for, it was not worth going to his certain death. After successfully escaping and seeing Patience, Joseph and the doctor safely away, Hawks goes back to the station to find Morales and Roque dead. He spreads the Texas flag on their graves and goes back to the main wagon train.

"The Jose Morales Story" is an insightful examination of the meaning of courage, particularly when bravery involves a thoughtful "understanding of the risk and an acceptance of the consequences of action." Roque demonstrates bravery when he understands that staying at the station will likely end in his death, but believes it is worth it to save the others, particularly the noble Olivers who were kind to him (although he takes delight in turning the tables on the judgmental Hawks). His death makes his reasoning for leaving the Alamo all the more credible. If he stayed at the Alamo, he wouldn't have saved anyone, unlike staying at the station. Roque mentions that often individuals have only a minute to make a decision that will affect them the rest of their lives. Colonel Travis didn't give Roque enough time to realize that by leaving the Alamo, he would be hated the rest of his life.

Aaron Oliver, on the other hand, did not show bravery in the sense that he was naively confident that he could reason with the Mescaleros and thus did not understand the risks and consequences of his actions. In that sense, he wasn't courageous. However, in facing the Mescaleros and thus being true to his Quaker beliefs, he was demonstrating integrity ("a regular pattern of behavior that is consistent with espoused values," "public justification of moral convictions, even if those convictions are not popular," and "treatment of others with care ... sensitivity to the needs of others") and in that sense was courageous.

Perhaps the Western film that most directly addresses the quality of courage is the very thoughtful, if somewhat flawed, *They Came to Cordura* (1959). The film begins with a rather heavy-handed prologue that explains the circumstances of the incursion into Mexico of a U.S. Army expedition to punish Pancho Villa for his raid on Columbus, New Mexico, in 1916. It ends with two questions: "What is courage? What is cowardice?"

1. The Quality of Courage

The action begins with Major Tom Thorn (Gary Cooper) introducing himself to Colonel DeRose (Edward Platt). Major Thorn, formerly a field officer, is now in charge of military awards. He tells DeRose that he wants to nominate a private, Andrew Hetherington (Michael Callan), for the Congressional Medal of Honor for his action in the fight against Villa's army at Guerrero. After Thorn leaves the camp, DeRose tells a newspaperman that the army is emphasizing awards to produce heroes going into America's probable entry into World War I.

When Thorn gets to the camp of Colonel Rogers (Robert Keith), Rogers is very excited about attacking Villa's men at Ojos Azules with an old-fashioned cavalry charge, "regiment in line," even though his men have never done or even seen it. Rogers insists on doing it because it may be the last time it is done and tells Thorn that he and Hetherington will take no part in the action. Thorn later asks Hetherington why he acted so bravely and what he felt and thought at the time. In response, Hetherington begins to cry and tells Thorn that the Lord took hold of him at Guerrero and he regained the evangelist faith beat into him by his father but that he's glad he didn't have to fight in the coming action.

The Mexicans are prepared in well-fortified positions at Ojo Azules, the rancho of Adelaide Geary (Rita Hayworth). The U.S. troopers charge the rancho while Thorn and Hetherington watch safely from a distance. Suddenly the Mexicans open fire and tear apart the troopers' "regiment in line." Just as it appears that the Americans will be soundly defeated, individual acts of heroism take place. Lieutenant William Fowler (Tab Hunter) leads his men over some breastworks and scatters the Mexicans behind it. Corporal Milo Trubee (Richard Conte) breaks into the rancho, causing havoc inside. Sergeant John Chawk (Van Heflin) pushes a cart next to the wall of the rancho in order to jump into the rancho. Private Wilbur Renziehausen (Dick York) climbs over the main gate to open it and admit the other troopers. The Mexicans abandon the rancho.

Rogers is elated about the success of the charge that will likely make him famous and end in a promotion. Rogers wants Thorn to recommend him for a citation, but Thorn refuses, saying that as a commander he was just doing what he was supposed to do. Instead he wants to recommend Fowler, Chawk, Trubee and Renziehausen for the Congressional Medal of Honor. An angry Rogers tells Thorn he's done a great deal for him, that he could have court-martialed Thorn for cowardice at Columbus. Despite this, Thorn refuses to cite Rogers for a citation. Thorn wants to go on with Rogers' unit as they continue to fight Villa's army to determine whether there are any other soldiers worthy of a citation for future actions.

However, an angry Rogers orders Thorn to take Hetherington, Fowler, Chawk, Renziehausen and Trubee to Cordura where Thorn's recommendations will be recorded. Rogers also orders Thorn to take along Adelaide Geary, whom Rogers, despite Thorn's objections, wants to charge with treason since Villa's men were using her rancho as a fortress. As Thorn leaves, an upset Rogers informs Thorn that he didn't court-martial him for the sake of Thorn's dead father, a famous and highly respected soldier who died in battle.

While en route to Cordura, Geary tries to convince Thorn to let her go because Rogers' charges are rather tenuous since she had no choice but to quarter anyone fighting in Mexico or they would quarter themselves at her rancho, anyway. Thorn refuses to let her go and tells her to stay away from the men. Chawk and Trubee are upset about Geary smoking in front of them when they don't have any tobacco. When Fowler asks Thorn what he thought of the action at Ojos Azules, Thorn tells him it was a reckless "farce." Fowler responds that a commander has to take chances. But according to Thorn, a commander should not attack with only hearsay knowledge of the terrain and enemy positions the way Rogers did. Fowler counters that the objectives were nevertheless achieved. Thorn retorts that that was only because the Mexicans didn't have rapid-fire weapons and a few men, like Fowler, took the initiative.

Geary tries to bribe Thorn to let her go, afraid that even if she is not convicted of a crime, the newspapers will "hang" her due to the bad reputation of her family. When Thorn refuses, she tries to run away. Thorn stops Chawk from shooting her as Fowler catches up to her. The men begin to wonder about the purpose of their journey to Cordura and why they haven't been told. Instead of telling them, Thorn takes Renziehausen aside and asks him why he vaulted the gate. Renziehausen responds that he was nearest to the gate and wasn't scared, or at least not aware of it. Thorn later tells Fowler that he is recommending all five men for the Congressional Medal of Honor, but he shouldn't tell Chawk, Trubee and Renziehausen about it, since if they began to think of themselves as heroes, they might not answer truthfully why they acted bravely. The conversation of Fowler and Thorn is interrupted when Chawk tries to take Geary's liquor from her and Thorn has to break it up. Thorn feels now he needs to tell the men the truth about recommending them for the Medal of Honor, which he does.

The next morning, Geary finds her beloved pet bird dead, apparently killed by one of the five men, none of whom are willing to admit it. An angry Thorn pushes them hard as a punishment. Fowler tells Thorn he doesn't want the medal because it would make the older officers jealous and vindictive towards a young and ambitious officer like him. Villa's men attack the men and they hide out in a canyon. While there, Thorn asks Chawk why he got on the roof of the rancho. Chawk says he just wanted to kill a couple of Mexicans and says that all the medal means to him is that he will get two extra bucks a month. Trubee asks Thorn to try and get him a transfer to the quartermaster corps, to get him out of fighting. He adds that he charged the corral as a self-sacrifice for the troops, but Thorn realizes that this isn't the truth. Trubee admits that he's only saying this because this is what he thinks Thorn wants to hear.

At daybreak, the soldiers are still trapped in the canyon. Despite Fowler's opposition (the cavalry never gives up its horses, according to him), Thorn releases his horses to Villa's men as an inducement for them to leave the canyon. The ploy works and the men walk out of there. Thorn tells the men that he released the horses because that was their best chance to stay alive, and that the coming war in Europe needs live heroes.

Trubee tells Thorn that he knows that Thorn ran at Columbus and asks that Thorn *not* recommend him for the medal (he doesn't want to be a "lead mule") and that Thorn turn Geary over to him. Thorn refuses. Hetherington collapses from typhoid and has to be carried on a litter, despite Chawk and Fowler suggesting that they leave him behind.

When they are camped out at night, Thorn stops Chawk and Trubee from assaulting Geary. Trubee tells everyone that Thorn hid in a ditch at Columbus. Thorn feels compelled to have Fowler throw away the men's guns. Later, Fowler says he is not going to back him up, claiming that Thorn only wants to give the men medals to make himself feel less guilty about hiding in a ditch in Columbus. Chawk tells Thorn he doesn't need the publicity of a medal because he is wanted for murder and threatens to kill Thorn if he insists on citing them for a medal since this would result in Chawk being hanged.

Thorn tells Geary what happened at Columbus: When Villa unexpectedly attacked, resulting in firing, Thorn, who had never seen combat, took his pistol and ran for the regimental headquarters. Bullets came close and he jumped into a culvert. When he left the culvert, he felt he was a coward and others labeled him as such as well. During the fight, he wasn't thinking of anything. Geary responds that one act of cowardice doesn't make a man a coward, just as one act of bravery doesn't make a man a hero. Thorn reveals that if Trubee talks, he will be dishonorably discharged. Geary says he should give in to the other men, but Thorn insists on writing his citations for their sake, to show them that they have something good in them that they didn't realize they had.

They reach the railroad they need to follow to get to Cordura, and a handcar to carry them down the tracks. Renziehausen admits he was scared at Ojos Azules and doesn't want the medal since his ear was shot off in the fight at the canyon and a medal would just make his disfigurement more visible. As the group presses on, they become more miserable. Chawk says that his father abused him and reveals how he paid him back. Geary confides in Thorn that she is worried that Chawk will kill him, but Thorn tells her how proud he is of what he is doing. At night, Geary "occupies" Chawk so Thorn can sleep instead of being on guard to prevent the other men from harming him. Geary reveals to Thorn the next morning that her Ojos Azules rancho was where she went to hide from a life she was ashamed of, losing the custody of her two children because of poor choices she made. Thorn gives his notebook with his comments about the citations and the men to Geary to hand in to the commander at Cordura if something happens to him.

Hetherington recovers from the typhoid. Chawk taunts Renziehausen about his ear and they get into a fight. Chawk, Fowler and Hetherington refuse to get in the handcar and walk ahead while the other members of the group get on the handcar. It begins to slide backwards. A desperate and exhausted Thorn tries to pull it with a rope but he collapses as the others (except Geary) refuse to help. When Thorn gets back up, Fowler throws a rock that hits his leg and causes him to collapse; the handcar slides backwards, pulling Thorn with it. Fowler grabs Thorn's gun and makes up a cover story to absolve the other soldiers of any wrongdoing. Fowler takes Thorn's notebook from Geary. In it, the men read about their heroism, but also about the fact that all of them, including Thorn, has a "crippled child" in them, and despite being "treacherous, vicious, dishonest," they can also be brave and noble. The notebook goes on to say that making it to Cordura proves something "beyond the limit of human conduct" and ends with "Judge not, lest ye be judged." Hetherington sees Cordura over the hill. They all go to Cordura, led by a revived Thorn.

They Came to Cordura is an ambitious film with psychologically complicated characters and some very profound philosophical ideas. Sometimes its ambition exceeds its reach, with a transformation of the characters (including a suddenly revived Thorn) at the end of the film that can appear too sudden, *à la* Tom Dunson in *Red River* (see Chapter 6). However, more than any other Western film and more than most other films, it directly investigates the quality of courage. The four soldiers to whom Thorn wants to award the Medal of Honor all clearly exhibit physical bravery, but their rejection of the medal shows that they are lacking in moral and/or psychological bravery. The ambitious Fowler wants to reject the medal because it would evoke jealousy in possibly vindictive senior officers. The lazy Trubee rejects the medal because it might result in giving him more responsibility than he wants. Renziehausen doesn't want it because it would bring attention to his disfigured ear. Chawk wants to reject the medal because the publicity might force him to face a murder charge. Even Geary is hiding out in Mexico because she doesn't have the moral or psychological bravery to face her past and the condemnation from others because of it.

On the other hand, Thorn clearly lacked physical bravery at Columbus only to redeem himself through his bravery in the fight in the canyon and his refusal to give up taking the five soldiers to Cordura despite their reluctance and Chawk's vow to kill him if he does. He demonstrates moral bravery by eventually refusing to give a citation to Rogers even though Rogers implies that he could expose him as a coward at Columbus and insists on taking the reluctant and angry soldiers to Cordura even though they also could expose him as a coward at Columbus. He also shows psychological bravery in his willingness to confront his actions at Columbus head on instead of rationalizing them.

Ironically, Thorn, the only man on the way to Cordura who doesn't deserve the Medal of Honor, turns out to be the bravest of them all. As Peterson and Seligman (2004) state, a requirement for courage is that it involves thoughtfulness. Thorn didn't have time to think about what was happening at Columbus, but by the time he started out on his journey to Cordura he had time to reflect on how he should act in a situation where he needed to risk his life to be brave. Jess Harper says it this way in the ".45 Calibre" episode of *Laramie* (see Chapter 2): "The way I see it, there's a time anybody can be afraid. It's the first time a man has to decide between living and dying. I kind of respect a fellow who's honest enough to admit he wants to go on living.... If a man's really yellow, he doesn't want to worry about a second time because he knows he'll never have to go that route again." Thorn insists he wants to give the men citations despite the fact that they can be "treacherous, vicious, dishonest," because their actions at Ojos Azules and Guerrero show that they can overcome the "crippled child" within them to act bravely and nobly, even if they didn't realize it at the time.

Chapter 2

Redemption

"I was wrong. He wasn't just half a man."—*7 Men from Now*

In the classic Western film *Ride the High Country* (1962), Steve Judd (Joel McCrea) is approaching the end of his life. He takes a job transporting gold from the gold fields in the mountains of California to a town below. For him, this assignment is a chance to redeem himself after going through a rough patch in his life. He puts it this way: "All I want to do is to enter my house justified." He enlists his old friend Gil Westrum (Randolph Scott) and young Heck Longtree (Ron Starr) to help him carry the gold, but Gil, who also has fallen on hard times, decides to steal the gold from Steve and enlists Heck in the plot. After an unsuccessful try, Gil and Heck redeem themselves by helping Steve fight the lecherous Hammond brothers, who seek revenge against Steve, Gil and Heck because they helped Elsa Knudsen (Mariette Hartley) escape from the brothers. When Gil assures a dying Steve that he will make sure the gold is delivered, his old friend says, "Hell, I know that. I always did. You just forgot it for a while, that's all."

Ride the High Country is just one of the many examples of the importance of redemption in Western films and television. According to Jim Kitses (2004), one of the major characteristics of the Western is the promise of "open horizons": The vastness and open vistas of the landscapes in the West reflect the "open options" and possibilities that the West presented at the time. Someone could come out West from the East and start over, becoming rich or famous or developing a whole new identity. This fresh start also means one's ability to redeem oneself is greatly enhanced in this

Journey through the mountains. The old men, Randolph Scott as Gil Westrum (far right) and Joel McCrea as Steve Judd (second from right), turn around to counsel Mariette Hartley as Elsa Knudsen (far left) and Ron Starr as Heck Longtree in Sam Peckinpah's *Ride the High Country* (1962, Metro-Goldwyn-Mayer).

new country: The coward can prove he is brave, the drunkard can sober up, and someone who is running away from himself, or from others, can stop running. Redemption can be made easier by leaving behind those you have disappointed or failed, to go to somewhere fresh where you can get a clean second chance at proving you are brave, honest, sober or competent.

Redemption in these films and television shows can be broken down into three categories: redeeming oneself for physical cowardice, redeeming oneself for an immoral past, and redeeming oneself for failures, losses and weaknesses.

Courage, what the psychologists Martin Seligman and Christopher Peterson (2004) define as emotional strengths that require someone to reach his or her objectives in the face of internal or external opposition, is at the heart of the Western ethos. This conflict means that if individuals fail to face physical danger to achieve their objectives when it is necessary, they need courage in order to redeem themselves. This dynamic also could mean a battle within oneself, because courage ultimately means overcoming the fear within oneself. In "Journey to San Carlos" (1957), one of the more perceptive episodes of *The Lone Ranger*, Ben Murray (Myron Healey) is a disgraced guide who ran when an Indian war party attacked the wagon train he was leading, resulting in the deaths of 18 people in the party. Murray loses his confidence and self-respect and decides to quit guiding. The Lone Ranger (Clayton Moore) tries to enlist Murray to guide a young sister and brother through hostile Indian country to San Carlos in order to help Murray redeem himself. Murray at first refuses, wallowing in self-pity, telling the Masked Man that the reason why he no longer guides is simple: He is a coward. The Ranger responds, "Cowardice is the most complicated thing on Earth," and challenges him to stop feeling sorry for himself and guide the young couple. Murray reluctantly agrees and, with the help of Lone Ranger and Tonto (Jay Silverheels), sets out for San Carlos. When the party is threatened, Murray starts to desert his companions in the middle of the night, but after agonizing over it, he overcomes his fear and decides to come back. When Murray asks the Lone Ranger why he didn't do or say anything when he saw him start to leave, the Ranger replies, "It was a contest within yourself. Nobody else had any business in it." The next day, they fight off the Indians and continue on their journey.

Ben Murray has to agonize over his cowardice before mustering up the courage to face it, a theme that is repeated in other Western films and shows. In one of the more serious episodes of *Maverick*, "The Day of Reckoning" (1958), Bret Maverick (James Garner) has to decide whether to come to the aid of a town threatened by a trail boss and his gun hand. A foolish newspaper editor, George Buckner (Willard Sage), needlessly antagonizes the trail boss and then hides, refusing to come to the aid of his printer when the trail boss and gun hand beat the printer to death while interrogating him about the whereabouts of the editor. The editor is confronted by Lil (Jean Willes) and forced to face his cowardice. He then redeems himself when he joins Bret and the rest of the townspeople in a showdown with the trail boss, his crew and the gunman.

According to Bandy and Stoehr (2012, p. 220), the director Budd Boetticher "gives his characters rare but telling opportunities for individuation and character transformation—where the choices are not, as in many traditional Westerns, primarily conditioned by concern with social norms, political ideals, historical goals or shared codes of honor. Their choices are occasioned primarily by personal moral awakenings and chances for self-realization." Interestingly, these choices are often made by secondary characters. In *7 Men from Now* (1956), John Greer (Walter Reed) is a passive, weak-willed man who has to be rescued by the brave and resolute Ben Stride (Randolph Scott) and even shrinks from confronting Bill Masters (Lee Marvin) when Masters insults Mrs. Greer (Gail Russell). Stride comes to his aid once again by knocking down the insolent Masters. Later, however, when Stride is hurt and needs help, Greer seeks the help of the town sheriff, even though he has to pass by a threatening outlaw, who shoots Greer in the back. As Masters witnesses the murder, he admits, "I was wrong. He wasn't just half a man."

Sometimes the cowardice of a person is enabled by those around him. In *Gun for a Coward* (1957), the naturally timid Bless Keough (Jeffrey Hunter) is protected from confrontational situations by his older brother Will (Fred MacMurray). When Bless is accused of running away from a fight with rustlers, leaving his younger brother Hade (Dean Stockwell) to die, Bless feels he has to stand up to a man who is bullying him to prove to himself and others he is no coward. Will steps in yet again in the middle of this confrontation to defeat the bully. Bless then challenges Will to a fistfight when he realizes this is the only way he can redeem himself and become his own man. After his fight with Will, Bless has the confidence to lead the Keough cowhands out after the rustlers. Now that Bless has become his own man, Will is free to leave town to explore other parts of the West.

In "Closer than a Brother," a 1961 episode of *The Rifleman*, reformed alcoholic Micah Torrance (Paul Fix) is so afraid of confronting gunslinger Ansel Bain (Berry Kroeger), who faced him down 16 years before, that he goes back to drinking. He bitterly tells Lucas McCain (Chuck Connors) that the only reason he has been able to be sober and function as marshal is that Lucas was there to back him up. Lucas realizes that he has to shame Micah into facing his tormenter alone, just as he had to challenge Micah to face his alcoholism when years ago he first came to the town of North Fork. When Micah does face his tormentor, he finds out, as is often true, that the real person is a lot less frightening than the nightmares he's had about him. Micah sends the man packing, realizing that for 16 years he has been "living in fear of his own weakness."

In ".45 Calibre," a 1960 episode of *Laramie*, Wes Torrey (Lee Van Cleef), his brother Al and a member of their gang kill the marshal of Laramie, Cole Blanton (Don Harvey), in order to clear the way to rob the town bank. A few hours later, a stagecoach brings Blanton's new deputy Vern Clark (George Nader) and his wife Louisa (Anna-Lisa) into the relay station run by Slim Sherman (John Smith), who has gone to Denver, and

Jess Harper (Robert Fuller). Harper informs Clark that Blanton is dead and the Torrey gang is on the loose, a situation which prompts Clark to ask Harper to be his deputy. Harper refuses. However, when a neighbor brings her dead husband, who has been killed by the Torrey gang, to the relay station, Harper changes his mind and goes to town to tell Clark he will accept his offer of being a deputy.

Clark calls a town meeting to get deputies, but gets only three men, one of whom is the town drunk, Charley Wilkes (Charley Briggs), to help Harper and him. The five men chase the Torrey gang, but in the ensuing fight they get away, and two of the deputies are killed as Wilkes and Clark, who is nicked by a bullet in the neck, run away, leaving only Harper, who kills Al Torrey, to face the gang. Back in Laramie, Harper lies to the townspeople that Clark killed Al Torrey so they won't lose respect for the man who is now the town marshal. But this doesn't keep Clark from feeling sorry for himself for being "yellow." With great insight, Harper tells Clark that whether someone is yellow depends on whether he runs a second time: "The way I see it, there's a time anybody can be afraid. It's the first time a man has to decide between living and dying. I kind of respect a fellow who's honest enough to admit he wants to go on living.... If a man's really yellow, he doesn't want to worry about a second time because he knows he'll never have to go that route again." When Clark tells him there won't be a second time for him because he's a coward, Harper responds insightfully that it's hard to believe that he's a coward because if Clark were yellow, running away wouldn't bother him so much.

Harper leaves Clark so he can rally the townspeople to fight off the impending attack by the Torrey gang. However, only two men agree to join Harper: Wilkes, who wants to redeem himself for running away the first time, and Sloane (John Pickard), who regrets not joining the posse earlier. Back in the Clarks' hotel room, Louisa criticizes Vern for running away and tries to coax him to join Harper and the men willing to stand up to the Torrey gang. After she leaves, Vern decides to join Harper in fighting the Torrey gang, but not before Louisa has gone to Harper's room to make Vern jealous enough to fight not only Harper, but also the Torrey gang. Louisa's ploy works, as the infuriated Vern goes into the streets not only to man the barricades erected to stop the Torrey gang, but also to challenge Harper. However, before he can draw on Harper, the Torrey gang rides in on a stage. In the ensuing gunfight, all of the gang members are killed except the wounded Wes Torrey, who hides out somewhere in the town.

While Harper, Sloane and Wilkes look for Torrey, Louisa admits she

2. Redemption

was very frightened during the gunfight and now empathizes with Vern's fear. She asks Vern to forgive her for trying to make him jealous and the two of them reconcile. Vern spots Torrey, but not before he escapes into Louisa's room. Louisa, overcoming her own fear, tries to stab Torrey, but he fights her off. Vern goes up to the room but is warned off by Louisa. Torrey tries to use Louisa as a shield, threatening Vern, but Harper breaks in and kills Torrey.

In some cases, a "coward" redeems himself out of love or friendship. In *The Fastest Gun Alive* (1956), George Kelby, Jr. (Glenn Ford), is a timid shopkeeper who was too scared to go after the man who killed his father, a famous marshal. Since then, he and his wife Dora (Jeanne Crain) have been drifting from town to town repeating the same pattern: As soon as a gunman hears about George being "the fastest gun alive," even faster than his famous father, and challenges him, George and Dora leave town to start fresh somewhere else so George won't have to face him.

They end up in Cross Creek, where George assumes the alias George Temple. To his wife's dismay, when George feels the townspeople don't respect him enough, he demonstrates his speed and accuracy with a gun, which gains him respect among the townspeople. But gunman Vinnie Harald (Broderick Crawford) hears about George and goes to Cross Creek to challenge him. Vinnie and his two henchmen, Dink Wells (Noah Beery, Jr.) and Taylor Swope (John Dehner), intimidate the townspeople into holing up in the church, and Harald tells them that unless George comes out to face him, he will burn the town. George reveals to the townspeople that he is really too afraid to face Harald. To keep the town from burning, townsman Lou Glover (Leif Erickson) decides to pretend he is George and face Harald, even though he has very little chance of besting Harald. At this point, George musters up the courage to go out and meet Vinnie to keep Glover from almost certain death and to save the town. George wins the gunfight and his self-respect.

Love plays a role in the 1960 episode of *Bonanza* entitled "The Last Trophy." An Englishman, Lord Marion Dunsford (Edward Ashley), is ridiculed by his wife, Lady Beatrice Dunsford (Hazel Court), for cowardly acts on different hunts around the world. When they are kidnapped by thug Solomon Belcher (Bert Freed) and his gang of Indians, Marion risks his life to save the woman he loves as he and the Cartwrights overcome Belcher and his gang. At this point, Beatrice not only recognizes Marion's courage, but empathizes with Marion when she understands for the first time in her life what fear of a deadly threat is like (Belcher put a knife to her throat).

Sometimes redemption takes the form of making up for an immoral past. The theme of the reformed gunfighter is a familiar plot in many Westerns. Five examples come from *The Rifleman*. In the 1961 episode "Death Trap," Lucas McCain (Chuck Connors) and his son Mark (Johnny Crawford) pick up a wounded man and take him into town. To Lucas' disgust, the only doctor in town is Simon Battle (Phil Carey), who is passing through North Fork with his daughter on their way to another town to become the doctor there. Lucas recognizes him as the gunman he had shot and thought he killed ten years before, and agrees to let Battle stay only to help the wounded man. Meanwhile, Spicer (James Drury), the outlaw who shot the man, finds out he is still alive and confronts Lucas and Battle and tries to intimidate them into turning the wounded man over to him so he can finish the job. While Lucas holds off Spicer and his three companions and Battle operates on the wounded man, Battle and McCain talk about their pasts, Lucas admitting that he could be a bit wild himself in his younger days. Later Battle's daughter explains to McCain that after he shot Battle, Battle's wife nursed him back to health, losing her own health and life in the process. As a result, Battle vowed to his wife he would become a doctor to save lives rather than take them. After saving the man's life, Battle and Lucas go out and overcome Spicer and his three companions. Battle leaves town, and both men admit they were wrong about the other.

In a more complicated episode from *The Rifleman*, "The Day of Reckoning" (1962), Jamison (Royal Dano) arrives with his son to become a preacher in a North Fork church. Lucas recognizes him from the days Jamison would burn down farms to take over the tenants' lands and claims that Jamison's conversion to religion is false and his role as a preacher hypocritical. Jamison tries to explain to Lucas that he decided to change his ways when he couldn't bring himself to kill an old man: In the old man, "I saw myself, and from that day forward, I ... I found myself becoming a part of every person I met.... Feeling their hurt and their joy. If I said an unkind word, I felt the hurt of it—as though the word was spoken to me." Lucas still wonders whether Jamison became a preacher because he truly believes in his religious mission or because he is a burned-out criminal too cowardly to continue his outlaw ways and hiding behind his preacher's collar. Jamison begins to doubt himself as well and decides he has to strap on a gun to face the gunmen brothers Charley (L.Q. Jones) and Willie Sheen (Warren Oates), both of whom have been hounding and threatening him from town to town, in order to prove to himself that he has not become a preacher because of physical cowardice. Although he goes out to face the Sheens, it is Lucas who kills them. Because he put on his guns,

Jamison feels he is not fit to be a preacher, but now convinced of Jamison's sincerity, Lucas persuades him to continue as a preacher.

In the 1959 episode "The Blowout," Lucas encounters Al Walker (John Dehner), who was once a reputable lawyer. Through a series of unfortunate events, he now has a reputation as a gunslinger. Dying of an incurable disease, he tells Lucas, "For the first time in my life, I thought of someone other than myself ... my family. And I knew that at least I owed it to them to know I died fittingly with a reputable doctor in attendance. That's one of the reasons I'm here. Lucas, I want your doctor to do it properly. I want a death certificate stating I died of natural causes. I owe it to my family—it would mean a lot to them ... and what I once stood for...." Lucas and acting Marshal Ben Waller (Hugh Sanders) get into a gunfight with the Porter brothers, who have come to kill Al. Before the Porter brothers are killed, one of them manages to kill Al. Lucas promises to make sure that the death certificate says Al died of natural causes.

A recurring subplot in the reformed gunfighter theme is that the former gunfighter is continually provoked into taking up his guns by those who want revenge or a "reputation" for killing the gunfighter. In 1959 episode "The Retired Gun," ex-gunfighter Wes Carney (Robert Webber) hung up his guns when he married Clair Wheatley (Eileen Harley), an old friend of Lucas'. They plan to settle down in North Fork, despite the objections of Micah Torrance, who tells Wes that he doesn't relish the idea of someone with Wes' reputation residing in North Fork after he stops a confrontation between Owny Kincaid (John Anderson) and Wes. Wes and Clair decide to buy a feed store. Meanwhile, Kincaid sends word to Clyde Bailey (Jack Kruschen), Morgan Bailey (Herman Rudin), Jeff Wallace (Duke Snider) and Phil Norton (Milan Smith) that Wes is in North Fork. Clyde has had a long-standing grudge against Wes and decides to pay him back, despite Lucas warning him against it. One day Kincaid, Wallace, Clyde and Morgan beat up Wes and tear apart his store. A badly mauled Wes admits to Lucas that he only gave up his gun and is running the feed store to please Clair, who fills a lonely place in his life. Meanwhile, the emboldened badmen have gone on a rampage, tearing up North Fork. The only men in town willing to go after the gang, besides Marshal Micah Torrance (Paul Fix), are Lucas and Wes. When Clair objects to Wes strapping on his gun again, Lucas gently confronts Clair, telling her a story about an Indian fighter who hung up his guns to please his wife, only to lose his self-respect and ruin his marriage, implying that Wes needs to be free to use his gun again. Wes joins Lucas and Micah in facing down the gang, vanquishing all five of them. Wes is wounded, but Clair surprises him by announcing that Wes is going to take a marshal's job in Bolton City, thus seeking redemption more consistent with his personality and skills.

In the 1959 episode "The Trade," outlaw Sam Morley (Paul Richards) asks Lucas for help. He wants to turn himself in for the reward money, so he can give it to the woman he loves, Beth Landis (Katherine Bard), so she can go back East for the proper medical care for her illness. He asks Lucas to raise the money, intending to pay him back with the reward money. Beth is reluctant to take the money since, as it turns out, she has only a month to live. Lucas convinces her to take the money and go back East by telling her, "You know, getting this money for you is a justification for Sam Morley's whole life. Don't rob him of giving it." Beth gets on the stage, not knowing how Sam got the money and Sam not knowing that she has only a month to live.

In the 1963 *Rifleman* episode "Old Man Running," the sin is of a different order than that of the former gunfighter or criminal. Lucas' father-in-law, Samuel Gibbs (John Anderson), has come to North Fork to seek help from Lucas against the three Sherman brothers, who are out to kill him (Gibbs turned in their brother Jeb for the reward). Lucas refuses because Gibbs years ago deserted his daughter (Lucas' wife) when she was ailing, a desertion which resulted in her death. Gibbs also has come to ask forgiveness from Mark, his grandson, and to make out his will giving his reward money to Mark. Mark refuses, but after Lucas disposes of the Shermans, Mark relents and forgives him.

In *Ride Lonesome* (1959), Ben Brigade (Randolph Scott) and two drifters, Sam Boone (Pernell Roberts) and Whit (James Coburn), are taking in Billy John (James Best) to Santa Cruz. Sam and Whit plot to take Billy John from Brigade, who they think is out for the reward for Billy John, because they will get amnesty for their crimes by taking Billy John to the law, planning afterwards to settle down as law-abiding citizens. Before Sam and Whit can take Billy John away from Brigade, Billy John's brother Frank (Lee Van Cleef) arrives to rescue Billy John. It turns out that Brigade was never after the reward, but after Frank, who killed his wife. Brigade kills Frank and turns Billy John over to Sam and Whit, telling them that he will hunt them down if they don't use their amnesty as an opportunity to become law-abiding.

Sometimes becoming part of a family helps the outlaw redeem himself. In *The Outlaw Josey Wales* (1976), the title character (Clint Eastwood) exacts revenge as a Confederate border raider and later as an outlaw, when the Unionist "redlegs," led by Captain Terrill (Bill McKinney), burn his farm and kill his wife and son. In his travels, he slowly acquires a "family" that replaces the one he lost: Cherokee Chief Lone Wattie (Chief Dan George), a Navajo girl (Geraldine Kearns), a grandmother (Paula Trueman) and her granddaughter (Sandra Locke). His newly formed relationships lead him to forsake his outlaw ways to return to his previous life as a farmer with his new family, although not before they help him in a confrontation with Captain Terrill and his redlegs.

An interesting variation on the theme of outlaws redeeming themselves is found in a 1959 episode of *Laramie*, "Night of the Quiet Men." Marshal John McCambridge (Lyle Bettger) feels remorse after killing two criminals who had tried to kill him. He has come to hate the killing, even though justified, that comes with the job and begins to feel he is turning into a man like the criminals he pursues. He quits his job and comes to the Sherman ranch to ask Slim Sherman (John Smith) to lease him a piece of land, although he doesn't tell Slim why he wants it. McCambridge brings a group of outlaws, none of whom are currently wanted by the law, to help build a ranch on the property. When Cole Rogers (Carl Benton Reid), a local rancher, hears what McCambridge is doing, he tries to pressure the sheriff (Bartlett Robinson), to get them off Slim's land. The sheriff tells Slim what McCambridge is doing with the land. Slim confronts McCambridge, who explains that he wants to rehabilitate ex-outlaws and that they are his partners in the ranching enterprise. Otherwise, they could end up in jail or dead. He reveals to Slim that he reached a point where he wanted to stop killing and start helping the outlaws he pursued as a marshal. Meanwhile, a homesteader's farm is burned and a stagecoach robbed. Rogers accuses McCambridge and his ex-outlaws, but it turns out two of his own men committed the crimes. A chastened Rogers offers McCambridge and his men the opportunity to start over again in Oregon on land that Rogers owns. McCambridge and his men ride off towards Oregon to start new lives.

The theme that the reformed gunfighter can use his past to help others avoid the same fate is the basis of a 1957 episode of *Zane Grey Theater*, "Gift from a Gunman." Gunfighter Will Gorman (Howard Keel) wants to go straight, but his efforts are complicated by former lover Marcy (Jean Willes), who married the colonel (John Dehner), one of Will's former partners in crime, when she thought Will was dead. Will has come back to the town of Tres Robles where Marcy, the colonel and the colonel's nephew, 17-year-old Dan (Michael Landon), are living, in order to start a freight line. Will stops a gunfight between young Dan, who is anxious to prove how fast he is with a gun, and another man who has implied that Will has gone legitimate because he has lost his nerve. Will lectures Dan about the futility of being a gunfighter. He tells Dan that when he (Will) was shot and almost died two years ago, he had "somehow become every man I ever killed." Will explains he started out being like Dan, trying to prove how fast he was with a gun. This resulted in Will being forced to kill to survive, trapping him in a deadly lifestyle. Instead of taking Will's talk to heart, Dan becomes disillusioned with his former idol, Will.

Marcy provokes the colonel by saying that she is going to run away with Will, neglecting to mention that Will has not agreed to go with her. The colonel wants to fight Will to keep Marcy from running away with him, even after Will says he is uninterested in her. Will shoots the colonel and then is confronted by Dan. Will realizes that Dan is challenging him because he wants to prove how fast he is and not really to avenge his uncle. Will shoots the gun out of Dan's hand, and Dan walks away sobered by the realization he is not that fast and that he could have been killed. After Dan leaves, Will reveals to Marcy that Dan actually was faster than Will and that Will, unbeknownst to Dan, was seriously wounded. To keep Dan from finding out, Will leaves town after getting Marcy to promise not to tell anyone the truth. Leaving town without telling Dan he was shot was Will's "gift" to Dan.

The lack of acceptance of the gunfighter turning a new leaf is the theme of a 1958 episode of *Zane Grey Theater*, "A Threat of Violence." Clay Culhane (Chris Alcaide), a reformed gunfighter turned lawyer, journeys 100 miles to the town of Contention to accept a job as a lawyer for the Topaz Mining Company. But the truth about Culhane's past has already reached company manager James Ballinger (Alex Gerry), who rescinds Culhane's job offer.

Culhane befriends Carlos Pindar (Cesar Romero), who saved him from horse thieves. Pindar is accused of killing Verge Cheney, a man he had threatened. Culhane decides to defend Pindar, partly because it is the only case offered to him and partly because he sees Pindar as a kindred spirit who, like Culhane, is trying to live down his past. In court, Culhane apparently proves that Pindar was not at the scene of the crime when it was committed. As a result, the sheriff (Lyle Bettger) allows Pindar to go free. Then Culhane learns that Cheney's widow and Pindar fabricated Pindar's alibi and Pindar *was* the killer. Culhane confronts Pindar about it and is forced to kill him. Culhane is left with mixed emotions: successfully winning his first case as a lawyer but being forced to use his gun once again and thus unable to entirely escape his past.

Warren Masters (Regis Parton) travels a rather unusual road to redemption in a 1959 episode of *The Texan*, "The Ringer." While impersonating

Bill Longley (Rory Calhoun), Masters chases a saloon girl and smashes up a saloon and hotel. The sheriff and townspeople are so afraid of the reputation of the man they think is Longley that they let him go if he promises to leave town. The next day, the real Longley learns from the frightened townspeople what happened and is chased out of town for what he allegedly did. Masters, continuing his impersonation, romances and then deserts Mary Lou Martin (Olive Sturgess), the daughter of Longley's old friend, Ed Martin (Grant Withers).

Professional gambler Jebb Kilmer (Adam Williams) and two of his gun hands meet with Masters. Kilmer reveals that he has arranged for Masters to impersonate Longley in a complicated ploy to get Longley in a vulnerable position and kill him to get revenge against Longley for previously shooting Kilmer in his right hand and ending Kilmer's crooked gambling career. Ed Martin gets Longley jailed for supposedly deserting his daughter. When Mary Lou appears at the jail, she exclaims that Longley is not the man who deserted her. Longley, released from jail, goes after Masters.

The more Masters learns about Longley from his friends, the more he decides to act like the honorable Longley. As a result, he begins to redeem himself by standing up for a bartender who is threatened by a hooligan. He continues to redeem himself by taking Longley's side against Kilmer and his two gunmen and dispatching all three of them. Masters completes his redemption by marrying Mary Lou in the presence of Longley and Ed Martin.

The reformed gunfighter is not the only Western character seeking redemption. Another is the bounty hunter, whom many despise for earning a living by bringing criminals, dead as well as alive, to the Law. Despite having high moral standards, Josh Randall of *Wanted: Dead or Alive* is often loathed simply for being a bounty hunter. The 1963 *Laramie* episode "Badge of Glory" deals with redemption on a number of different levels. Jess Harper (Robert Fuller) decides to ride guard on a stagecoach he suspects will be robbed and ends up breaking up the robbery, wounding one of the bandits, Sam Logan (Sheldon Allman), who makes it to the home of John Holby (Lin McCarthy). Holby has forsaken his former life as a bounty hunter to become a preacher but previously used to ride with Sam. As Sam lies dying, he begs Holby to turn in his body and claim the $5000 reward by pretending to be the one who shot him as a way for Sam to redeem himself for all the bad he has done and for Holby to have the money to build a church. Holby claims the reward despite the objections of his wife Amelia (Jean Allison), in order to use the money for his church and give Sam a chance to redeem himself.

Chuck Logan (Gregg Palmer) and the other two members of the Logan gang want revenge after finding out that Holby has claimed he killed Sam. They go to Holby's farm and shoot a churchgoer, Laurie Adams (Laraine Stephens), when trying to kill Holby, before being chased off by Harper and Sheriff Mason (George Wallace). Holby attempts to redeem himself by admitting to Laurie's fiancé, Bob Talmadge (Russell Johnson), that he lied about killing Logan. An angry Talmadge blames him for Laurie being shot and gets the town council to ask Holby to leave town. The sheriff is left alone to guard Holby and his wife while Jess tries to get the townspeople to help protect the Holbys. He is unsuccessful. While Harper is in town, the sheriff is shot by the Logan gang. Harper takes the wounded sheriff to town while Talmadge goes to the Holby farm to force Holby to leave. While they are talking, Harper arrives, and then the three Logan gang members arrive to kill Holby. In an attempt to redeem himself, Holby goes out to meet the badmen by himself in order to spare the lives of Harper, Talmadge and his wife, and is shot down. After refusing to help Harper and Holby, but now realizing Holby's good intentions, Talmadge attempts to redeem himself by helping Harper confront the bandits.

The road to redemption is often not a straight one. In the 1970 *Gunsmoke* episode "Hackett," Quentin Sargent (Morgan Woodward) is confronted on his farm by Will Hackett (Earl Holliman). Ten years before, Hackett, Quentin, Bronk and Telly attempted to rob a train. Quentin escaped in the middle of the robbery, but Hackett, Bronk and Telly were captured and served ten years in prison. Hackett coerces Quentin into buying the horses and dynamite that Hackett, Bronk and Telly need to rob a train. Quentin goes along with the plan since he fears that Hackett would otherwise kill him or reveal to authorities Quentin's role in the previous train robbery.

During his stay at the Sargent homestead, Hackett humiliates Quentin as much as he can. While Quentin is coming back from town after buying the dynamite and horses, Hackett makes amorous advances towards Geneva, Quentin's wife (Jennifer West), just as Quentin arrives home. Quentin backs down even though the scratch marks on Geneva's face indicate that Hackett accosted her. Quentin later explains to Geneva why he is afraid of Hackett and his role in the upcoming robbery. Quentin admits to his wife that he is a coward. Geneva tries to console him, but he decides to do something about the planned robbery. He leaves an anonymous note about the impending bank robbery for Festus Haggen (Ken Curtis), who is acting as marshal while Matt Dillon (James Arness) is out of town. Festus wires Dillon, who stops the robbery and shoots Bronk and Telly. Hackett gets away.

2. Redemption

Hackett goes back to Quentin's homestead to exact revenge on Quentin for upsetting his plans. Quentin and Geneva try to hide. Quentin finally decides to attack Hackett with a scythe but is unsuccessful, and Hackett shoots him in the leg. Hackett is about to attack Geneva just as Dillon arrives. Hackett tries to shoot Dillon, but Quentin tackles him, and Dillon captures Hackett. As Hackett is being away, he tells Quentin that he will get back at him someday. The now emboldened Quentin tells Hackett he won't be hiding if he does. Now that he has redeemed himself for his physical cowardice, Quentin lets Matt know he is ready to tell him about his past crimes, thus redeeming himself for those past transgressions as well.

Love can also play a role in the redemption for an immoral past. In "Gunfighter R.I.P.," a 1966 *Gunsmoke* episode, Joe Bascome (Darren McGavin) defends a Chinese man, Ching Fa (H.T. Tsiang), against three racists who are beating him up. One of the racists challenges Bascome, who kills him and his two friends, but not before Ching Fa dies and Bascome is wounded severely in the shoulder and the leg. Ching Fa's daughter, Ching Lee (France Nuyen), is so grateful to Bascome for fighting for her father, she takes him to her home where she does laundry and rides to Dodge to get Doc Adams (Milburn Stone). Doc gives Ching Lee instructions to keep Bascome in bed, but he proves to be a difficult patient.

After Doc leaves, brothers Mark (Stefan Gierasch) and Paul Douglas (Michael Conrad) come to see Bascome. They have hired Bascome to kill Matt Dillon (James Arness) and want to know what Bascome is going to do now that he is injured. Bascome convinces them he can do the job once he is fully recovered. During Bascome's slow recuperation, he and Ching Lee grow close. When he is fully recovered, the Douglas brothers tell Bascome he has to go to Dodge the next day, or the deal is off. Bascome agrees, accepting $500 with $500 more to be paid after he has killed Dillon. When Ching Lee tells Bascome not to go and that she loves him, Bascome laughs and says he didn't face the three racists to save her father and that he stayed with her because it was convenient. He leaves Ching Lee distraught and crying.

But Bascome leaves a letter for Ching Lee explaining why he is going to Dodge. Ching Lee goes to Dodge to give the two brothers their down payment back so Bascome doesn't have to do the job, but they hit her and refuse to call off the deal. When Bascome hears about the brothers hurting Ching Lee, he angrily confronts them, hitting Paul with a bottle and telling them the deal is off. Later the brothers break in on Ching Lee and Bascome at gunpoint, telling them that either Bascome kills Dillon or they will kill

Ching Lee. When Dillon's stage comes in, Bascome challenges Dillon, but before they can fire at each other, Ching Lee jumps through the window of the second-floor room where she is being held in order to stop Bascome from killing Dillon. As she tumbles to the ground, Dillon and Bascome turn around and kill the brothers, who were about to shoot them. Ching Lee is badly hurt, and Bascome decides to put up his guns to help her recover.

True to the realistic nature of *Gunsmoke*, one of the less sentimental television Westerns, it is not clear how successful Bascome's reformation and his relationship with Ching Lee will be. In one scene when Ching Lee tries to convince Bascome to give up his work as a paid killer and live with her, he tells her that doing that wouldn't work since there will always be someone who wants to confront Bascome because of his past and Bascome doesn't know any other vocation. However, for the time being, Bascome's devotion to the injured Ching Lee is believable.

Redemption of a different kind of outlaw occurs in the 1975 *Gunsmoke* episode, "The Squaw." Charley Dent (Tom Reese) and three outlaws try to kill Gristy Calhoun (John Saxon), even though Calhoun has helped them rob a stage. Calhoun turns the tables on them and at gunpoint leaves the four outlaws without their horses as he rides away with the loot. Gristy has very little water and has to ride through the desert to avoid the law and his former partners-in-crime. Festus Haggen (Ken Curtis) and Matt Dillon (James Arness) capture one of the outlaws, and Matt continues on the trail of the gang as Festus takes the captured outlaw back to Dodge.

Calhoun's horse dies of thirst while the three outlaws gather their horses and go after him. Calhoun is surprised by Comanches, who offer to give him water, a horse and a woman, Quanah (Arlene Martel), in exchange for some of his money so they can buy tobacco and other things they want. Calhoun is amenable to the trade, but doesn't want Quanah. The Comanches insist that he take her since she is considered "bad medicine" because they hold her responsible for her two husbands dying (she isn't). Calhoun verbally abuses Quanah, insisting that she always stay behind him as they travel together, and tries to abandon her, giving her a horse and water, but she clings to him. He reluctantly agrees to let her go with him, although he doesn't "trust Injuns."

Dillon captures Calhoun, whose gun has been taken by Quanah to keep him from killing or being killed. She explains to Calhoun that she wanted to stay with him since the Comanches would kill her, not only because she was "bad medicine," but also because her mother was a Cherokee and she wasn't Comanche. Her mother had been ostracized from her tribe for having given birth to Quanah; and until Quanah was 12, when she was traded to the Comanches by some buffalo hunters her mother had reluctantly joined, she and her mother made their way the best they could away from other Indians. Until she married a Comanche, Quanah was treated as a slave by the Comanches. Her sad story prompts Calhoun to tell her they are both losers. Despite his treatment of her, Quanah develops empathy for Calhoun, telling Dillon that Calhoun's bravado is an attempt to cover up his fear. When Calhoun tries to convince her to help him escape with the money, she refuses, responding that the money will not change him and that only people can change people.

Dent and his two outlaw companions find Dillon, Quanah and Calhoun. As they run from the bandits, Calhoun rescues Quanah when her horse stumbles. By the time they reach a cabin, the outlaws have deprived them of water. Dent yells down to Dillon, Quanah, and Calhoun in the cabin that he will give them a horse and water if they give him the loot. Dillon refuses, despite Calhoun and Quanah trying to convince him to take the offer. A discouraged Calhoun tells Quanah that losers are always losers, but she tells him that a man can be what he wants to be. Calhoun relates how his overbearing father robbed him of "spine and spirit" and how he hated his father for treating his mother badly. Even after his father died, he felt he had to prove himself to him, which is the reason why the money was so important to him. Quanah tells Calhoun she will wait for him as long as necessary even if he is locked up.

The outlaws spook the horses, and Dillon is trapped under one of them when he tries to calm them. Calhoun goes out to help Dillon and kills Dent. Quanah tells the two outlaws who are left that she will give them the money for two horses and the water. The two outlaws ride away with the money. Calhoun tells Quanah, "No need to stay behind me. A woman's a woman. I learned that the hard way, like everything else." He now realizes that with the love of Quanah, he is no longer a loser. Dillon, apparently believing that Calhoun has reformed, wishes Quanah and Calhoun luck and chases the two outlaws.

In the Anthony Mann film *Bend of the River* (1952), James Stewart plays a former outlaw and border raider, Glyn McLyntock, who is trying to run away from his past. His attempt to escape his past is symbolized by the bandanna he hangs around his neck to hide rope burn scars (an attempt was made to lynch him for one of his crimes). To redeem himself, he guides a wagon train carrying settlers who want to homestead on the Oregon frontier. In several violent confrontations with enemies of the wagon train, McLyntock comes dangerously close to reverting to his savage ways but resists, only killing when he has to kill. He saves the wagon train by killing Emerson Cole (Arthur Kennedy), another former border raider and criminal who, unlike Glyn, is not interested in redemption. Glyn's allegiance to the settlers has saved him from himself.

The importance of Emerson Cole (played well by Arthur Kennedy), who helps the wagon train until he is tempted to betray it, to the development of both the plot and the growth of Glyn McLyntock (played equally well by Stewart) is emphasized by Jeanne Basinger (2007, p. 90):

> The link between the hero and the villain is specifically acknowledged through the dialogue. As the two men ride side by side, Kennedy observes to Stewart (whose character name is Glyn McClintock *sic*): "McClintock [*sic*] of the border. A rancher. I don't get it. What are you running from?" Stewart: "A man named Glyn McClintock" [*sic*]. Kennedy: "What happens when he catches up with you?" Stewart: "He died on the Missouri border." Kennedy: "No. He'll catch up with you one day." The irony is that he has, of course, already caught up with him, in the form of Kennedy.

Basinger explains that this sets up the final confrontation:

> Ultimately, Stewart frees himself of his "other self." He fights and destroys Kennedy in a conflict which takes place in water and light, two purifying elements. The two men struggle inside a supply wagon, and then fall outward in a violent movement into the rushing river. After a prolonged fight in the water underneath the bright sunlight of the day, Stewart emerges triumphant as Kennedy's body is borne off downstream. The evil self is washed away in a violent purification rite [p. 90].

McLyntock has shown the courage to face his evil self and triumph over it.

Sometimes individuals need to redeem themselves for past failures or losses. A recurring theme in Westerns is the alcoholic, often someone in a position of authority (e.g., a sheriff, doctor or lawyer), whose disease has robbed him of his self-respect and the respect of the community and thus needs to stop drinking in order to redeem himself. *The Rifleman's* Micah Torrance is one example of this theme. Another especially insightful example can be found in a 1957 episode of *Cheyenne*, "Deadline." It begins with Cheyenne (Clint Walker) helping his good friend, reformed alcoholic Charley Dolan (John Qualen), with his homestead. When Charley is evicted by the unscrupulous Len Garth (Bruce Cowling), Cheyenne implies that it is because Charley foolishly signed his homestead away while on a bender. An incensed Charley shows Cheyenne his "conscience bottle," a full bottle sealed with a government stamp that is proof that Charley hasn't taken a drop of alcohol in three years, ever since someone picked him up from the gutter after a drunken binge and helped him get back on his feet. Charley explains that alcoholism is something that the alcoholic has to face every day, something Charley has done by staring down the "conscience bottle" on a daily basis.

When Cheyenne goes to town, he befriends a young drunkard, Boyd Copeland (Mark Roberts). Boyd's uncle John is killed and his newspaper office burned down by Garth because he was attacking Garth in his newspaper. This prompts Boyd to take up his uncle's crusade against the power-hungry Garth, but he needs money to buy new equipment. Charley gives Boyd $2000, trying to help Boyd the way he was helped three years ago, explaining to Cheyenne, "Whiskey's made us [Charley and Boyd] brothers." Charley, Cheyenne, and Boyd take a wagon trip to the railhead to pick up the newspaper equipment. When they are camped out, Cheyenne stops Boyd from taking a drink, and Cheyenne tells Charley that Boyd is nothing but a drunk. Charley responds that only an alcoholic like Charley knows what it means to be a drunk and that alcoholism is a battle that Cheyenne never had to face. A chastened Cheyenne goes to talk to Boyd, who explains that he drinks because he is a physical coward. Cheyenne asks who's to say what courage is and adds that it took a special kind of courage for Boyd to admit he's a coward.

During the trip home after picking up the equipment, Fred Murkle (John Truax), who has been traveling with the wagon but secretly working for Garth, entices Boyd to drink after he has surreptitiously greased the brakes on the wagon. When the runaway wagon won't stop because of the greased brakes, it overturns on Charley, who with his dying words tells Cheyenne not to blame Boyd for the accident but to help him. Cheyenne loses his temper when he smells liquor on Boyd's breath and slaps him, claiming that Boyd's professed cowardice is just an excuse for drinking and implying that Boyd is responsible for the accident. When they get to town, Cheyenne finds out the accident occurred because the brakes were greased by Murkle and tells Boyd it wasn't his fault. Garth comes after Boyd when he uses his new newspaper press to attack Garth with the help of the testimony of a witness who reveals Garth's criminal activities. Boyd and Cheyenne go out to face Garth, who wounds Boyd, but is killed by Cheyenne. Boyd has redeemed himself by facing down Garth and his alcoholism.

The 1973 *Gunsmoke* episode "Lynch Town" provides another example of alcoholics who need some help. In Kingsville, a derelict, thief and child beater, Jake Fielder (Ken Swofford), is falsely accused of killing a woman, Kate Geer (Nancy Jeris). Jake finds her apparently drunk and she falls and hits her head on a doorstep. The accident kills her, and Jake takes the opportunity to steal from her safe. Sheriff Ridder (Warren J. Kammerling) asks Judge Warfield (David Wayne), a drunk, and Matt Dillon (James Arness) to come to Kingsville to prevent Jake's lynching. But before they can get there, the townspeople kick the sheriff out of town and lynch Jake.

Dillon asks for an inquest into the death of Kate to determine Jake's role in her death. The town boss, appropriately named John King (Scott Brady), tells Judge Warfield, used to taking the orders of bosses like King, to make sure the inquest finds Fielder guilty as a way of exonerating the lynch mob members, or King will force him to retire.

King also forces the judge to room with Fielder's tattered and dirty son, Rob (Mitch Vogel), to keep the boy from disrupting the "judicial" process. As he gets to know Rob, the judge begins to appreciate the intelligence of the self-taught boy. At the inquest, Minnie Nolan (Julie Cobb) and the sheriff say that Kate never drank and Jake had previously threatened Kate. But Dillon testifies that he found a broken liquor bottle at the scene of the crime. The judge is about to close the inquest and declare Jake guilty when Dillon asks bartender Tom Hart (Norman Alden) to testify. To keep Hart from testifying, King gets the judge to call a recess.

Afterwards, Rob tells the judge he is kind and trustworthy, the kind of person people like, something that moves the judge deeply. When Rob is on the witness stand the next day, the judge gets him to realize that Jake stole and even beat Rob for what Jake thought were Rob's best interests, resulting in Rob realizing how much his father loved him. On the witness stand, the bartender is forced to admit that the night of Kate's death, King and Kate argued over the receipts of the saloon, which King secretly owned along with Kate, and that in the ensuing argument Kate fell and hit her head. However, King claims that Kate was still alive when he and the bartender left. Dillon surmises that Kate could have fallen later due to her injury when Fielder was there. The judge rules that Kate died of causes unknown, exonerating Jake. The judge accuses King of corrupting the judicial process and admits his role in that corruption. With that act of courage, Warfield has ended his career as a judge but decides to go back to practice law with Rob, who apparently will keep him sober as his clerk.

In the 1959 film *Rio Bravo*, Dude (Dean Martin) has fallen on hard times because of his alcoholism. When Dude, who is known for his prowess with a gun, aids Sheriff John T. Chance (John Wayne) in the apprehension of Joe Burdette (Claude Akins), Chance decides to give Dude an opportunity to redeem himself by deputizing him. Chance needs help guarding Joe until a U.S. marshal can come and take him to the Presidio. However, Joe's powerful brother, Nathan (John Russell), and his henchmen plan to free Joe. Dude manages to stay sober long enough to help Chance, Stumpy

(Walter Brennan) and Colorado Ryan (Ricky Nelson) overcome Burdette and his gang so the U.S. Marshal can take Joe away.

In a 1960 episode of *Wagon Train*, "The Colter Craven Story," directed by John Ford, it is an alcoholic doctor who needs to be redeemed. Dr. Craven's (Carleton Young) memories of his inability to save scores of soldiers during the Civil War have driven him to the bottle. During a trip that Craven is taking on the wagon train of Seth Adams (Ward Bond), a woman about to have a baby needs a Caesarean. Craven thinks he is too shaky due to his Civil War memories and alcoholism to perform the operation. To give Craven the courage to do it, Seth relates to him the story of someone he knew back in Illinois, Ulysses Grant, who overcame his drinking problem and led the Union to victory. Grant's story encourages Craven enough to successfully perform the operation.

A similar plot characterizes "The Journal of Death," a 1970 episode of *The High Chaparral*. Marshal Garnett (Morgan Woodward) brings a prisoner, Dr. Matthew Kendall (John Colicos), to the ranch of John Cannon (Leif Erickson). Garnett accuses Kendall of drunkenly butchering Union prisoners while operating on them at a Confederate prisoner of war camp, something that Garnett witnessed himself. When Kendall tries to escape, Victoria Cannon (Linda Cristal) is accidentally injured. Her only hope is if Kendall operates. Kendall agrees to help, but only if Cannon allows him to escape. Cannon agrees to those terms over Garnett's objections.

When it is time to begin the operation, Kendall hesitates out of fear, but he continues with Cannon's encouragement, and the operation is a success. Afterwards, Kendall admits to Cannon that he operated in the prisoner of war camp under horrendous conditions and inadequate resources. He was drunk to be able to give him the strength to continue under such circumstances and forget the results of his operations. He swore that after the war was over, he would never again be responsible for another human being. Cannon tells Kendall he is holding up his end of the bargain, giving Kendall his best horse, supplies, $500 and a two day start on Garnett, whom Cannon has held prisoner. When Garnett protests, Kendall tells him how much he suffered when he couldn't save the men he operated on in the Civil War. Because of Kendall's revelations and Victoria's recovery, Garnett decides not to pursue Kendall any longer. Kendall tells John that what happened in the Civil War is now in the past. He just wants to be alone and find himself. John assures him that he can.

The Searchers (1956) begins in Texas in 1868 with the return of Ethan Edwards (John Wayne) to visit his brother Aaron (Walter Coy), Aaron's wife Martha (Dorothy Jordan) and their children Lucy (Pippa Scott), Debbie

(Lana Wood) and Ben (Robert Lyden) and to give Debbie one of his war medals. Martin Pawley (Jeffrey Hunter), who lives at the Edwards household, arrives there soon after to the dismay of the Indian-hating Ethan (Martin is one-eighth Cherokee). Consequently, Ethan dismisses the fact that he found Martin as a baby after his folks had been massacred and that he was raised by Aaron's family. Aaron tells Ethan that many neighbors are leaving the area (apparently because of the Indian threat) and that before the Civil War, Ethan wanted to leave but didn't. Ethan gives Aaron 180 "Yankee dollars" that Aaron says are freshly minted, the implication being that they were stolen.

The Reverend Samuel Johnson Clayton (Ward Bond), aka Captain Clayton of the Texas Rangers, visits the Edwards homestead with Lars Jorgensen (John Qualen), whose cows were stolen. Clayton swears Martin into the Rangers to help chase down the thieves, but Ethan convinces Aaron to stay home to protect his family instead of leaving with the Rangers. Ethan himself volunteers to go with the Rangers but refuses to take the oath since he took an oath to the Confederacy and he only takes one oath at a time, apparently never surrendering after the war was over. The Rangers find one of Jorgensen's cows killed by Comanches. Ethan surmises that stealing the cows was a tactic to divert the Rangers while the Comanches attacked one of the homesteads. Ethan and Martin rush back to the Edwards homestead to find it burning, Martha, Aaron and Ben dead, and Lucy and Debbie missing. Clayton, Ethan, Brad Jorgensen (Harry Carey, Jr.), the son of Lars and boyfriend of Lucy, and Martin go after Lucy and Debbie with a group of Rangers. As they leave, Mrs. Jorgensen (Olive Carey) begs Ethan not to let Martin and Brad seek vengeance on the Comanches. On the trail of the Comanches, the Rangers find a Comanche buried in a shallow grave. They dig him up and Ethan shoots him in the eyes to keep him from ascending to the "Spirit Land" and thus condemn his soul to wander for eternity, according to Comanche beliefs.

The Ranger party eventually finds the Comanche camp. Ethan wants to directly attack, despite the danger to Lucy and Debbie if they are there, but Clayton insists on stealing their pony herd to make the Comanches more amenable to trading for the girls. Clayton wins the argument, but the Comanches escape before they can be engaged. As the Rangers ride away, they are surrounded by the Comanches but successfully beat off an attack. This is a baptism of fire for Martin, who fights despite his fear. When Clayton stops Ethan from needlessly firing at a retreating Comanche, Ethan, sick of Clayton bossing him around, leaves the Rangers, defiantly shooting across the river at the Comanches as he leaves. Ethan wants to look for Lucy and Debbie alone, but Brad and Martin insist on going along. Ethan consents, but only if they obey his orders.

Ethan goes off scouting by himself and comes back shaken and uncommunicative. Brad and Martin force Ethan to tell them that he is upset because he found Lucy dead and refuses to say what she looked like when he found her. An unhinged Brad rides off to attack the Comanches in a wild charge and is killed. Ethan promises Martin that they will find Debbie as sure as the "turnin' of the earth." After they lose the trail of the Comanches, Ethan and Martin go back to the Jorgensens, who already know about Brad's death. Laurie Jorgensen (Vera Miles), who is attracted to Martin, greets him enthusiastically. Ethan tells Martin that he wants to go on alone looking for Debbie, and that Martin could stay and work for the Jorgensens, who are partners with Ethan in the cattle business. To make sure he goes alone, Ethan leaves very early, before Martin wakes up, but Martin goes after him to stop him from hurting Debbie out of an irrational hatred for the Comanches, even though he has declared to Laurie that he wants to develop a serious relationship with her.

Ethan and Martin go to the trading post of Jerem Futterman (Peter Mamakos), who shows them Debbie's dress and wants money for more information about how he got it. When Ethan pays him, Futterman tells him that the dress belonged to a captive of Chief Scar (Henry Brandon), who was headed to Fort Wingate to get agency beef. When Ethan and Martin are camped out, Ethan uses Martin as bait to attract somebody lurking about. Futterman and two of his men attack the camp, but a hidden Ethan kills them. Martin is upset that Ethan used him as bait, but they move on. In a letter to Laurie, Martin tells her that he accidentally bought an Indian "bride," Look, and cannot leave her without provoking the Indians. When Ethan asks his "bride" where Scar is, she runs away frightened.

In the winter, Ethan and Martin come upon a buffalo herd and a crazed Ethan kills as many of them as he can to prevent the Comanches from eating them. Afterwards they find the camp of the Comanche group that has held Debbie destroyed by the army with dead Comanches, including Martin's "bride," all around. Ethan and Martin ask the army's commanders if they know about any white women recaptured from the Comanches by the army. None of the frightened and crazed women Ethan and Martin are shown are Debbie. Ethan claims that they are no longer white but are Comanche.

In a cantina, Old Mose (Hank Worden) tells Ethan and Martin that Emilio Gabriel Fernandez y Figueroa (Antonio Moreno) knows something about Scar's whereabouts. Emilio agrees to take Martin and Ethan along with his vaqueros to Scar's camp. When they get there, Ethan, Martin, Emilio and Scar go into Scar's tepee where Ethan wants to negotiate Debbie's release, but before they can begin to talk about Debbie, they see her there. Ethan leaves and tells Scar he will see him the next day. Emilio tells Ethan that Scar knows why Ethan is there. Ethan tells Martin that this means that Scar means to kill them. Debbie comes to the camp of Martin and Ethan and tells Martin that the Comanches are her people now and to let her be. Ethan pulls out his gun as though he is going to kill Debbie, but Martin stands in front of her. A Comanche shoots Ethan with an arrow and Comanches led by Scar chase Martin and Ethan into a cave, where they defend themselves. Ethan, badly wounded, makes out his will, which would give his property to Martin. Instead of being grateful, Martin is angry that Debbie is not in his will because it implies Ethan doesn't consider Debbie kinfolk any more, but a Comanche.

Ethan and Martin go back to the Jorgensens just as an impatient Laurie, after five years of waiting, is about to marry Charlie McCrory (Ken Curtis). When Laurie and Martin are alone, Laurie softens towards him when Martin tells her he loves her. This precipitates a farcical fight between McCrory and Martin, which results in a cancellation of the Laurie-Charlie nuptials. Old Mose, who has been captured and beaten up by Scar, is brought to the Jorgensens by soldiers. Old Mose tells the wedding party, which includes Clayton and his Rangers, where Scar is located. Clayton, the Rangers, Martin and Ethan prepare to go and attack Scar's camp. Laurie tries to dissuade Martin from going because Debbie is now an Indian and Martin will be killed by Scar. Martin, who still considers Debbie his sister, insists on going.

When the Rangers reach Scar's camp, Clayton agrees to let Martin go in before the attack to locate Debbie. When Martin finds Debbie, she agrees to go with him, but Martin has to kill Scar as he enters their tepee. At the same time, the Ranger company attacks the Comanche camp and Ethan takes Scar's scalp. Ethan chases after Debbie and Martin, who tries to stop him before he can kill Debbie. However, instead of killing her, Ethan gently picks her up and brings her back to the Jorgensens. As the Jorgensens, Debbie, Martin and Laurie go into the house, Ethan goes off by himself, apparently doomed to roam, just like the dead Comanche whose eyes he shot.

Up to the end of the film, Ethan has shown every indication of possibly wanting to harm Debbie. Ethan wants to search for Debbie by himself without the help or influence of anyone else, possibly because of his extreme independence, possibly because he doesn't want anyone around when he exacts his revenge on Scar, the Comanches and perhaps Debbie. His hatred for the Comanches is so excessive that he irrationally tries to kill an entire buffalo herd to deprive the Comanches of food. He shoots at Comanches running away. He shoots the eyes of a dead Comanche to keep him from going to the Spirit Land. He scalps the dead Scar. He leaves Debbie, his only living blood relation, out of his will. At the very end of the film, he pushes aside Martin as he rushes towards her with a crazed look in his eye. The question remains, why does he lovingly take Debbie up in his arms when, up to that point, he has no signs that he will do so? Indick (2008, pp. 170–71) explains it this way:

> Ethan's final acceptance of Debbie as a white woman is linked to his acceptance of Martin as a white man.... In doing so he has accepted him as a full-fledged family member—not just as an adoptive nephew, but as his son and heir. In doing so, he has softened.

This explanation is not totally convincing. After all, Martin was raised by white people. His parents were killed by Indians, and he's only one-eighth Cherokee, one of the "civilized" tribes. However, Indick goes on to give another reason:

> [I]n scalping Scar, Ethan has fulfilled his vengeance quest and satiated his bloodlust. Having exorcised his psychological demons, he no longer needs to shed the blood of his niece. Having killed her captor and corrupter, having exorcised his psychological demons, he no longer needs to shed the blood of his niece.... We can understand Ethan's change of heart as a natural development of his journey, a transformative passage through the wilderness that softened his hatred and rekindled the desperate need for personal connections that brought him back to his brother's homestead in the first place.

Bandy and Stoehr (2012, p. 197) provide another explanation for Ethan's behavior when opposing an enemy like Scar, who, according to Indick (2008) is a fierce racist and savage warrior:

> We witness Ethan's fury unleashed, but it is this type of anger that drives him continuously toward his goal of finding Debbie and killing Scar. It is also the kind of passion and determination, no matter how excessive it may become, that was sometimes required in eliminating a threat from a savage land and in clearing a way for the arrival of civilization. In conquering a wilderness and building a nation, the power of ideals is inherently limited, even fragile, given the resistance of reality.

In other words, Ethan's savagery is a means to the end of survival. The fundamental problem with Ethan is that he, unlike Clayton, has lost the distinction between brutal means and the end of survival to which it is directed, because he has no connections, now that Martha is dead, to the community or anyone in it. As a result, he becomes not only vengeful, but unhinged. In this respect he is like Tom Dunson in *Red River* (see Chapter

The searchers. In foreground (from left to right) Harry Carey, Jr., as Brad Jorgensen, Jeffrey Hunter as Martin Pawley and John Wayne as Ethan Edwards show their determination in their quest to find the captive girls in John Ford's *The Searchers* (1956, Warner Brothers).

6) and unlike Hunter Boyd in *From Hell to Texas* (see Chapter 4), whose vengeance, although misguided, is at least tempered by his "queer sense of justice" and ultimately the life of a surviving son. According to Indick, it's the killing (albeit not by Ethan) and Ethan's scalping of Scar that allows him to exorcise his demons. That's certainly a part of it, but it is also the case that it's the physical connection with Debbie that allows him to regain his understanding that his savagery is only a means to keep alive those personal connections. Love has redeemed Ethan just as it does Howard Kemp in *The Naked Spur* (See Chapter 3). Bandy and Stoehr (2012, pp. 197–98) explain Ethan's redemption this way:

> After his Comanche enemies have been eliminated, Ethan brings Debbie home; he does not, as Martin fears, kill her. It is as if the physical act of picking up Debbie in his arms once again, as he did during his homecoming when she was a little girl, is enough to convince Ethan that he has been wrong in wanting "Debbie" (i.e., her defiled body) dead. According to such an interpretation, this is a moral awakening triggered by a nostalgic remembrance that is in turn occasioned by the physical embrace of a specific individual. Ideologies and stereotypes do not matter here as much as direct

human contact and the value of a unique person, especially if she is the daughter of a loved one. And Ethan and Marty are, at the end of their long journey, reconciled.

If Scar appears more savage than Ethan, it is because his people are the losers in the conflict and Ethan's people are the winners. Although Ethan loses loved ones in the conflict, he knows that eventually his community and some of his loved ones will not only survive, but flourish, whereas Scar's community and loved ones will continue to be devastated.

There is an issue that John Ford skirts or sugarcoats: the problematic reception that Debbie will receive when she returns to the white community. At the end, Debbie is welcomed into the Jorgensen household by Lars (interestingly, the Swedish-born Lars would not have been exposed to the racism of the American frontier when he was growing up) and the warm and empathic Mrs. Jorgensen. However, Ford does indicate at times that virulent white racism is not confined to Ethan. The most glaring example of this is the massacre, reminiscent of Sand Creek, that takes the lives of Look and other innocent Indians. However, you don't have to look past the Jorgensen household to see what Debbie will face when she returns home in this rather chilling exchange between Laurie and Martin:

LAURIE: Marty ... You're not going. Not this time.

MARTIN (staring): You crazy?

LAURIE: It's too late.... She's a woman grown now...

MARTIN : I got to go. I got to fetch her home.

LAURIE : Fetch *what* home? ... The leavin's of Comanche bucks—sold time an' again to the highest bidder? ... With savage brats of her own, most like?...

MARTIN (shouting it): *Laurie!* Shut your mouth!

LAURIE : Do you know what Ethan will do if he has a chance? ... He'll put a bullet in her brain! And I tell you Martha would want him to!

MARTIN: Only if I'm dead!

He strides out past her.

It's possible that Laurie, desperate to keep Martin from leaving, doesn't mean what she says or doesn't know what she is talking about (the idea that Martha would want Ethan to kill her own child is especially disturbing). But it's likely others would mean it and believe it, whether she was "defiled" or not, which would greatly reduce her prospects for marriage or even friendship in the white community. Debbie's position in the community would be like that of the "half-breed" depicted in so many

Westerns, somebody who doesn't fit in the Indian *or* the white world. Perhaps that is why she is initially reluctant to go back with Ethan and Martin. (As mentioned above, Martin is only one-eighth Cherokee, a "civilized tribe," who has suffered the loss of his parents and hasn't been "defiled" by any physical contact with the Comanches.)

Redemption also plays a part at the societal level in television and film Westerns. Although John Lenihan (1980) agrees that the films of the late 1960s and 1970s have a more jaundiced view of society than earlier films, he states that the idea that politicians, businessmen, law enforcement, the army and society in general can be cowardly, corrupt and/or racist goes back well before the late 1960s in both films and television. The disreputable passengers in the film *Stagecoach* (1939)—the drunken doctor, the prostitute and outlaw—prove to be more honorable than the town which has rejected them and the banker traveling with them. Tom Jeffords (James Stewart) has to contend with racist townspeople in trying to broker peace between Cochise (Jeff Chandler) and the white population in *Broken Arrow* (1950). Will Kane (Gary Cooper) famously throws his marshal's badge in the dirt in *High Noon* (1952) when the cowardly, greedy and corrupt townspeople refuse to help him against the Miller gang.

These moral failings mean that cowardly, corrupt and/or racist townspeople have a chance to redeem themselves after they prove themselves unworthy, although it often involves a brave man or two setting an example before the townspeople can redeem themselves. In the *Maverick* episode "Day of Reckoning," the townspeople refuse to stand up to the trail boss and his trail hands who have killed an innocent printer and threaten to tear the town apart unless the townspeople give up a cowardly newspaper publisher who has offended the cowboys. However, goaded and led by the self-professed "coward" Bret Maverick, the townspeople and cowardly newspaper publisher face down the badmen.

Similarly, in the 1961 *Rifleman* episode "The Long Gun from Tucson," John Tolliver (Peter Whitney) and three members of his gang plan to go to North Fork to exact revenge on the townspeople. Five years earlier, professional killer Holliver provoked a 19-year-old boy, whom he had been paid to kill, into a gunfight which ended in the boy's death. The townspeople couldn't arrest Holliver for the killing since technically it was self-defense. However, since Holliver was alone and there were many of them, the townspeople were able to ride him out of town on a rail, humiliating him in the process. When Tolliver returns with his gang, most of the townspeople and the marshal, Micah Torrance, are at an out-of-town celebration, leaving the town vulnerable to Holliver and his gang. Gunsmith

Henry Waller (Whit Bissell) recognizes Holliver when he and his cohorts ride into town. Henry, Nils Swenson (Joe Higgins), Eddie Halstead (John Harmon) and Lucas McCain (Chuck Connors), acting as deputy marshal in Micah's absence, unite to face Holliver and his gang. However, when Holliver tells Lucas that he would be satisfied to face only one person, Henry cites poor health, and Nils and Eddie back down from helping Lucas since the three men claim it is Lucas' responsibility as deputy marshal to face the Holliver gang alone. The next morning, Lucas goes out alone to face Holliver and his gunmen. But before any of them can draw a gun, Henry, then Eddie and Nils, join Lucas in the street. In the ensuing gunfight, Holliver and his cohorts are killed. Henry, Eddie and Nils have redeemed themselves after refusing to help Lucas.

Another example is the 1960 *Laramie* episode "Hour After Dawn." Four bandits ride into Laramie to rob the bank but are stopped by the townspeople. Three get away, but Billy Pardee (Ben Johnson) is shot off his horse and jailed after killing a deputy. Sheriff Mort Corey (Robert Osterloh) becomes nervous when he finds out that Pardee is the half-brother of Con Creighton (Bruce Bennett), the head of a large gang. Mort is wounded when helping to stop an attempt to rescue Pardee from jail. As a result, he deputizes Slim Sherman (John Smith) and Jess Harper (Robert Fuller).

Tough-looking men, apparently members of Creighton's gang, stream into town. Judge Oliver (S. John Launer) comes to town and tries, convicts and sentences Pardee to hang the next morning for the deputy's murder. After the judge leaves, Creighton's men seal off the town. That evening, egged on by his wife, Corey lets Sherman and Harper know that he will not help them the next morning. Two leading citizens try to convince Slim and Jess to take Pardee out of town and hang him in a foolhardy attempt to keep Creighton and his men from attacking the next morning.

Sherman and Harper refuse to perform this violation of due process of law. It becomes obvious to Sherman and Harper that the two of them and a deputy, Tooey (Irving Bacon), are the only ones who will face the Creighton gang. Creighton and his gang walk down the street, ready to attack the next morning as Pardee is being led to the gallows. However, Corey and a large number of townspeople, including the two townspeople who came to see Harper and Sherman the night before, redeem themselves by backing up Sherman and Harper. In the ensuing gunfight, Creighton and Pardee are killed and the gang members defeated. Corey decides to stay as sheriff, going against his wife's wishes.

A town's road to redemption is often not a straight one. In a 1963 episode of *The Virginian*, "Siege," Trampas (Doug McClure) travels to Logan, New Mexico, to pay off his debts and confront Duke Logan (Philip Carey), who ran him out of town because he was interested in Duke's sister, Carol (Elinor Donohue); Duke didn't think Trampas was good enough for her. When he checks into a hotel run by Charley Sanchez (Nestor Paiva), he has a confrontation with Pablo Lopez (Joseph Campanella), leader of the Comancheros staying in town. Duke and Marshal Brett Cole (Ron Hayes) visit Trampas in his hotel room to tell him to leave town. Trampas says he wants first to see Carole, but Brett tells Trampas that she is married to him. His hopes of reconciliation with Carole dashed, Trampas decides to leave town but wants to visit some friends, Fred and Sarah Hall, on his way to Shiloh. He finds the Halls dead and their place ransacked. He follows the tracks leading from the Halls' place to a campsite with three Comancheros, who have four of the Halls' horses. Trampas confronts them and in the ensuing gunfight kills one and takes the other two back to Logan to stand trial for the murder of the Halls.

The marshal only reluctantly locks up the two Comancheros due to the power the outlaw band has over the town. Brett tells Trampas he has no authority to hold the Comancheros since his jurisdiction extends only to the town limits and the Halls were killed out of town. He can hold them only until the county sheriff comes to Logan in two weeks to take them to trial, and only then if Trampas signs a complaint and waits around until the trial to testify against them. At this point, Duke steps in and tries to convince Trampas to drop his charges. The Comancheros spend a great deal of money locally and have previously reached an agreement with the townspeople not to cause trouble in town. Duke is afraid that if the two Comancheros go on trial, the rest of them will cause trouble. Trampas will not back down.

Lopez comes to town to get his two men freed, telling Duke and Brett that he will punish the two men if they have done anything wrong. Brett refuses, and Lopez menacingly tells the marshal he will come back the next day. Duke, afraid of what will happen, tries to bribe Trampas to leave. Trampas refuses. Duke and Carole try to persuade Brett to release the two Comancheros, but he refuses, even when Carole threatens to leave him if he doesn't. Brett explains to her that he cannot live with himself knowing what both he and Carole will think of him if he lets the Comancheros go. Afterwards, the townspeople let Trampas and Brett know they won't get involved in a confrontation with the Comancheros.

The next day, a large group of Comancheros ride into town. Duke tells Brett that the town council has fired him, and Duke releases the prisoners.

Trampas decides to leave, now that he sees his efforts to see justice done are in vain. Carole goes to see Brett and apologizes for not backing him. Wanting revenge on Trampas, Lopez tells the townspeople to stay in their homes as Lopez apparently plans to kill Trampas. Brett goes to Trampas' hotel room to tell him he will help Trampas, but Trampas turns down his offer. As Trampas walks to the livery stable to get his horse to leave town, many Comancheros appear in the street, and they begin to fire on Trampas. First Brett, and then Duke and the rest of the townspeople begin shooting at the Comancheros and subdue them. Trampas goes back to Shiloh knowing that the townspeople have, if belatedly, redeemed themselves.

However, redemption cannot entirely wipe out the past. In 1956's *The Fastest Gun Alive*, George Kelby will never entirely get over the fact that he didn't go after the man who killed his father. In the *Maverick* episode "The Day of Reckoning," George Buckner can never forget that he stood by while his newspaper employee was beaten to death. Even though Ethan in *The Searchers* redeems himself by saving Debbie, he knows that he can never overcome his past and is doomed to be a lonely wanderer. To his dismay, Clay Culhane, in "A Threat of Violence," is forced to use his gun again despite his desire to hang it up now that he is a lawyer. In the film *The Naked Spur* (1953), Howie Kemp will never completely get over losing his ranch and his wife (see Chapter 3).

The consequences of redemption are shown clearly in the Westerns of Anthony Mann. As Jim Kitses points out, the Mann heroes often have to kill their friends or family members before they can be fully redeemed. In *Bend of the River*, before the former Missouri border raider Glyn McLyntock (James Stewart) can redeem himself, he has to kill his former ally and Missouri border raider Cole Emerson (Arthur Kennedy), whom he hoped would join him in leaving his criminal past behind. In *Man of the West*, Link Jones (Gary Cooper) has to kill his stepfather, Dock Tobin (Lee J. Cobb), and stepbrother, Claude (John Dehner), before fully redeeming himself after a criminal career. What separates the hero from the villain is that the hero has a moral dimension that allows for the possibility of redemption; the villain does not. The best that the villain can do is to seek revenge, a degrading, meaningless act, but not redemption, a regenerative and insightful act. In TV Westerns, especially the early ones before the onset of the "adult" Westerns, lead characters are often so morally pure that it seems they don't need to redeem themselves. However, sometimes they show an empathy and understanding that makes it seem that they too had to seek redemption somewhere in their lives. In "Journey to San

Trapped. The congenial salesman, Sam Beasley, played by Arthur O'Connell (center), the reformed Link Jones, played by Gary Cooper (second from right), and singer Billie Ellis, played by Julie London (far right), are held captive by the outlaws (far left), Coaley (Jack Lord) and (second from left) Dock Tobin (Lee J. Cobb), in Anthony Mann's *Man of the West* (1958, United Artists).

Carlos," the extraordinarily noble Lone Ranger empathizes with Ben Murray and tells him, "Cowardice is the most complicated thing on Earth." How could he know that cowardice is complicated without having acted cowardly, or at least been tempted to act cowardly, in the past? How could he empathize with Ben Murray's internal struggles over his cowardice unless he himself had struggled the same way? In *Tension at Table Rock*, Wes Tancred's cowardice (see Chapter 7) in trying to cover up his identity allows him to empathize with Fred Miller.

The empathy of the hero also stems from the fact that in a moral sense he is similar enough to those who have transgressed to understand them. In *Laramie*'s "Night of the Quiet Men," John McCambridge is appalled by how similar he is to the criminals he has brought to justice. In *The Searchers*, Ethan Edwards' ferocity matches that of the Indian he pursues, Scar. In *Bend of the River*, Glyn McLyntock struggles to escape his connection to the villain Emerson Cole, demonstrated by McLyntock losing control of himself and almost killing a man who crosses him. In *Man of the West*, Link Jones (Gary Cooper) has to break the connections to his villainous family to redeem himself. Kitses (2004, p. 144) puts it this way:

> Mann often deceives by introducing his men as simple, uncluttered heroes, the mood slowly darkening as we notice similarities in temperament and behavior between hero and villain. Hence Link Jones…, who appears as a country bumpkin at the outset, only to emerge later as capable of the most brutal of acts, savagely beating and tearing the pants of the wolfish young Coaley. The extraordinary power of this famous scene, which culminates in Link not being quite able to strangle his beaten and humiliated opponent with his bare hands, flows again from what I have called the psychological structure in Mann's work. For in attempting to destroy the past that holds him in ransom—tangibly here, in that Coaley is created in the film as Link's successor—the hero is driven inescapably to relive it, the violence and evil that he has tried to bury forced to the surface by the situation he finds himself in.

The empathy of those who redeem themselves also extends to their victims. Preacher Jamison in *The Rifleman*'s "Day of Reckoning" episode states that he refused to shoot down an old man because in the old man, "I saw myself, and from that day forward, I … I found myself becoming a part of every person I met … feeling their hurt and their joy. If I said an unkind word, I felt the hurt of it—as though the word was spoken to me." Will Gorman in "Gift from a Gunman" says after he was shot that he had "somehow become every man I ever killed."

Chapter 3

Love, Friendship and Bonds to the Community

"Do something right, not out of hatin', but out of likin'.... I mean this town, these people."—*Posse from Hell*

Although westerns traditionally emphasize the importance of rugged individualism, the themes of honor and justice, love, friendship and bonds to a community are often powerful motivating forces. Peterson and Seligman (2004, p. 219) put the connections between courage and relationships this way:

> Entering and sustaining high-quality connections with others can be a consequence of bravery (Worline, Wrzesniewski and Rafaeli, 2002). In a medical context, Shelp (1984) suggested that a true physician-patient relationship involves bravery because doctor and patient must together negotiate disease, pain and suffering to promote healing. In a family context, Fowers (1998) suggested that bravery is required to surrender to vulnerability within marriage. Because self-disclosure and honesty go hand in hand with the potential to be hurt and rejected, bravery may help to sustain close relationships (Fowers, 1998; Prince, 1984). Way (1995, 1998) linked the daily practice of bravery with the development of authenticity in relation to others and youths' ability to enter into rewarding relationships.

According to John Cawelti (1999, p. 29), there are basically three types of individuals in the Western genre: "The townspeople or agents of civilization, the savages or outlaws who threaten this first group, and the heroes who are above all 'men in the middle,' possessing many qualities and skills of the savages but fundamentally committed to the townspeople." The action in the Western revolves around various "communities," a fort or ranch, but most likely the town. Cawelti (1999, p. 29) explains that the community of the town provides for all kinds of interactions between the three types of individuals:

> It is out of the multiple variations possible on the relationship between these groups that the various Western plots are concocted. For example, the simplest version of all has the hero protecting the townspeople from the savages, using his own savage skills against the denizens of the wilderness. A second more complex variation shows the hero initially indifferent to the plight of the townspeople and more inclined to identify with the savages. However, in the course of the story his position changes and he becomes the ally of the townspeople. This variation can generate a number of different plots. There is the revenge Western: a hero seeks revenge against the outlaws or Indians who have wronged him. In order to accomplish his vengeance, he rejects the pacifistic ideals of the townspeople, but in the end, he discovers that he is really committed to their way of life (John Ford's *The Searchers*). A related plot is that of the hero who initially seeks his own selfish material gain, using his savage skills as a means to his end; but, as the story progresses, he recognizes his moral involvement with the townspeople and becomes their champion (cf. Anthony Mann's *The Far Country*).

Sometimes the welfare of others in the community or love of another individual spurs individuals towards their courageous acts. *The Fastest Gun Alive* and *Bonanza*'s "The Last Trophy," mentioned in Chapter 2, are examples of this type of motivation.

Another example is the Anthony Mann Western *The Far Country* (1955). Jeff Webster (James Stewart) is the ultimate tough loner, asking nothing from anyone and giving nothing in return; his social isolation is apparently due to a woman who spurned and hurt him. His friend Ben (Walter Brennan) is his only connection to humanity. Jeff begins to change when he meets Renee (Corinne Calvert) who, along with Ben, acts as his conscience and prompts him to save the survivors of an avalanche. His journey back to humanity continues when, in an ambush, Ben is killed and Jeff shot in the hand. Renee shows her devotion to him by nursing him back to health, in the process helping him overcome his fear of intimacy and regain his ability to trust and love again. Jeff completes his redemption by killing the criminals who threaten the community in order to restore it to peace and harmony and as a result rejoins the community.

Sometimes the lesson that needs to be learned is that not everybody in the community has to be "good people" or as good as oneself in order to be loyal to that community. In 1961's *Posse from Hell*, four men, led by Crip (Vic Morrow), ride into Paradise, take over the saloon and shoot Marshal Isaac Webb (Ward Ramsey). Holding hostages, they intimidate the townspeople into letting them rob the bank, but not before killing four other townspeople and taking a young girl, Helen Caldwell (Zohra Lampert), as a hostage.

Soon after Banner Cole (Audie Murphy) rides into town. Marshal Webb asked him there to become his deputy; now shot and dying, Webb asks him to organize a posse and to chase the bandits, doing something right for once. The misanthropic Cole, embittered and cynical about being badly treated in his life, tries to refuse, but out of loyalty to Webb, the only man he likes, he agrees. Before he dies, Webb tells him that he should do it out of "likin'," not out of "hatin'," and that the townspeople are hurt and there are some good people in the town worth helping.

Unfortunately for Cole, the posse doesn't live up to his standards. It consists of town drunk Billy Caldwell (Royal Dano), who believes he has to join the posse only because it's his niece who was abducted; an arrogant old ex-soldier, Captain Jeremiah Brown (Robert Keith), out to prove himself; Jock Wiley (Paul Carr), fast with his gun when it comes to shooting bottles, but untested in a gunfight; Seymour Kern (John Saxon), who is going only because his banker boss insists he stay close to the stolen money; Burt Hogan (Frank Overton), who wants to avenge the death of his brother at the hands of the gang, and an Indian, Johnny Caddo (Rodolfo Acosta).

After the posse members leave town, they find Helen abandoned by the gang after apparently being sexually assaulted. Kern begins to show he might be worth more than Cole thought when he helps kill a rattlesnake threatening Helen. However, she is so distraught about being violated and fearing what people will think about her, that she tries to kill herself. She is stopped by Cole, who sends her back to Paradise with her Uncle Billy, even though she doesn't want to face the townspeople.

The posse members move on and spot four horsemen, who the posse thinks might be the gang who terrorized Paradise. They find out that the horsemen are innocent cowhands who have been attacked by the four bandits, but the impetuous Brown starts to shoot at them before they are identified as harmless and Cole has to wound Brown to stop him. After Brown leaves the posse to go back to Paradise, they go on and surround a cabin where the four bandits are holed up. After shooting erupts, Wiley freezes when confronted by a fleeing gang member and is killed, but one gang member, Chunk, is killed, and Kern proves his courage under fire. Hogan claims that he killed Chunk and, since Chunk killed his brother, that he has avenged his brother, although it was really Cole who killed Chunk and another gang member who killed Hogan's brother. Having deceived himself into thinking he has killed his brother's murderer and thus in his mind done his duty, Hogan leaves the posse.

Having newfound respect for them, Cole tells Caddo and Kern they have done enough and they can go back to Paradise, but they refuse. When

3. Love, Friendship and Bonds to the Community 53

Hiding in a cabin. Audie Murphy as Banner Cole (left) finds Zohra Lampert as the ashamed Helen Caldwell (center) and Royal Dano as the alcoholic Uncle Billy (right) hunkered down in a shack in Herbert Coleman's *Posse from Hell* (1961, Universal-International).

Cole asks Caddo, someone the other townspeople have ostracized because he is an Indian, why he joined the posse, Caddo responds that it's what a man should do. Kern tells Cole the trip has taught him to understand a whole new set of values that have convinced him to leave his status-seeking past behind. Cole admits that he has learned something as well, that Webb was right about being part of a community. The three of them track the gang through the desert as they circle back to Paradise and shoot one of them, Leo (Lee Van Cleef). As he lies dying, Leo claims that Crip is crazy and is going back to Paradise to shoot up the town and the townspeople. The three posse members continue on, but Caddo is killed by Crip when he goes off by himself to warn Paradise about Crip and his surviving gang member.

Cole finds Helen and Billy in a cabin while Kern waits outside. They are there because Helen, still ashamed of what happened to her, refuses to go back to Paradise. The two bandits sneak up on the cabin and kill Billy, but Kern shoots one of them, Hash (Charles Horvath), and in self-defense Helen finishes him off. Cole goes after Crip and kills him. In the melee, Cole and Kern are wounded. Cole convinces Helen that she should go back to Paradise and to learn to live with what happened to her, and assures her that not everyone will look down on her.

Back in Paradise, some of the townspeople, suspicious of Cole's gunfighter reputation and that the money from the bank wasn't recovered, are less than congratulatory towards him. But Benson (James Bell), Dr. Welles (Forrest Lewis) and others are appreciative. Despite the skepticism of some of the townspeople, the marshal's badge is offered to Cole. Upset by the attitude of some of them, Cole hesitates taking it. Benson remarks to Cole and the town citizens that some of them have a negative attitude towards Cole because deep down they are ashamed that they didn't chase the bandits as Cole did. Benson wisely tells Cole that even though some people might not be able to live up to Cole's standards, they can still be good people.

As Cole walks through the town with Helen, she tells him that despite the way some people (especially the women) now treat her, she will stay in Paradise and can live with what happened to her on the trail. Cole says that what Webb told him was true, that there are some good people in Paradise and worthwhile people can be found when someone looks hard enough for them. They have both learned that it is better to live in an imperfect community than outside it.

In another Anthony Mann Western, *The Tin Star* (1957), Morg Hickman (Henry Fonda) nurses a grudge that alienates him from other people. Hickman is a bounty hunter who was once a sheriff who needed $1000 for his sick wife and child to relocate to a drier climate. None of the townspeople whom he had faithfully served over the years were willing to loan him the money, so he tried to get it by hunting a man down for the bounty. However, his wife and child died anyway. Embittered, Morg became a bounty hunter only looking out for himself. He comes across a young sheriff, Ben (Anthony Perkins), desperately in need of guidance, and develops a relationship with Nona (Betsy Palmer) and her son Kip (Michael Ray), both of whom are outcasts because Kip's father was an Indian. Through his successful mentoring of Ben and developing love for Nona and Kip, he reintegrates himself back into the community, leaving town with Nona and Kip and seeking out another sheriff's job. Referring to Perkins and Fonda, Jeanne Basinger (2007, p. 114) states:

> The tin star itself is a symbol of force in both of their lives. Just as Perkins must learn how to be worthy of the star, Fonda must learn to reaccept the responsibility it carries

with it for other people. Fonda's picking up the star to wear it again is his reentry into organized society. This is borne out by his finding a new family, a wife (Betsy Palmer) and a son, to replace those he has lost. By putting on the star, he finds what he has lost. Or, as Perkins says, "Once a man pins it on, he can't take it off."

Love also is key to the characters in "The Hangman," a 1960 episode of *The Rifleman*. Ex-convict Volney Adams (Whit Bissell) is wrongly accused of killing his employer. Largely due to the efforts of a stranger in town, "Colonel" Sims (Richard Deacon), the townspeople overwhelmingly believe that Adams committed the crime, and the hangman, Harold Tenner (Denver Pyle), even begins to build a gallows before Adams is found guilty. In an emotional scene, the woman Adams loves, Ellie Aikens (Betty Lou Gerson), brings him breakfast in his jail cell to keep up his strength. They hear pounding in the background. Ellie tries to convince Adams they're replacing the hotel roof, but Adams knows that it's Tenner building the gallows. He tells Ellie, "What's the sense in keeping up my strength? It won't keep me from stretching a rope." Ellie responds, "Volney, all my life I've been a lonely woman. I've had few friends and no one to love. Since I met you.... I've had something to be proud of. A man who loved me, who's kind to me, who's given me the strength I never knew. You've got to have that strength for me. Please?" Volney replies, "Ellie, if it wasn't for you, I wouldn't care if I lived or died." He now has the strength to continue. Lucas McCain (Chuck Connors), who doesn't believe that "anyone gentle enough to see the real beauty in Ellie Aikens could ever raise his hands against another human being," decides to interrogate Tenner. He finds out that Tenner was the killer and takes him into custody, as Adams returns to Ellie.

In "Memories of Monica," a 1962 episode of *Have Gun—Will Travel*, love is put to the test when Ben Turner (Larry Ward), out of prison after six years, threatens to come to town with his "Texas men" and take Monica (Judi Meredith), his former girlfriend, away from her current husband, Sheriff Reagan (Bing Russell), killing Reagan if need be. Paladin (Richard Boone) agrees to help Reagan face Turner and his men since Reagan once saved his life. The townspeople are either friends of Turner or afraid of him, so only Paladin, Reagan and his deputy will face him. As the pressure mounts, Reagan is clearly rattled, needlessly beating the deputy when he refuses to help and insulting Monica. Reagan decides to run away, telling Monica and Paladin that Monica is not worth dying for. Turner comes to town and only Paladin, townsman Charlie (Garry Wahlberg) and Monica, armed with a shotgun, face him and his six men. Monica, unlike Reagan, has been true to her marriage and spouse and will not let Turner take her away. In the ensuing gunfight, Monica kills Turner, Charlie and Paladin kill three others, and the other three give up. Monica is shot but before dying she tells Paladin (in reference to Reagan), "Don't judge him too harshly. He's a good man." When Reagan comes back, he is a broken man who realizes how much Monica loved him and what he has lost by not standing up for her.

An example of finding the courage to overcome the fear of being hurt in order to be able to love again is the 1959 film *The Hanging Tree*. Dr. Joseph Frail (Gary Cooper) sets up an office in the mining town of Skull Creek, Montana. A strange combination of kindness and cruelty, Frail rescues and treats Rune (Ben Piazza) after he has been shot but coerces Rune to be his servant by threatening to tell the community that he is a thief, all the time treating Rune harshly. He tends to Elizabeth Mahler (Maria Schell), a Swiss immigrant who has been badly hurt in an accident, and lets her stay in the house next to him. Frail later beats up Frenchy Plante (Karl Malden) for trying to force himself on Elizabeth. The doctor also secretly finances the gold claim of Plante, Elizabeth and Rune. However, Frail rebuffs the romantic advances that Elizabeth makes towards him. When Elizabeth asks him why, Frail tells her that he was scarred by his brother having an affair with his wife, finding the two of them dead from a murder-suicide, and then burning his house down with the bodies in it. Ever since, the memory of those events has kept him from getting close to anyone.

Elizabeth, Plante and Rune strike it rich, and the town celebration turns into a riot. Plante again sexually assaults Elizabeth, but she is saved by Frail, who shoots Plante. The pious hypocrite Dr. Grubb (George C. Scott), an enemy of Frail, takes advantage of the situation by forming a lynch mob to hang Frail. They take him to the "hanging tree" and put a rope around his neck. But before he can be hanged, Rune and Elizabeth offer their claim to the mob if they let Frail go. The town lets Elizabeth release Frail. As she walks away, Frail calls her. He cups her chin with both hands, and their foreheads touch. Frail has found someone who is able to help him forget the trauma in his past and to find the courage to show the love that he feels.

Another example is *The Naked Spur* (1953). Howard Kemp (James Stewart) captures outlaw Ben Vandergroat (Robert Ryan) but has to transport him back to Abilene for trial to get the $5000 reward. Along the way he reluctantly accepts the aid of Roy Anderson (Ralph Meeker) and Jessie Tate (Millard Mitchell), both of whom are interested in sharing the reward. Kemp wants the money to buy back his ranch, which he lost when his wife sold it and ran away with another man while Kemp was fighting in the Civil

3. Love, Friendship and Bonds to the Community

Love at last. Gary Cooper as Dr. Joseph Frail finally finds the courage to show his love for Maria Schell as Elizabeth Mahler in Delmar Daves' *The Hanging Tree* (1959, Warner Brothers).

War. Vandergroat realizes how tormented Kemp is about his personal and financial losses and plans to use the woman he is traveling with, Lina Patch (Janet Leigh), to cause dissension between the three partners.

As the journey proceeds, Lina becomes closer to Kemp and more distant from Vandergroat. Vandegroat convinces Tate to free him, only then to kill Tate. Vandegroat tries to kill Kemp, but Anderson ends up killing Vandergroat. Anderson drowns when he tries to retrieve Vandergroat's body, which has fallen into a river. Kemp, left alone with Lina, with great effort retrieves the body, but then lets it drift downstream when he realizes that the love of Lina, and not the reward money or the ranch he can buy with it, is what will truly redeem his past losses. Kemp has the courage to love again despite how badly his wife once hurt him. When Kemp releases Vandergroat's body downstream, he also has released his obsession with his tortured past. Jeanne Basinger (2007, p. 95) points out that in his final struggle with Vandergroat, Kemp:

climbs the rocks himself. Using the "naked spur" from his boot, he laboriously chips out places for his hands to grip the edge of the solid rock as he climbs. (Those high rocks on the location used for the setting are in reality known as "the naked spur.") Far below him thunders the roaring water. Above him waits Ryan, ready to kill. Stewart is in the position of the Mann hero, suspended between two physical dangers, having to make his own way to solid ground. Complicated set-ups reveal a maplike view of the space: Ryan on the mountain top, waiting, the river rushing below, and Stewart tortuously chipping his way up the cliff at a dangerous height ... pursued and pursuer in one image. Stewart reaches the top, tossing his spur into Ryan's face, *à la* Stanwyck tossing the scissors at [Judith] Anderson in *The Furies*. In his own eyes, and in the eyes of the audience, Stewart has overcome and endured. He has earned the right to a better life, as his physical triumph marks the beginning of his ability to come to terms with himself.

Two people helping each other to love can make it easier for each to find the courage to do it. In the 1961 film *The Deadly Companions*, "Yellowleg" (Brian Keith) comes into a bar and finds Turk (Chill Wills) at the end of a rope, his feet propped up by a barrel because the patrons found him to be a card cheat. Yellowleg and Billy (Steve Cochran), Turk's companion, rescue him and the three of them go to Gila City to rob a bank. When they reach Gila City, Billy and Yellowleg, the name Turk has given him because he is a Yankee, go into the bar which is doubling that day as a church. Kit Tildon (Maureen O'Hara) and her son Mead (Bill Vaughan) come into the "church," but she is chastised by the women there as a fallen woman. The preacher (Strother Martin) tells Yellowleg to take off his hat, but instead he leaves the "church."

Turk tells Billy of his bizarre plan to form his own republic with his own army, the reason he is robbing the bank. A doctor tells Yellowleg that the bullet in his neck has to come out because it is keeping him from raising his right arm. Yellowleg decides not to have the operation because the recovery period is too long. It dawns on the doctor that Yellowleg was a man he knew five years before who had been cut up and scalped (the reason he won't remove his hat) by another man, whom Yellowleg reveals as Turk. Yellowleg lets the doctor know he plans to take revenge on that man.

Some bandits try to rob the bank, but Billy kills them. However, due to his bad arm, when Yellowleg tries to kill the bandits, he accidentally kills Mead. The distraught Kit wants to bury her son in Siringo near his father since the Gila City townswomen treat her so badly. Unfortunately, Siringo is in Apache country and the townsmen are scared to go there. A guilty Yellowleg asks Kit to escort her there but she refuses. Despite this, Yellowleg forces Turk (whom he wants to kill) to join him in following Kit. The ladies man Billy, infatuated with Kit, also decides to tag along. Turk

A determined bounty hunter. James Stewart as the obsessive Howard Kemp (far right) gets tough with the devious Ben Vandegroat, played by Robert Ryan (second from left), while Vandegroat's girlfriend, Lina Patch, played by Janet Leigh, holds him close and the avaricious Roy Anderson, played by Ralph Meeker (second from right), and Jesse Tate, played by Millard Mitchell (far left), look on in Anthony Mann's *The Naked Spur* **(1953, Metro-Goldwyn-Mayer).**

would like to kill Yellowleg for frustrating his bank plans but is too scared to do it. When the three men spot Kit, she tries to get away and gets stuck in a stream where a man has died with an Apache arrow in him. Yellowleg tries to let Kit know he understands how she feels since he "knows" a man who wanted revenge for five years and the worst day of his life was when he got it and lost the one thing he was living for.

At night when Yellowleg is asleep, Billy sneaks off to molest Kit, who tries to resist him before Yellowleg stops him. In the fight, Yellowleg's hat falls off, revealing his scalp wound. Yellowleg chases Billy out of the camp but insists that Turk stay. Turk sneaks away from Kit and Yellowleg as well. Yellowleg continues to Siringo with Kit, managing to avoid a stage stolen by the Apaches. Kit reveals she was only married for two weeks when her husband was killed, leading people in Siringo to believe Kit was a "fallen woman" months later when Mead was born. Yellowleg steals a horse from the Apaches to replace one that they lost, in the process hitting an Apache. Yellowleg buries their wagon to throw the Apaches off their trail, but Kit refuses to bury Mead's coffin as well. They continue on to Siringo on a travois. The Apache whom Yellowleg had hit harasses Kit and Yellowleg, stopping short of killing either one. When Yellowleg is asleep, Kit says she knows him better than any man she's ever known, but still has conflicted feelings about the man who killed her son. The Apache kills Yellowleg's and Kit's mule, forcing them to carry the coffin themselves, but later Kit kills the Apache.

When Kit and Yellowleg finally get to Siringo, now a ghost town, they find her husband's grave just as Turk and Billy show up and disarm them. Yellowleg guesses correctly that Billy and Turk have stolen money from the Gila City Bank. Billy asks Yellowleg to kill Turk so he doesn't have to share the money with him. Kit tells Yellowleg she can forgive him for accidentally killing her son, but not for killing Turk in cold blood. She reveals to Yellowleg she has psychological scars from needing to survive after her husband's death by letting men touch her for money and questions whether Yellowleg could love a woman like that. He responds by kissing her. Turk appears and Yellowleg and Turk shoot at each other. Billy wounds Turk, but Turk kills Billy. Yellowleg can kill the wounded and helpless Turk but forgoes killing or scalping him when Kit begs him not to do it. The parson (Strother Martin) and the posse chasing Billy and Turk arrive in Siringo and take Turk prisoner and give Mead a decent burial. Kit and Yellowlegs go off together.

Kitses (2004, p. 207) explains the evolution of Yellowleg and Kit:

> Frozen in a posture of righteousness, unable to give or take, Yellowleg and Kit tear at each other like animals. "You don't know me well enough to hate me!" shouts Yellowleg when Kit lashes out at him with a whip. The slow and exhausting process by which the two come to know each other and themselves is the bedrock of the film, Peckinpah building on this action surely to flesh out his theme. Alone in a wild and primitive landscape, the man and woman gradually recognize their need, each other's humanity, and begin tentatively to reach out to each other.

In other words, both characters have to find the courage to fight past their hate and their shame to love again. Fortunately, each of them provides the other one a reason to make that psychological journey as surely as they support each other on the way to Siringo. According to Dostoyevsky, Hell is the suffering of being unable to love.

Bonds of brother with brother, and brother with parents can also motivate individuals to find the courage to sacrifice themselves for their

3. Love, Friendship and Bonds to the Community   61

family members. In the 1957 film *Night Passage*, Grant McLaine (James Stewart) is a railroad troubleshooter. He was unjustly fired from his job by Ben Kimball (Jay C. Flippen) because of his suspicions of McLaine tipping off the Utica Kid (Audie Murphy) about a big payroll that the Kid and his gang stole from the railroad. However, Ben desperately needs to get the payroll through to the end of the line, or his workers will quit. Therefore, he decides to trick the thieves by giving Grant the payroll of $10,000 instead of putting it in the train safe. To ensure that the thieves will be thwarted, Kimball arranges for his second in command, Jeff Kurth (Hugh Beaumont), to be in a boxcar with 12 men ready to attack the bandits when they approach the train.

Grant boards the train with Joey (Brandon DeWilde), an orphan he has rescued from Concho (Robert Wilke), who was literally dragging Joey back to the gang headed by Whitey Harbin (Dan Duryea) that includes the Utica Kid (Audie Murphy). Joey reveals that before he ran off, the Utica Kid kept the other members of the gang from harming him. Concho later boards the train as part of the plot to rob it. Previously Harbin's men have been told by railroad employee Will Tenner (Herbert Andersen) that the money would be on the train, but Tenner does not have the time to tell the gang members the money is not in the safe and that Grant has it. Harbin's gang manages to lock Kurth and his men in their boxcar and decouple it from the rest of the speeding train. One of his men opens the safe, and when they see the money is not there Harbin kidnaps Verna Kimball (Elaine Stewart), telling her husband Ben, who is also on the train, that he will get her back when Harbin gets the $10,000. Meanwhile, McLaine has secretly put the $10,000 in Joey's lunch box. McLaine is kicked off the train by Concho, and Joey and his lunch box are swept up by the Utica Kid, who meets the rest of the gang and Verna at the gang's hideout.

McLaine makes it to the hideout and tells Harbin he wants to join the gang since he is angry about being fired from the railroad. The Utica Kid reveals that he and McLaine are brothers and he doesn't trust him to be in the gang. Concho doesn't like the idea of McLaine joining the gang, pulls a gun on him, but is killed by McLaine. Harbin, who doesn't like the Utica Kid, decides to let McLaine join the gang. While they are alone, McLaine takes a chance and tells the Kid that the money is in Joey's lunch box and asks the Kid to let Joey and him leave the hideout with the money so Joey won't end up an outlaw, a situation which he suspects will happen if Joey stays with the gang. He refuses and tells McLaine he will give him a ten-minute head start to get away without the money. Instead, McLaine decides to go to where the rest of the gang is congregated. When the Kid gets there as well, McLaine plays a railroad song sung by their father that appears to soften up the Kid. However, at that point Renner reaches the hideout and reveals that McLaine had been carrying the money and is working for the railroad.

McLaine causes a commotion that allows him to escape with Verna. The Kid grabs Joey and the money and heads out separately. The other gang members go after all of them. Harbin's gang catches up with McLaine and Verna. McLaine manages to send Verna off safely but is badly outnumbered by the gang. The Kid and Joey watch the gunfight safely from above. Joey tells the Kid they have to help McLaine, but he refuses. Joey rides down there and is shot off his horse and rescued by McLaine. Although the Kid could safely ride away with the money, he decides to go down and help McLaine. Apparently, the ties that bind him to his brother, parents and Joey are stronger than his selfish interests and his resentment towards his "good" older brother being held up as a role model for him. The two of them kill all of the gang members except Harbin, who kills the Kid before McLaine kills him. Before he dies, the Kid reveals how much the railroad song affected him.

Sometimes family ties allow a person the courage to overcome the racism of the community or even his own racism. In the 1960 film *The Unforgiven*, brothers Ben (Burt Lancaster), Andy (Doug McClure) and Cash Zachary (Audie Murphy) live with their mother, Mattilda (Lillian Gish), and sister, Rachel (Audrey Hepburn), on their Texas ranch. Ben and Cash are alarmed by a mysterious stranger who shows up outside their ranch. They go out to find him, but he gets away in a sandstorm. The next day, Kiowas come ominously close to the house, demanding that they receive Rachel in a trade, but Ben tells the Kiowas that she belongs with them, not the Kiowas.

When Charley Rawlins (Albert Salmi), Rachel's fiancé, is killed by the Kiowas, Rachel is accused of being a Kiowa, something the mysterious old man who appeared earlier, Abe Kelsey (Joseph Wiseman), has been telling the settlers in the area. To prove that the old man is lying, Ben, Cash and a group of men go after the old man, bring him back and put a rope around his neck. The old man still claims that Rachel was an Indian baby that Mattilda and her deceased husband Bill took from a Kiowa village after it was raided by white settlers. Kelsey wanted Mattilda and Bill to trade the baby for Kelsey's son held captive by the Kiowas, but the Zacharys refused, resulting in the death of Kelsey's son. Since then, Kelsey has hounded the Zacharys with an obsessiveness bordering on madness.

Mattilda is so incensed by what Kelsey is telling the settlers that she whips the horse underneath Kelsey, and he hangs.

Zeb Rawlins (Charles Bickford), the father of Charley, insists that the women examine Rachel to see if she is dark all over and not just tan from the sun to determine whether she is an Indian or not. Ben refuses, even though his refusal means Rawlins and the other settlers will have nothing to do with his family just before all of them are to start on a very important cattle drive. Back at the Zachary home, Mattilda admits to her family that Rachel is a Kiowa she took as a replacement for a baby she lost. Because of his hatred for Indians, Cash is so disgusted at finding out that Rachel is one he deserts the family when Ben refuses to get rid of her. After Cash leaves, the Kiowas come for Rachel. She tries to give herself up to avoid a fight, but Ben and Andy won't let her, preferring to fight and die rather than give her up.

The Zacharys repel the first two attacks of the Kiowas, but Mattilda suffers a wound. The Kiowas drive the Zacharys' cattle straight towards their house, destroying much of it and forcing Ben, Andy, Rachel and a prostrate Mattilda to the root cellar. Just as it seems the Zacharys will be overcome, Cash redeems himself by returning to the family to help fend off the Kiowas. For Cash, as well as the rest of the Zacharys, Indian or not, Rachel is part of the family and worth fighting for. By supporting each other and Cash overcoming his racism, the Zacharys survive.

A classic Western that illustrates the love of family as a motivator of courage is *3:10 to Yuma* (1957). Ben Wade (Glenn Ford) and his gang rob a stagecoach, while Dan Evans (Van Heflin) and his two young sons watch from afar. When Wade sees them, he warns them not to interfere with the holdup even though Evans' cattle are being inadvertently driven off by Wade's gang and Wade temporarily takes Evans' horses. Evans' sons beg their father to help the stagecoach, but Dan realizes he would only be killed if he tried. When the stagecoach driver tells Wade he will kill one of his men if he doesn't stop the robbery, Wade shows his ruthlessness by shooting his man in order to kill the stagecoach driver. However, Wade shows that he is not totally callous by telling the passengers to take the dead driver back to Bisbee to be buried because that is his home town.

When he gets home, Evans becomes defensive when his wife Alice (Leona Dora) says it is a shame that Dan and the boys only looked on during the robbery. Dan goes into Bisbee to borrow money to buy the water he desperately needs for his ranch due to a three-year drought. Meanwhile, Wade and his gang have gone into Bisbee, where they see the marshal (Ford Rainey), who suspects that Wade and his gang are outlaws, but without proof the marshal and his posse ride out of town. Afterwards everyone in Wade's gang expect him leave town, but Wade stays to romance the barmaid. Outside of town, the marshal encounters Evans and Mr. Butterfield (Robert Emhardt), the owner of the stagecoach line, who inform the marshal of the robbery. All of them go back into town to capture Wade, which they do when the very nervous Evans gathers the courage to keep Wade talking to him as the marshal sneaks up on Wade with a shotgun.

To get the $200 paid to each man by Butterfield to guard Wade, Evans, who needs the money to save his ranch and thus provide for his family, and Alex Potter (Henry Jones), the town drunk, volunteer to take Wade to Contention where they will put him on a train to Yuma prison while the marshal and the posse use the stagecoach as a decoy. Evans and Potter, along with Wade, split off from the stagecoach once they reach Evans' ranch. While at the ranch, the charming Wade flirts with Alice, who is obviously flattered, which irritates the jealous Evans. Before Dan, Potter and Wade leave, Alice tells Dan that she and the boys are proud of him.

When they reach Contention, Wade tries to bribe Dan with $10,000 to let him go, but Dan refuses. Bob, a friend of the murdered stagecoach driver, tries to kill Wade, but Evans stops him. But during the melee a gun goes off, which alerts gang member Charley Prince (Richard Jaeckel) that Wade is in Contention. Prince comes back with the rest of the gang. The gang hangs Potter, which scares the other townspeople away, prompting Butterfield to try to convince Wade that holding him is hopeless and even tells Evans he can have the $200 even if he lets Wade go. By this time, Alice has reached Contention and also tries to convince Dan to give Wade up in order to save his life. Dan refuses, telling Alice that he owes it to Potter to take Wade to the train since Potter sacrificed his life trying to do it. He adds that it's something that Alice and the boys will remember about him with pride. As the train pulls into town, Evans takes Wade to the train, using Wade as a shield to protect him from Prince and the gang who have him surrounded. Prince tells Wade to duck so the gang can kill Evans, but instead Wade jumps on the train with Evans, explaining to Evans he did it since he owed Evans for saving Wade's life when Bob tried to kill him. Some critics have complained that the surprise ending is contrived, but David Meuel (2015, p. 161) disagrees:

> Over the years, some critics have viewed Ben Wade's unexpected change of heart at the end of the story as weakness of the film. It's true that *3:10 to Yuma* would have been more uncompromising as a noir if Wade hadn't changed. But the change is also consistent with Wade's personal code, something that's been well established. Evans saved Wade's life earlier in the story. So, by Wade's estimation, he owes Evans one.

3. Love, Friendship and Bonds to the Community 65

The journey to the train station. Van Heflin as the desperate but determined Dan Evans (left) forces the smooth villain, Ben Wade, played by Glenn Ford (right), to go with him to the train to Yuma in Delmer Daves' *3:10 to Yuma* (1957, Columbia Pictures).

> Besides, as we learn, sparing Evans isn't such a big deal in Wade's mind, because he will most likely bust out of Yuma, anyway.

I agree that the ending works, but for a different reason, or at least an additional reason: Wade's vanity. He's not the type to let anyone else be "one up" him, even when it comes to saving a life. Even the opportunity to show how great he is by busting out of Yuma plays into his vanity. However, this film is mainly about Dan Evans, whose transformation is explained by Meuel (2015, p. 159):

> As Western heroes go, Dan Evans is also quite different. Far from the strong, silent, supremely self-confident type, he is a struggling rancher who feels that he's let his wife and sons down—that he's been a failure as a family man and provider. He's also envious of Wade, especially of his money and his charm, things he can't give his wife. In addition, he struggles with committing to the posse that plans to take Wade to Contention City. Initially, he doesn't want to get involved. Later, he agrees to help simply for the money. Finally, he follows through on the commitment not for the

money but because he sees this course of action as something he must do to reclaim his own self-respect. He, too, is a dynamic character who grows and changes as the story unfolds. An interesting catalyst in his change, incidentally, is Alex Potter, who is eager to prove his worth as part of the posse and meets a sad end. As Dan tells Alice: "The town drunk gave his life because he believed that people should be able to live in decency and peace together. Do you think I can do less?"

Meuel captures Evans' road to redemption well. However, it's possible that Wade is as envious of Evans as Evans is of him. After all, who is to be more admired: the fearless man who acts bravely and sometimes recklessly or the frightened man who acts bravely despite his fear? In fact, despite Wade's reckless decision to stay behind in Bisbee to romance the barmaid, he's always had his gang to back him up. Evans is truly a man who was more willing to face danger alone. Though momentarily swayed by Wade's superficial charm, Alice is mature enough to understand this and love Dan all the more deeply for it, a kind of love a man like Wade can only envy.

Another classic Western that involves finding the courage to do what is best for those close to you is *Shane* (1953). The film begins when Shane (Alan Ladd) asks to cross the land of Joe Starrett (Van Heflin), who lives there with his wife Marian (Jean Arthur) and son Joey (Brandon DeWilde). Joe suspects that Shane is a hired gun working for the Rykers, who want to chase the Starretts off their lands. However, when Rufus (Emile Meyer) and Morgan Ryker (John Dierkes) along with their cowhand Chris Calloway (Ben Johnson) confront Joe, trampling his garden and telling him to vacate his property so that the Rykers have more range for their cattle, Shane says he is a friend of the Starretts. This prompts the Rykers to leave, but not before they again trample the vegetable garden.

Joe invites Shane inside their cabin for dinner, and tells Shane that the only way he will leave his land is in a pine box. The friendship between Joe and Shane is cemented when the two of them remove a tree stump that Joe has been unable to remove by himself. As a result, Shane decides to stay with the Starretts, at least for a while. Later the two men go into town to buy supplies from Grafton's Mercantile, which also has a bar. While they are there, Grafton's man, Chris Calloway, comes in for a drink. He humiliates Shane, even to the point of throwing whiskey on him, but Shane restrains himself from fighting even though it makes him look like a coward. Back at the Starrett homestead, Marion and Joey let Shane know they don't believe he is a coward.

The following Saturday, the homesteaders go to Grafton's together for supplies. Again, Calloway verbally insults Shane, but this time Shane

3. Love, Friendship and Bonds to the Community

throws whiskey on Calloway's chest and face, leading to a fight that Shane wins. This prompts Rufus Ryker to offer Shane a job, which Shane refuses. An angry Rufus threatens Shane, but he won't back down, even though Rufus has his men with him. Joey runs to get his father, who is nearby, and the two of them fight off Rufus and his men, further strengthening the bonds between them. A frustrated Rufus at this point decides to get a professional gunman and killer, Wilson (Jack Palance), to take care of Shane, which would leave the homesteaders vulnerable.

When Marion objects to Shane teaching Joey how to shoot, Shane responds that a gun is nothing more than a tool, "as good or bad as the man using it," although this doesn't convince her that Joey should be able to handle one. Morgan Ryker rides up to the Starrett homestead with Wilson along, but this time Morgan is polite, using persuasion to try to get Joe to sell him his homestead. Morgan argues that the ranchers, like the Rykers, came to the land before the homesteaders and did the dirty work of fighting rustlers and Indians. However, Joe doesn't budge from his refusal to sell. Morgan and Wilson leave. Wilson later baits a hot-headed homesteader, "Stonewall" Torrey (Elisha Cook, Jr.), into a gunfight that the outmatched Torrey loses.

Morgan and two of his men go to Joe's to invite him to Grafton's to have a reasonable talk about their conflict with Rufus only in attendance while Morgan and his men go "home." Calloway rides out to the Starrett homestead and lets Shane know that Joe will be facing the Rykers and Wilson. This setup has so disgusted Calloway that he has quit the Rykers. Thus, Calloway redeems himself for siding earlier with the Rykers. Joe decides he will go to meet Rufus, even though he doesn't really believe Rufus will be at Grafton's by himself. Marion tries to convince Joe that going to Grafton's will be suicidal. Joe responds that he has to do it so she and Joey will not think him a coward and that he knows she will be well taken care of if he dies, obviously referring to Shane. When Marion begs Shane to convince Joe not to go, Shane refuses to intervene, but later offers to go in his place. When Joe refuses Shane's help, Shane fights him and subdues the strong Joe only by hitting him over the head with a gun butt. This infuriates and disillusions Joey, who says he hates Shane for fighting dirty.

When Shane gets to Grafton's, he shoots and kills Wilson and the Rykers but is badly wounded himself. Joey has followed Shane to Grafton's and apologizes to Shane and asks him to stay, but Shane refuses, telling Joey that a man has to be what he is and not someone else: "You can't break the mold." Leaving also makes it an easier family situation for his friend

Two ambivalent characters. Marian Starrett, played by Jean Arthur (left), and Shane, played by Alan Ladd (right), ponder how to handle their complicated feelings for each other in George Stevens' *Shane* (1953, Paramount Pictures).

Starrett, whose wife is secretly attracted to Shane and whose son idolizes him.

In "The Men of Defiance," a 1960 episode of *Laramie*, Jess Harper (Robert Fuller) rides with Marshal Stewart (Mort Mills) in pursuit of Frank Bannister (John Anderson), the man who killed four members of Jess' family years ago. Bannister and his gang ambush Stewart and Harper outside of Fort Defiance, a civilian fort and trading post run by three men who formed a close bond fighting for the South during the Civil War: Clint Gentry (Don Megowan), Reb O'Neil (Bing Russell) and Gabe Kert (John Pickard). O'Neil is captured by the Bannister gang after saving the marshal and a wounded Harper, both of whom reach the fort. Bannister tells Gentry that he will kill O'Neil if he doesn't give up the marshal and Harper.

Bannister's ultimatum puts Gentry in a difficult dilemma when Harper asks him to have his men deputized so they can go out and capture

Bannister and his gang. Gentry explains to Harper that the laws that condemn Bannister and his gang have no sway out in the middle of nowhere, where the men of the fort make their own laws designed to protect their own community. Gentry refuses to put the men of the fort in danger. However, he realizes that the only way he can save O'Neil and remain loyal to the men of the fort is for the marshal and him to rush the Bannister gang in a wagon and save O'Neil, which they do.

Chapter 4

Justice

"I gave you your life because you saved my last son. If you grant me that, I don't mind going to Hell for the rest of it."—*From Hell to Texas*

The virtue of justice promotes healthy community life and as such can be broken down into citizenship, fairness and leadership. Citizenship involves social responsibility, loyalty to a group, and teamwork. Fairness involves treating all people equally in accordance with what is morally right. Leadership is taking the initiative to encourage the group to accomplish necessary goals (Peterson and Seligman, 2004).

An example of fairness is the film *From Hell to Texas* (1958). It begins with young Tod Lohman (Don Murray) being chased by Tom Boyd (Dennis Hopper) and Otis Boyd (Ken Scott) and their range hands for the alleged killing of the Boyds' brother Shorty. Lohman gets away when he stampedes horses through his pursuers, accidentally seriously hurting Otis, who dies later. Tom decides to track down Lohman, but Lohman gets the drop on him and lets him go, explaining that the death of Shorty was an accident. As Tom is leaving, he tries to kill Lohman but misses, shooting Lohman's horse instead. Lohman again gets the upper hand but lets Tom go because he hates killing and doesn't believe morally it would be right to kill Tom, although he risks Tom coming after him again.

Tom then goes back to report what has happened to his father, powerful rancher Hunter Boyd (R.G. Armstrong), who chastises Tom for going after Lohman alone. When Tom says that his father would have done the same thing, his father, a man with more temperance than his son, responds, "Who do you think I am? One of those fools who wants to be the big man with a quicker trigger?" Hunter is also upset that Tom killed Lohman's horse.

Lohman wanders through the desert on foot until he reaches a river and the aid of Amos Bradley (Chill Wills) and his daughter Juanita (Diane Varsi), who becomes smitten with Lohman. When Lohman tells Amos what has happened to him, Amos mentions that Hunter is a "powerfully wicked man," but has a "queer sense of justice." Hunter's unusual moral code is demonstrated the next day when Hunter, Tom and the ranch hands catch up with Lohman, Amos and Juanita. Hunter and Tom do not accept Lohman's defense that the death of Shorty and crippling of Otis were accidental. However, even though Hunter and Tom desperately want to exact revenge on Lohman, Hunter, with his "queer sense of justice," lets the cornered Lohman get a several-hour head start with a fresh horse, much to Tom's displeasure. As far as Hunter is concerned, it isn't fair that Tom killed Lohman's horse and left him on foot in the desert. However, despite letting Lohman escape in this instance, Hunter is still determined to bring Lohman to his brand of justice.

After a skirmish in which Lohman kills ranch hand Carmody (John Larch) and a fight with Comanches, which leaves two other ranch hands dead, Lohman makes it to the ranch of Amos. However, Hunter, Tom and a ranch hand arrive and shoot, but don't kill, Amos, while Lohman escapes. Lohman comes back to the ranch and then to town to face Hunter, Tom and the ranch hand. In the ensuing gunfight, Tom gets caught in a fire and is badly burned, prompting Lohman to save his life. Hunter then refuses to kill Lohman, explaining, "I gave you your life because you saved my last son. If you grant me that, I don't mind going to Hell for the rest of it." Lohman responds, "I'll grant you that and I have no doubt that you will, Mr. Boyd." Although Hunter does have a sense of fairness, it has its limits, and it doesn't keep him from causing a number of needless deaths. Lohman goes back to Juanita and the Bradleys.

Peterson and Seligman explain the relationship between fairness and identity (2004, p. 402):

> The sensitivity to fairness that comes with a commitment to justice, the exposure to alternative interpretations of reality that one gets in negotiating equitable solutions, and the insights and emotional responsiveness that develop with each act of compassion are elements of moral experience that constantly change who you are and how you perceive and engage morally. This dynamic makes moral identity formation an ongoing, ever-changing part of one's larger identity and sense of self. This is deep identity, not simply a claim to be a caring person or a professed devotion to fairness, but identity as integral, even foundational, to who one is and how one defines oneself to oneself.

Peterson and Seligman add that once a person integrates a sense of fairness into his or her identity, that person's self-esteem depends on maintaining that sense of fairness. A sense of fairness also involves perspective-taking empathy (the ability to understand the thoughts and feelings of another person), self-reflection (the ability to look closely at one's own assumptions, views, beliefs and values), along with relationship problem-solving skills and the desire and ability to address conflicts between oneself and others with a solution as equitable as possible to all parties involved. Both Hunter Boyd's and Tod Lohman's sense of justice is an integral part of the identity of each man, but Lohman's sense of justice differs from Boyd's because of Lohman's greater empathy and relationship problem-solving ability. This difference is why in Lohman's mind "the powerfully wicked" Hunter will end up going to Hell for what he did.

Sometimes justice has to be tempered so the letter of the law matches its spirit. In the 1960 *Laramie* episode "The Track of the Jackal," a bounty hunter, Luke Wiley (Stephen McNally) comes to town looking for Sumner Campbell (Robert Wilke), who as Vernon Bates is wanted for murder in Rawlings. Campbell-Bates has a wife and a son and a good reputation since settling in Laramie two years previously. Wiley sets out to ambush Campbell and get the $800 reward, but Campbell gets the drop on him and is about to shoot him but decides not to do it. When Wiley asks Jess Harper (Robert Fuller) for help in capturing Campbell, Harper refuses because of Wiley's reputation as someone who would like to bring back his quarry dead rather than alive.

Wiley tries a different tactic, telling the townspeople that Campbell is wanted in Rawlins because he beat a boy to death there. Some of the townspeople, led by Jimmy Foster (Steven Terrell) and Firth (Stacy Harris), demand that Harper cooperate in Wiley's capture of Campbell. Jess instead goes out to Campbell's place and stops Foster and a friend from trying to capture Campbell. Campbell explains to Harper that he killed the 23-year-old Andrew McIntire in self-defense, but Andrew's father was powerful enough to intimidate the jury to convict Campbell. Stirred up by Wiley, some townspeople, including Foster and Firth, come to help Wiley take Campbell, now in jail, back to Rawlins. Realizing that if Campbell is taken back to Rawlins he will be executed by a populace biased against him, Harper resists the townspeople and shoots Foster in the leg. Not willing to give up, Wiley invites the McIntires and their henchmen to Laramie to come to town to kill Campbell if they can't take him back to Rawlins. Slim Sherman (John Smith) arrives to help Harper and Campbell fight off the McIntires and their hired guns. Wiley is killed in the gunfight, and

Sherman and Harper go back with Campbell to Rawlins to see that he gets a fair trial now that the McIntires are no longer in power.

A 1958 episode of *Have Gun—Will Travel*, "The Hanging of Roy Carter," involves a conflict between the letter of the law and its spirit, or to put it another way, a conflict with a sense of justice without empathy or a sense of justice with empathy. Keno Smith (John Duke) steals Paladin's guns while he is asleep, but Paladin (Richard Boone) wakes up and subdues him before he can leave. A posse rides up and becomes intent on lynching Smith, but Paladin steps in. Posse leader Sidney Carter (Robert Armstrong) says that Smith is guilty of robbery and murder and has framed Roy, Sidney's son. Paladin convinces the posse to take Smith in and get a confession from him to stop the execution of Roy, who will be hanged the next day. Even though the posse gets Smith's confession that states that Roy had nothing to do with the crimes, it appears that it is too late to get the governor to halt the execution.

Paladin decides to go to the prison as a witness of the execution to see if he can stop it. He goes to see the warden, John Bullock (Paul Birch), who adamantly refuses to delay the execution despite Paladin's signed affidavit that Smith has exonerated Roy. The chaplain (John Larch) wants to delay the execution but refuses to do anything about it, saying that he sometimes has to be practical and compromise with what he believes when the warden is inflexible. Roy is led to the scaffold, but the mechanism doesn't work because Paladin has jammed a piece of wood into it. In the confusion, Paladin grabs Roy and pushes him into his cell, pulling the door behind them and breaking the locks. When the guard has almost sawed through the bars, the chaplain gathers the courage to grab the worn-out hacksaw and break it into pieces, even though he is breaking the letter of the law by interfering. The warden has no choice but to go to town to get another hacksaw, a trip which will give the governor time to stop the execution. As soon as the warden and guards leave Roy's cell, Paladin easily breaks open the door of the cell. He realizes that the warden, to his credit, also understood how easy it would be to break open the cell, but he didn't do it in order to give Roy more time.

When Roy is released, his autocratic father orders him to come with him, but Roy refuses and says he wants to go with the chaplain to buy more books for the prison inmates. After his ordeal, he not only has been liberated from the prison but has found the courage to liberate himself from his father's oppressive control.

Yet another example of the courage to decipher between the spirit of the law and the letter of the law, as well as the courage to redeem oneself, is the 1957 *Gunsmoke* episode "Gone Straight." A "deputy" acting for a Stockraiser's Association in New Mexico comes to Dodge with a warrant for Jim Glass, a former member of Billy the Kid's gang. The "deputy" suspects that Glass is in Tascosa and expects Marshal Matt Dillon (James Arness) to go there to serve the warrant since Tascosa is in his jurisdiction. When Dillon and Chester (Dennis Weaver) go to Tascosa, they encounter a man named Nate Timble (Carl Betz), who is building a school for the town. Timble tells Dillon that he doesn't know anything about a Jim Glass, but mentions that he is helping Mike Postil (Tige Andrews) break away from the cattle rustler Gunter (Joe De Santis) and his gang and go straight. At Timble's house, his wife (Marianne Stewart) tells Dillon and Chester that Timble is going to construct more needed buildings once he finishes the school.

Gunter and two of his men ride into town and try to get Postil to come back with them. When Postil refuses, Gunter threatens him. Before anyone can draw a gun, Timble and Dillon confront Gunter and his men, and they back down. Mrs. Timble asks Dillon if Timble was right to stand up for Postil to give him a chance to go straight and Dillon responds yes.

The next day, Dillon and Chester wait for Gunter and his men on the way to town where they are going to confront Timble and Postil. Timble and Postil join Dillon and Chester when they confront Gunter and his men. In the ensuing gunfight, Gunter and one of his men is killed, and Timble is wounded, as the rest of Gunter's men ride away after being warned by Dillon to never bother Timble or Postil again. Afterwards, when Chester takes off Timble's shirt to look at his wound, it reveals a scar that clearly identifies him as Jim Glass. Despite knowing Trimble's true identity, Dillon claims that the dead Gunter is really Glass, apparently something he will report to the "deputy" waiting back in Dodge. Since Dillon recognizes that Timble has had the courage to redeem himself by going straight, he should have the courage to follow the spirit rather than the letter of the law.

The conflict between following the spirit of the law vs. the letter of the law is something often exemplified in a military setting, where adherence to the rules and regulations is required. In a 1956 episode of *Cheyenne*, "Decision," Captain Quinlan (Richard Denning) is a by-the-book soldier who supports his commanding officer, Major Heffler (Ray Teal), even though he is leading the cavalry troop and a wagon train full of civilians to certain death through the desert because he is excessively afraid of confronting hostile Indians by going another way. Cheyenne (Clint Walker), a scout, and the soldiers mutiny and decide to take over command from the major and the captain in order to travel through Indian country rather than facing sure death in the desert. The captain, despite his doubts about the major's decisions, sides with the major when the soldiers mutiny and they relieve the major and captain of their commands. Successfully making it through Indian country after a fight which leaves the major dead, the soldiers reach the fort. Although just before getting to the fort he vowed to report the mutiny as army regulations dictate, the captain shows mercy by not reporting it, realizing that prudence and humanity dictate that even in the army, regulations can be a poor substitute for a conscience.

Sometimes justice hurried is justice denied. In the 1962 *Laramie* episode "Justice in a Hurry," Ev Keleher (Hugh Sanders) comes upon the overnight campsite of Slim Sherman (John Smith), on his way home to his ranch near Laramie. At gunpoint, Keleher accuses Sherman of being hired by Arney Jackson to kill his cattle. Sherman manages to disarm Keleher and convinces him he has nothing to do with Jackson. The next day, Sherman travels to his ranch; but when Jackson is found murdered, Keleher is arrested for it. Not only was it well known that Keleher was feuding with Jackson and that Keleher is an ex-con, but two witnesses, Edna Holtzhoff (Kathleen Freeman) and Sam Norris (Paul Birch), swear they saw Keleher kill Jackson. Keleher claims that he was with Sherman at the time of the killing, but the sheriff (Robert Wilke) is skeptical when he takes Keleher out to the campsite and he can't tell the sheriff where Sherman was going or even his name. The judge (George Mitchell) decides to try Keleher the next day, despite the pleas of Keleher's daughter, Julie (Diana Millay), that she needs time to find Sherman and corroborate her father's story.

Julie manages to find Sherman at his ranch that night and brings him back to town the next morning, but they come upon the sheriff burying a casket that he says contains Keleher, convicted and hanged for the crime. An enraged Julie confronts the judge, but the judge and even Keleher's defense attorney claim it wouldn't have made any difference in the verdict. Julie vows to get even. Soon after Norris is found dead, the sheriff jails Julie as a suspect. However, somebody takes a shot at Sherman, a situation which makes him think that someone besides Julie and Ev is behind the killings, especially after he finds out that Edna Holtzhoff is too nearsighted to have been a reliable witness. The sheriff seems reluctant to accept Sherman's suspicions.

Sherman suspects that Marv Jackson (George Wallace) might be behind the killings of his uncle Arney, because he inherited his ranch, and Norris, because Marv wanted to keep Norris from admitting he gave false eyewitness testimony. When he goes to Marv's ranch, he finds evidence that Marv was involved in the killings, something that Marv confirms when he confronts Sherman. When the sheriff appears unexpectedly on the scene to back up Sherman, Marv shoots the sheriff. Sherman subdues Marv so he can be brought to trial.

Before he went to the ranch, the sheriff went to the judge and turned in his badge, telling him that he no longer wanted to be involved in the judge's hurried justice. After Marv is subdued, the sheriff tells Julie and Sherman that he half-believed Ev's story to begin with, and, for that reason, told the judge and everyone else he had hanged Ev. In reality, he hid him away in a cabin until he could prove his suspicions. Although the sheriff had failed to follow the letter of the law, he was true to its spirit. As a result, a free Julie and Ev are reunited.

The basis of the social responsibility and loyalty to the group that makes up citizenship is the adherence to free and fair elections. Without those, justice cannot prevail. A number of Western films and television shows deal with the courage needed to make fair elections happen. In "The Taffeta Mayor," a 1958 episode of *Have Gun—Will Travel*, Paladin (Richard Boone) is hired by John Kellaway, an honest man running for mayor of Colton, Wyoming, against Ben Trask (Bobby Hall), a puppet of the corrupt town boss Arnold Oaklin (Edward Platt). When Paladin gets there, he finds that Kellaway has been murdered. Paladin goes to see his widow Lucy (Norma Crane), who rebuffs him as a cheap gunfighter who never would have been hired by her husband. Clay Morrow (Robert Karnes), clearly frightened by Oaklin, tries to explain to Paladin that, to avoid trouble, the townspeople have accepted the corruption of Oaklin and his henchmen.

Paladin goes to Oaklin's store to confront him, only to be beaten up by him, Trask and one of Oaklin's henchmen. Paladin convinces Lucy to have the courage to run for mayor despite the hostility and ridicule she will face, something that is possible since the Wyoming legislature has given women the right to vote. The prospects for her election look dim since nobody wants to listen to her campaign speeches. But the women of the town swing the vote in her favor. Paladin forces Oaklin at gunpoint to go to Lucy's store to congratulate her for her election win, realizing that an attempt is about to made on her life. Paladin foils the attempt, killing Trask in the process. Lucy decides to leave the town to go to Philadelphia, explaining to Morrow that she ran for mayor only to honor her honest husband, and she feels the craven townspeople aren't good enough to support her and to be represented by her.

For justice to prevail, trials also have to be fair and unbiased. Two episodes of *Have Gun—Will Travel* illustrate this. In the 1961 episode "The Last Judgment," an unwilling Paladin is assigned to be a defense attorney for Dr. Simon Loving (Donald Randolph) by Elroy P. Greenleaf (Harold J. Stone), a judge of questionable authority who rules the town in a tyrannical fashion. Because of the Hippocratic Oath, Loving had the temerity to treat a wounded man without informing the judge. When the wounded man kills the town sheriff, Greenleaf arrests Loving for the murder since it was Loving who helped him recover sufficiently to kill the sheriff.

During the trial, Paladin coerces the judge into making a bet: If Loving is found guilty, he will hang; but if he isn't found guilty, the judge will hang for conspiracy to murder. The judge amends the bet to include the hanging of Paladin as well as Loving if Loving is found guilty. The judge reminds jury members of the ways he has benefited them in an attempt to remind them how he can punish them if they return a not-guilty verdict. Paladin decides that the only way to counteract the judge is to use equally shady tactics: He bribes or threatens them with his prowess with a gun in order to get their votes. He adds that when a federal judge finally comes to town, he will not look kindly on a jury in an illegal trial that voted to hang the defendant. Now that the presiding judge sees that the trial is going against him, he signals his law enforcement henchmen to shoot Paladin, but Paladin shoots them instead, killing one and wounding the other. The doctor follows his Hippocratic Oath and treats the wounded man. At this point, Paladin stops the farce of a trial before it can validate the proceedings with a verdict. The deposed judge is shackled to wait for the federal judge to charge and try him, and the gallows are torn down.

In *Have Gun—Will Travel*'s "Deliver the Body" (1958), Paladin is hired by Silver Flat, Nevada, Mayor Lovett (R.G. Armstrong) to bring in Bert Tyler (Robert Gist), who is accused of killing the sheriff. Before Paladin can get to Silver Flat, Lovett verbally attacks Tom Nelson (James Franciscus) for successfully defending Tyler on a past murder charge, thus freeing him to kill the sheriff. When Paladin first meets Lovett, he gets the impression he wants Tyler brought in dead. Paladin convinces Nelson to help him find Tyler and assures him that he will do everything he can to bring Tyler in alive.

Paladin finds Tyler and, after fighting him, takes him into custody. Tyler tells Paladin he was with a girl 50 miles away when the sheriff was shot, and if the girl can come to Silver Flat she will verify this. After Paladin brings him in, Tyler tells Paladin that Lovett and the sheriff were enemies, implying that Lovett had a motive for killing the sheriff. Even though

Paladin has fulfilled his obligation to Lovett, he decides to stick around to see that justice is done for Tyler, even offering a reluctant Nelson $500 to represent Tyler. Lovett appears to be even more determined not to give Tyler a fair trial by making himself judge and not waiting for the girl who is Tyler's alibi to make it to Silver Flat. Lovett becomes so upset by Paladin trying to get Tyler a fair trial that he sends his henchmen out to kill him, but Paladin gets the drop on them instead. Nelson comes back with a court order changing the venue of the trial from Silver Flat to another town where Tyler can get a fair trial. Lovett tries to kill Paladin, Nelson and Tyler, but Paladin kills him instead.

Even in a fair trial, sometimes it takes courage to go against the wishes of one's community and even one's own family to pursue one's own perception of justice. In a 1965 episode of *The Big Valley*, "The Murdered Party," Heath Barkley (Lee Majors) witnesses the murder of Colonel Ashby, a well-respected member of the community, by Korby Kyles (Warren Oates), a member of a disreputable family, and chases him down and captures him. Korby's father, Jacob (Larry D. Mann), asks Jarrod Barkley (Richard Long) to be Korby's lawyer since no other lawyer is willing to take the case. Jarrod refuses.

Jarrod starts to have second thoughts about not representing Korby when he gets the idea that not only the district attorney, Clem Greene (Paul Fix), but the townspeople and the newspaper in its editorial have all prejudged Korby. Jarrod develops more doubts when he talks to Korby, who proclaims his innocence. He tells Jarrod that he worked for Colonel Ashby's opium-smuggling ring and that a "Chinaman" involved in that trade killed the colonel.

It looks as if Jarrod will not have to represent Korby when the judge assigns young attorney Matt Cooper (Karl Held) that responsibility. At first Jarrod and his conscience are relieved. But when he talks to Matt, he finds out that he has already prejudged Korby. This revelation is the determining factor in Jarrod deciding to defend Korby. Jarrod throws himself energetically into the defense of Korby, going thoroughly over the scene of the crime, a railroad station.

At the trial, Jarrod calls to the witness stand government agent Asa Harmon (Stacy Harris), who corroborates Korby's contention that Ashby was deeply involved in the opium trade. Jarrod then calls Heath and so rattles him about his testimony that he saw Korby kill Ashby even though it was a very dark night and the railroad station area was poorly lighted, that Heath finally admits that he wasn't sure it was Korby who he saw kill Ashby. District Attorney Greene calls a surprise witness, railroad worker

Henry Bingham (Clegg Hoyt), who testifies that from his angle the headlight of the train provided enough light for him to see clearly that Korby killed Ashby. Shaken by this testimony, Korby blurts out a denial that clearly implicates him. As a result, he is found guilty.

Jarrod, chastened by the guilt of Korby, returns to the Barkley mansion. When he expresses his remorse about defending Korby, the rest of the family, including Heath, act as if they don't know what he is talking about, thus indicating that they accept him and what he did and embracing him as they go off to dinner. They understand that Jarrod has been true to his ingrained sense of fairness and social responsibility.

In some cases, it is the ordinary citizen who needs to have the courage to see that justice is done. In a 1962 *Bonanza* episode, "The Jury," Hoss Cartwright (Dan Blocker) is the only juror voting "not guilty" due to "reasonable doubt" in the murder trial of Jamie Wrenn (Jack Betts), someone who has alienated the community with his obnoxious behavior. Hoss is bothered by the fact that the case against Wrenn hinges on one eyewitness, Hjalmer Olson (James Bell), who claims he saw Wrenn kill his brother and steal their money in the dark of night. Despite the judge's warnings about the jury members not discussing their deliberations, word leaks that Hoss is the only one holding out against a conviction, a situation which angers the community. In an attempt to rid the jury of Hoss, jury member Bud Murdoch (Don Haggerty) tries to get the judge to dismiss the jury and start over, but the judge refuses. One day when Hoss is in the saloon, Olson says he recognizes a bill that Hoss has used to pay for his beer as one of the stolen bills. Hoss says he doesn't know where it came from, but Murdoch claims that Hoss' possession of the bill makes it look as if he was bribed and that the only way he can clear himself is to vote Wrenn guilty. Hoss becomes even more convinced that Wrenn might not be guilty when Junior (Bobs Watson) reveals that he (Junior) offered to be Wrenn's alibi for the night of the murder, but Wrenn refused.

With the help of Junior, Wrenn unsuccessfully tries to break out of jail and run away, behavior which further incriminates him. Despite this attempted escape, Hoss asks Adam to talk to Olson to see how good his eyesight is. Adam (Pernell Roberts) sees that Olson's eyesight is fine; but before Adam leaves Olson's place, Adam becomes suspicious that Olson is hiding something. When Adam surreptitiously comes back, he finds Olson with the stolen money. Olson confesses to killing his brother and admits he put the stolen bill in Hoss' pocket. Like Jarrod Barkley, Hoss has had the courage to be true to his sense of fairness and social responsibility.

Sometimes justice needs to occur after a lynching has taken place. In the 1966 *Gunsmoke* episode "The Good People," Ben Rucker (Morgan Woodward) and his sons Gabe (Allen Case) and Seth (Tom Simcox) pursue suspected rustlers. Ben and Gabe, separated from Seth, go after one of the suspected rustlers, Jed Bailey (Steve Gravers). Convinced that he is guilty, Ben and Gabe hang him despite Bailey protesting he is innocent. Seth joins Ben and Gabe at the hanging tree with the unsettling news that he has proof that Bailey couldn't have been one of the rustlers despite his poor reputation. Ben and Gabe decide not to say anything about it, despite Seth's misgivings.

After the Rucker father and sons return to their ranch, Silas Shute (Shug Fisher) comes upon Bailey hanging from the tree. He believes he is an outlaw, Jake Daniels, with a $500 reward offered for his capture, dead or alive. He brings the body to Dodge to collect the reward. He has shot the dead man to make it look as if he captured him. Matt Dillon (James Arness) sees that the dead man looks like Jake Daniels but is really Jed Bailey. Since he won't get the reward, Shute decides to tell the truth about finding the man hanging from the tree, but it is too late. Since the man has Shute's bullet hole in him, Shute is put in jail for the murder of Bailey. Shute is further incriminated when Dillon, Shute and Festus Haggen (Ken Curtis) go to the tree and find no rope there (the Ruckers having removed it), which contradicts Shute's story.

At the Rucker ranch, the father and sons tell Matt they shot two of the rustlers the day of the hanging but didn't see Bailey. Back in town, Matt tells Doc Adams (Milburn Stone) that he has his doubts about Shute's guilt. He wants to put Seth on the jury. If he is the only juror who votes not guilty, that vote could be a sign that Seth knows that Shute is innocent and the Ruckers had something to do with the hanging. Seth accepts a place on the jury and is the only one voting not guilty. Since Seth refuses to change his vote, the judge has no recourse but to declare a mistrial.

Back at the ranch, Seth tells Gabe he is leaving. Gabe, afraid that Seth is going to tell Dillon the truth of what happened, tries to stop him by beating him up. Ben stops the fight. Seth leaves, and the next day Ben gathers up the courage to convince Gabe that the two of them should go into town and confess. Ben feels guilty about covering up what they did and letting someone else take the blame when he was proud of the fact that he raised his boys to do the right thing. When Ben and Gabe get to town, they find that Seth has already gone there. To protect his father and brother and keep Shute or any other innocent person from being charged with the crime, he falsely confesses to the hanging himself. When the father and brother confess, it is obvious that Seth, who would find it very difficult if not impossible to hang a man by himself, is innocent and Ben and Gabe guilty. Ben tells Seth he is proud of him for doing the right thing and Gabe shakes his hand. Seth assures Ben that he will take care of the ranch until his father and brother get out of prison. Ben is finally able to get back his sense of fairness that Seth has always maintained.

Fairness also includes treating all people, regardless of differences in race, ethnicity, religion, or other differences in background, equally. An important part of this fair and equal treatment of others involves a person's perspective-taking ability or empathy, which keeps him or her from treating and viewing those of another race, ethnicity or religion as "the other." For Westerns, this approach often means pleading the case for the fair treatment of Native Americans. An early example of this approach is the 1950 film *Broken Arrow*, based on the historical figures of Cochise and Tom Jeffords. Before *Broken Arrow*, Native Americans were often portrayed as faceless enemies or in a negative light. An example of the latter is *My Darling Clementine* (1946). When Wyatt Earp's (Henry Fonda) shave is disturbed by bullets flying into the barber shop, Earp goes to the saloon where Injun Joe is shooting off his gun. Earp disarms the Indian with a blow to the head and exclaims, "What kind of town is this? Selling liquor to the Indians!" He then tells the culprit to "get outta town and stay out" and kicks him in the rear end to emphasize his point. The Indian at this point no longer has even the dignity of being an enemy but is a pathetic drunk.

In *Broken Arrow*, the portrayal of Native Americans is much more dignified. Tom Jeffords (James Stewart) comes across a wounded Apache boy and gives him water. Because of his act of kindness, the Apaches don't harm Jeffords, but he has to watch helplessly as they kill a group of prospectors and is warned not to return to Apache territory.

When he gets back to Tucson, he turns down a job scouting for the army and instead learns the Apache language and customs. Despite having been warned against it, he goes back to the Apaches to ask them to allow the mail service couriers to go through their territory. The chief, Cochise (Jeff Chandler), agrees. While with the Apaches, Jeffords falls in love with young Sonseeahary (Debra Paget). "Indian lover" Jeffords is almost lynched back in Tucson by whites angry over an attack on a wagon train by a few of Chochise's renegade warriors. He is saved by General O.O. Howard (Basil Ruysdael), the "Christian General," who states that the Bible "says nothing about the pigmentation of the skin."

Jeffords goes on the Butterfield stage, the first one to go through Apache territory in five years. It is attacked by renegade warriors. Jeffords rides off for help from Cochise, who arrives to save the stagecoach. After Jeffords and Sonseeahary are married, a group of whites set a trap for Cochise, Jeffords and Sonseeahary, killing Sonseeahary and wounding Jeffords before they are chased away. Jeffords burns with the desire for revenge but is stopped by Cochise from retaliating since the military was not involved in the killings and Geronimo's people broke the peace just as much as the whites who killed Sonseeahary. Jeffords agrees that peace is more important than revenge and that by keeping the peace, he can keep his memory of Sonseeahary alive. Although Cochise and the Apaches in the film accommodate themselves more to the wishes of the whites than vice versa, the presence of Jeffords and General Howard at least gives the impression that the Apaches deserve justice and might possibly receive it.

After *Broken Arrow*, there are numerous films with a sympathetic viewpoint of Native Americans with characters who treat them justly or advocate their just treatment (*Devil's Doorway*, 1950; *Broken Lance*, 1954; *White Feather*, 1955; *Reprisal!*, 1956; *The Last Hunt*, 1956; *Cheyenne Autumn*, 1964; *Tell Them Willie Boy Is Here*, 1969) and even films in which Indians are the salvation of a white man (*Run of the Arrow*, 1957; *A Man Called Horse*, 1970; *Little Big Man*, 1970; *Dances with Wolves*, 1990). But generally Native Americans remained a subjugated people whose best, if not totally desirable hope, was to assimilate to the white man's ways. Even then they could not count on white man's justice.

A complicated example of a white man helping a Native American is found in the 1957 *Have Gun—Will Travel* episode "Winchester Quarantine." At a stagecoach stop, rancher Clyde McNally (Leo Gordon) and his foreman, Peavey (Robert Karnes), kill the horse of a Cherokee, Joseph Whitehorse (Anthony Caruso), and beat him up. They have accused Whitehorse of having sick stock that are infecting the stock of the other ranchers. After the fight is over, Paladin (Richard Boone) shows Whitehorse his business card. Whitehorse later discovers the card and tells Paladin that because he is an Indian, the only person in town who will have anything to do with him is the pharmacist, Rheinhart (Vic Perrin). McNally has an irrational hatred for Whitehorse (McNally's father and brother were killed by the Sioux), despite the fact that Joseph is well-educated, was raised in a mission school, and has tried to assimilate to the white man's ways.

At the Whitehorse homestead, Joseph's wife Martha (Carol Thurston) tries to convince Paladin to protect Whitehorse, who is threatened with violence every time he leaves his ranch. But Whitehorse resists, and Paladin says he will not accept land in payment, the only way the Whitehorses can pay him. However, Paladin says he will give Whitehorse one of his horses in exchange for Whitehorse's dead horse, expecting that McNally will give him money as compensation because of having killed it.

In town, McNally, Peavey and the ranchers confront Paladin for standing up for Whitehorse, but McNally backs down when Paladin stands up to him. Paladin seemingly changes sides when he gets McNally to agree to give Paladin $2000 if he can convince the reluctant Whitehorses to sell their land to McNally, who covets it. When Paladin goes to the Whitehorse ranch and tells them the deal he has made with McNally, the couple feel he has betrayed them, but they reluctantly agree to the deal. However, it turns out that Paladin has suspected and then learned for sure from the pharmacist that the cattle are dying not because of disease, but because the soil on the Whitehorses land is poisoned with the natural chemical molybdenum, which, in turn, has poisoned the grass the cattle have eaten. When he explains about the poisoned land to McNally after the deal has been concluded, McNally draws on Paladin, but Paladin shoots him in the shoulder. After McNally and his men leave, another rancher feels sorry for the Whitehorses and says he will sell some of his land, presumably good, to them and even invites the couple to his house.

Often in films and television Westerns, the rights of Native Americans are respected only after they are dead and cannot pose a threat. In *The Magnificent Seven* (1960), Vin (Steve McQueen) and Chris (Yul Brynner) meet when they brave gunfire in order to drive a hearse up to Boot Hill so an Indian can be buried there. In a 1960 episode of *Cheyenne*, "Home of the Brave," the army gives Cheyenne (Clint Walker) the task of taking the body of Cole Prescott, a fallen decorated soldier, home to be buried. However, the town council of the aptly named "White River" refuses to allow him to be buried there because his mother was a Sioux. Cheyenne finds out that there is a town ordinance stating that three citizens can override the veto of the town council and allow Cole to be buried there. Cheyenne finds three citizens, Sheriff Dan Blaisdell (Brad Johnson), Dr. Henry Malcomb (Regis Toomey) and Ruth Thompson (Paula Raymond), willing to face the censure of the townspeople (including the spouses of Dr. Malcomb and Ruth Thompson) and even physical violence. In an attempt to stop the burial, John Thompson (John Howard) shoots the sheriff and tries to burn Prescott's body, but the sheriff kills him. At this point, an army detail rides into town to let the townspeople know that they will bury Prescott in Arlington National Cemetery with full military honors.

In the film *Tell Them Willie Boy Is Here* (1969), set in 1909, a Paiute

Indian, Willie (Robert Blake), kills the father of his lover, Lola (Katharine Ross), in self-defense, and the two of them flee. The white community blows the incident out of proportion, believing this could be the start of an Indian uprising. Deputy Sheriff Christopher Cooper (Robert Redford) and a posse chase after the couple. Cooper wants to capture Willie to prove that he (Cooper) is the equal of his famous lawman father. At the end of the chase, Cooper ends up facing Willie, who levels a rifle at him, but Cooper shoots him dead. Afterwards, Cooper checks the rifle and finds that it isn't loaded. Because of his newfound sympathy and respect for Willie, he carries the body down the mountain and gives it to the Paiutes, who will burn it as is their custom. When the county sheriff complains to Cooper that the white community wants to see Willie's body, he responds, "Tell them we are all out of souvenirs," another example of a Native American receiving justice only after death.

One way that an Indian can receive white man's justice in films and television Westerns is to become a law enforcement officer. In "The Indian," a 1959 *Rifleman* episode, Mark (Johnny Crawford) and Lucas McCain (Chuck Connors) come across Sam Buckhart (Michael Ansara), a Harvard-educated Apache and deputy marshal, taking his Indian prisoner to North Fork. In North Fork, he looks for an Indian suspected of burning down a farmhouse with a white Quaker couple in it. Fooling the townspeople by dressing as a white man, he is welcomed by the men in the saloon for bringing in an Indian for a crime. When Buckhart leaves, he tells McCain that when he was an Apache warrior, he came across a wounded officer, but instead of killing him, he nursed him back to health. After the man died, his will had a provision for Buckhart's way to be paid to attend Harvard. After Harvard, he felt he could best help his people by becoming a marshal.

After Buckhart leaves town, the townspeople learn that he is an Indian and, in an irrational prejudiced outburst, shoot up all the glasses in the saloon where Buckhart had been in order to make sure no one drank from the glass Buckhart touched. When Buckhart goes to the Indian encampment where the Indian suspected of burning the farmhouse is living, the accused man denies any wrongdoing and instead incriminates a white man named Slade (Lewis Charles).

McCain, letting Buckhart know that the townspeople will be worked up now that they know that he is an Indian, tries to keep him from going to town to question or arrest Slade. Refusing to be detained, Buckhart goes to town and takes Slade into custody. A mob led by Gorman (Herbert Rudley) and Tub (Mickey Simpson) try to stop Buckhart from taking away

Slade. They were pleased when the accused was an Indian but won't stand for an Indian arresting a white man. Micah Torrance (Paul Fix) faces the mob with his shotgun, letting them know that they would have to go through him to get at Buckhart. Lucas at first stays out of it, but then pretends to be on the mob's side. Using psychology, Lucas insinuates how much they would regret hurting Micah in order to save someone who burned two innocent people alive. The mob melts away, but Gorman and Tub pull their guns on Buckhart, who wounds them both. Before he is led away, Slade incriminates Gorman, and Buckhart leads him away as well.

There are also examples of the heroes of Westerns fighting for the rights of Mexicans and trying, if unsuccessfully, to get them fair treatment, such as *The Burning Hills* (1956), *The Badlanders* (1958) and *Buchanan Rides Alone* (1958). An early example is *The Strawberry Roan* (1948), where Gene Autry stands up for a Mexican-American student who is being prevented from speaking in a class about American history by a Caucasian student:

> Your friend Pedro has a right to speak here too.... Pedro's not new here, Lefty. He may be new to this school or this ranch, but so are you. And he has a right to be here, just the same as you and I have. Sure, you're an American, so am I. We were born here. So were our parents. But if you trace history far enough back, Lefty, you'll find that some of our ancestors were new here too, like Pedro. A man named Columbus discovered America with three ships. He was new here, but the Indians were here ahead of him ... and after the Indians came settlers, even before your family and mine. The early Spaniards brought some things to the West we can never forget. Not just horses and cattle.... They brought their missions and their faith. That's history, Lefty. So, stand up and shake hands with a fella whose ancestors date back farther than ours. Shake hands with Pedro Gonzales.

In a few instances, Mexican-Americans themselves have stood up for the rights of their people by using their positions in law enforcement. In "The Nine Lives of Elfego Baca," a 1958 episode of *Walt Disney's Wonderful World of Color*, Baca (Robert Loggia) enters Frisco, New Mexico, just as a cowboy is terrorizing the town. Its Mexican-American inhabitants are too frightened to do anything about the cowboy, so Baca gets a judge to swear him in as deputy sheriff so he can arrest the man. Baca arrests the man, who is fined $5 for being drunk and disorderly. Angered that the cowboy was even arrested, 80 of his friends chase Baca into an adobe house. To the delight of the Mexican-American populace, Baca is unharmed despite the mob shooting 4000 bullets into the house, dynamiting it, trying to burn it down, and losing four of their men killed and 13 badly wounded. Finally, a deputy marshal from Socorro, Ed Morgan (Robert F. Simon), sent for by the Mexican-American populace, arrives to take Baca to Socorro for trial. Baca agrees to go with Morgan if he can keep his guns to protect himself on the journey. At the trial, under examination from the prosecutor, Baca relates how he freed his father from jail (the father had been falsely accused of murder). The jury finds Baca not guilty.

Later Baca returns to Frisco to visit Anita Chavez (Lisa Montell), the woman whose house he used for a refuge during the gunfight. She says that her father's land was taken by a stranger who then sold it to a mining company. Baca tells her that he wants to become a lawyer to fight such injustices. During his stay, Baca learns that Dice Smith (Charles Maxwell) is gunning for him. Smith tries to shoot Baca as he is leaving town but hits only Baca's belt buckle as Baca shoots him in the arm. When Baca is back in Socorro, he is appointed sheriff of Socorro County and soon thereafter releases five Mexican-American sheepherders arrested due to an unjust law that puts people in jail for not paying their debts.

The 1970 film *Valdez Is Coming* deals with prejudice, primarily against Mexican-Americans, but also against blacks and Native Americans, and the way one man resists that prejudice. Bob Valdez (Burt Lancaster) comes upon a group of spectators watching another group of men shooting up a cabin. The shooters are led by Frank Tanner (Jon Cypher), who claims that the black man inside is an army deserter who killed his friend. Valdez, a part-time constable in the "Mexican part of town," despite being treated disrespectfully by Tanner and his men, tries to talk the alleged killer out of the cabin. It looks as if he will be successful until R.L. Davis (Richard Jordan), a young man trying to impress Tanner, shoots at the black man. The black man thinks Valdez has tricked him and tries to shoot Valdez, who kills him instead. When Tanner finally gets a good look at the dead man, he admits without any remorse that he's not the man he thought killed his friend, apparently having accused him before in part because he was a black man.

Valdez goes to the townspeople to gather a collection for the dead man's pregnant Apache woman. The townspeople gather only three or four dollars. An upset Valdez asks for at least $200. The townspeople say that if Tanner gives him $100, they will give him another $100. Valdez goes twice to Tanner to ask for the money. The first time, Tanner's men shoot all around Valdez out of pure meanness. The second time, Tanner responds with an ethnic slur and then has his men tie a large wooden cross to Valdez and force him to walk back home. Valdez is able to make it back to the house of his friend Diego Luz (Frank Silvera) due to the unexpected help of Davis, who unties Valdez from the cross. Diego and Valdez have a conversation about how condescending the Anglos of the region are towards them.

Valdez has had enough and sends word to Tanner that he is coming. Despite Tanner being guarded at his compound, Valdez sneaks into the bedroom of Tanner while he is in bed with his woman, Gay Erin (Susan Clark), the widow of the man who was murdered, and kidnaps her. Tanner's men chase Valdez and Gay through the mountains. During the chase, Gay admits that she killed her husband. Tanner's men corner Valdez, but not before he has killed ten of them. Tanner, apparently afraid to do it himself, asks his men to kill Valdez, but they all refuse to do it. The film ends when Valdez simply tells Tanner to either draw his gun or pay him the $100.

A film based on true events is 1982's *The Ballad of Gregorio Cortez*. Unlike Bob Valdez (Burt Lancaster) and Elfego Baca (Robert Loggia), Gregorio Cortez is portrayed by a Mexican-American actor, Edward James Olmos, whose authenticity is enhanced by actually speaking Spanish in situations one would expect him to speak Spanish.

The story begins in 1901 in Gonzales, Texas. Sheriff Morris (Timothy Scott) suspects that Mexican-Americans are involved in rustling. He goes to the home of Gregorio Cortez with his Spanish interpreter, Boone Choate (Tom Bower). Gregorio and his brother, Romaldo (Pepe Serna), are in the front of the house when Morris and Choate pull up in their buggy. Through his interpreter, Morris asks Gregorio if he traded a horse. Gregorio responds in Spanish he didn't trade a horse (caballo) but did trade a mare (yegua). According to Choate's translation, Cortez said that he didn't trade a horse. Choate's incomplete translation makes the sheriff suspicious because he believes Cortez did trade a horse, not realizing that Mexicans make a difference between a male horse (caballo) and a mare (yegua). Morris tells Cortez that he is going to arrest him, and Cortez refuses. The sheriff pulls a gun and shoots the unarmed Romaldo, a wound that later proves fatal. Cortez fatally shoots the sheriff and escapes.

Sheriff Glover (Michael McGuire) joins a posse that surrounds the house where Cortez is hiding. When Glover shoots at the house, Cortez kills him and pandemonium breaks out. A rancher with the posse, Henry Schnabel (Ben Zeller), is apparently accidentally killed by the posse in the chaotic situation. By this time, the whole incident has been blown out of proportion with false reports of a gang of Mexicans helping Cortez, a narrative which results in the shooting of innocent Mexicans and 600 men chasing after Cortez. Cortez is trapped in a box canyon but manages to escape, only to hear the distressing news that his wife and children have been jailed. Finally, after ten days in which he traveled 400 miles on horseback and 100 miles on foot, Gregorio is captured when a Mexican-American betrays his location for the $1000 reward.

Cortez is put in the same jail as his family but, to his dismay, not near them. Through an interpreter, Carlota Muñoz (Rosana DeSoto), Gregorio's lawyer, B.R. Abernathy (Barry Corbin), learns Cortez's version of events and defends him in court. But Gregorio is convicted of murder without malice and sentenced to 50 years. By this time, Cortez has reached legendary stature in the Mexican-American community and even has a ballad written about him. The Anglo community, however, is outraged he was not sentenced to hang and a mob tries to lynch him, only to be stopped by Sheriff Frank Fly (James Gammon). A postscript mentions that Cortez's conviction was reversed, but he was tried six more times. He was acquitted of killing Sheriff Morris and Henry Schnabel but convicted of stealing the horse on which he fled and killing Sheriff Glover, for which he was sentenced to life imprisonment. In 1913, he was pardoned by Texas' governor after serving 12 years, thanks in part to the organizations that had been formed to publicize the case and raise money for his defense. He died in 1916.

The Chinese also have been featured as victims of discrimination; one of the better accounts of that prejudice is the 2006 miniseries *Broken Trail*, based on true events. It begins with Prentice "Prent" Ritter (Robert Duvall) and his nephew Tom Harte (Thomas Haden Church) driving 500 horses from Oregon to Sheridan, Wyoming, to deliver them to the British army. An Irish fiddler, Heck Gilpin (Scott Cooper), joins them when Harte makes a stop to purchase supplies. The three men meet Captain Bill Fender (James Russo), who is taking five Chinese girls to sell to the madam Kate Becker (Rusty Schwimmer) in Caribou City, Idaho. Fender steals the cowboy's money and escapes with one of the Chinese girls, whom he rapes. Harte trails Fender, hangs him and takes the girl back to camp.

The girls and Ritter and Harte bridge the language gap, the two men teaching one of the girls how to drive a wagon and another how to ride a horse. Despite the best efforts of Harte and Ritter, one of the Chinese girls dies of tick fever. When they get to Caribou City, the cowboys intend to leave the girls with someone who will take care of them. However, they find out through interpreter Lung Hay (Donald Fong) that the girls want to stay with them. Meanwhile, Kate Becker demands that Ritter and Harte hand the girls over to her since she paid Fender for them. Harte and Gilpin beat off three men who have broken into the girls' room and attacked them. Harte, Gilpin, Ritter, prostitute Nola Johns (Greta Scacchi), Lung Hay and the girls flee town. Becker vows to get them back and exact revenge.

Nola explains to Ritter that she turned to prostitution when her husband died. The two of them get closer, as do Harte and Sun Fu (Gwendoline Yeo). Lung Hay reveals that he left his wife in China many years ago to look for gold in America. The group's idyllic time together is disturbed when the girl who was raped, Ye Fung (Olivia Feng), becomes so depressed that she kills herself.

On the trail, the group is confronted by Ed Bywaters (Chris Mulkey) and his gang, who have been hired by Becker to get the girls back. With Harte and Gilpin providing cover, Ritter pretends to be Smallpox Bob, a scoundrel who peddles smallpox-infected blankets to the Indians. Afraid of being infected, the gang leaves.

The group eventually reaches Sheridan, Wyoming, and sell their horses to the British Army. Afterwards, Bywaters and his gang appear in Sheridan while Harte is out on the range. They take Nola, Lung Hay and the girls hostage, and kill Gilpin, as Baywaters prepares to torture Ritter. But Ritter lets out a yell that alerts Harte, who shoots the other gang members. Despite being wounded, Bywaters takes aim at Harte, but Ritter saves him by killing Bywaters with a mallet. Nola starts to leave with the Chinese girls for San Francisco; but before the stagecoach can leave, Sun Fu, in love with Harte, gets out of the coach, and Harte smiles. We find out in a postscript that Harte and Sun Fu married and their grandchildren still ranch in Wyoming.

An interesting example of justice for a minority group and conflicting cultural conceptions of what justice means is the 1973 *Gunsmoke* episode "This Golden Land." The Ruxton brothers—Rouse (Victor French), Calvin (Kevin Coughlin) and Homer (Wayne McLaren)—come upon a Jewish father and son, Moshe Gorofsky (Paul Stevens) and Semel Gorofsky (Scott Selles), praying on the prairie. Even though the mother, Zisha (Bettye Ackerman), tells the three Rouses not to disturb the father and son at prayer, Rouse ropes Semel and drags him. Moshe, Zisha and their other two sons, Laibel (Joseph Hindy) and Gearshon (Richard Dreyfuss), later find Semel badly wounded. They take him to Doc Adams (Milburn Stone), but despite his best efforts, Semel dies.

Matt Dillon (James Arness) and Festus (Ken Curtis) visit the Gorofskys at their farm to find out what happened. Moshe refuses to identify the three men who dragged his son away because the Talmud says someone can accuse another person of a crime like murder only if the accuser saw him or her do it and not on circumstantial evidence, and neither Moshe nor Zisha saw the Ruxtons kill Semel. A frustrated Dillon warns Moshe that if the three men get away with it, they could kill someone else. Festus accuses Moshe of being afraid. Back at the farmhouse, Gearshon tells his father he is wrong not to identify the men.

In town, the Gorofskys meet the Ruxtons. By the look that Moshe gives the three men, Gearshon realizes they are the ones who dragged Semel away. Gearshon attacks them with Laibel joining in. The Ruxtons get the upper hand and start to beat the two boys up while Moshe yells for them to stop. Dillon arrives to break the fight up, but Moshe still refuses to identify the Ruxtons.

Back at the farm, Gearshon refuses to come to dinner, telling his mother that his family needs to fight back against people like the Ruxtons. When Gearshon finally joins the family dinner, he tells his father he is wrong; the father says that if Gearshon can't accept his truth, Gearshon can't accept him. Gearshon rides off. The mother, upset, tells her husband he is a coward and a dreamer. Moshe admits he is afraid, but of two things only: offending God and losing his wife's love. With increased understanding of her husband, she tells him she has never loved him more than now.

Wielding a shotgun, Gearshon goes to the Ruxton ranch to force them to come to town and confess their crime. When he sees one of them behind him, he shoots both barrels at one of the Ruxtons but misses, leaving him with an empty gun. The Ruxtons take Gearshon back to the Gorofsky farm, and Rouse tells Moshe to leave Kansas with his family within 24 hours. Moshe refuses, even though Rouse threatens to kill them. Rouse tells the Gorofskys that after dragging Semel, they let go of the rope and that as Semel ran away, the rope got caught in a rock and pulled him down with the other end of the rope around his neck. Moshe says he believes Rouse, and the Ruxtons give themselves up to face assault charges.

Even though a number of films in the late 1940s and 1950s are devoted to overcoming or trying to overcome prejudice against African-Americans, it wasn't until *Sergeant Rutledge* (1960) that a Western about racial prejudice against African-Americans featured an African-American in a leading role. In 1881 Arizona, at an army post, Lucy Dabney, after being beaten and raped, and her father, Major Dabney, are found dead. Circumstantial evidence points to Braxton Rutledge (Woody Strode). Rutledge says when he found Lucy already dead, a distraught Major Dabney, thinking Rutledge had killed her, shot at Rutledge, only to be shot by him. Rutledge flees, afraid as a black man he wouldn't get a fair trial, only to be apprehended when he warns an army patrol it is riding into an Apache ambush.

Rutledge is defended in the trial by Lt. Tom Cantrell (Jeffrey Hunter), under whom Rutledge served in the African-American Ninth Cavalry. Just when it appears the evidence will convict Rutledge, Cantrell reveals that he found Lucy's cross on a dead Apache who had killed Chris Hubble. Chris' father, Chandler Hubble (Fred Libby), blurts out that Chris killed

Lucy. However, Cantrell finds an inconsistency in Chandler's testimony that throws suspicion on him, and he confesses. Rutledge goes back to leading his unit.

By 1972, films had progressed to the point where African-Americans didn't need whites like Tom Cantrell to save them. *Buck and the Preacher* (1972) opens with a group of African-Americans, just freed from slavery, heading west to start a new life. They are attacked by a group of white men led by DeShay (Cameron Mitchell). An unsuspecting Buck (Sidney Poitier) approaches the scene thinking everything is all right but rides away when he is fired upon. Buck comes upon Preacher (Harry Belafonte), takes his horse and rides away. Preacher then rides Buck's horse into town and finds out that DeShay will pay him $500 for helping him to locate Buck or taking him in alive or dead. When Buck returns to the camp of the African-Americans and offers to help them move farther west, Preacher shows up as well. Buck does not trust Preacher, feeding him and giving him his horse back but asking him to leave the camp. Buck later makes a deal with some Native Americans to protect the African-Americans as they move west. As Preacher learns more about Buck's attempts to help the African-Americans, he begins to admire him for what he is doing. When DeShay and his men raid the camp again, Preacher gives up his plan to kill Buck for the reward. He decides to join forces with Buck and the African-Americans, advising Buck how they can ambush DeShay and his men. Buck concurs with Preacher's plan, killing DeShay and most of his men. However, the local sheriff (John Kelly) pursues them.

Preacher, Buck and Buck's wife Ruth (Ruby Dee) rob a bank in order to gain funds to help finance the African-Americans' move out west. The sheriff chases them to Indian Territory, where a Native American war party does not allow the sheriff and his posse to continue the chase. Later the sheriff decides not to attack the African-American camp. One of his men is so disgusted with this decision that he kills the sheriff and orders the posse to attack the African-American camp. Buck lures the posse away from the camp. In a gunfight, Preacher is wounded, but the posse is defeated with the help of the Native Americans. Buck, Preacher and Ruth are able to start their new lives.

Chapter 5

Temperance

"It takes a real man to keep his gun in his holster and his fists in his pockets."—"Silent Thunder" from *Desilu Playhouse*

One of the six virtues that the positive psychologists, Christopher Peterson and Martin Seligman (2004), discuss is temperance, which generally speaking is protecting against excess. Temperance can be broken down into four strengths: forgiveness and mercy, humility and modesty, prudence, and self-regulation. To demonstrate these virtues often demands courage.

According to Rye, Loiacono, Folck, Olszewski, Heim and Madia (2001), forgiveness involves a decrease in three dimensions: behavior towards the offender (e.g., verbal aggression), negative affect towards the offender (e.g., hostility) and cognitions towards the offender (e.g., thoughts of revenge). Forgiveness is associated with empathy and perspective-taking (McCullough, Worthington and Rachal, 1997).

Peterson and Seligman (2004, p. 463) explain the difference between humility and modesty:

> [H]umility involves the non-defensive willingness to see the self accurately, including both strengths and limitations. Humble individuals don't see themselves as better or worse than they really are and have no interest in dominating others. Although it is not always easy to see oneself accurately, a distinguishing characteristic is that humble people welcome accurate information and are open to using that information to learn about and improve themselves. Modesty is a social virtue in which the person in the presence of others downplays their successes and positive characteristics, whether they believe this to be true or not.

Peterson and Seligman (2004, p. 478) go on to define prudence:

> Prudence is a cognitive orientation to the personal future, a form of practical reasoning and self-management that helps to achieve the individual's long-term goals effectively. Prudent individuals show a far-sighted and deliberative concern for the consequences of their actions and decisions, successfully resist impulses and other choices that satisfy shorter term goals at the expense of longer term ones, have a flexible and moderate approach to life, and strive for balance among their goals and ends.

Self-regulation refers to the ability to control one's emotions, thoughts, impulses and behaviors in accordance with one's standards and in pursuit of one's goals. Prudence and self-regulation overlap, although self-regulation is the broader concept (Peterson and Seligman, 2004).

Forgiveness and mercy are often featured in Westerns. In *The Searchers*, when Ethan (John Wayne) rescues Debbie, he not only redeems himself but shows mercy towards someone who has adopted Indian ways. In the *Rifleman* episode "Old Man Running," Mark, but not Lucas, forgives his grandfather (John Anderson) for deserting his mother when she was extremely ill and ended up dying. Self-regulation, the ability to exercise control over one's actions, is exemplified in many different ways in Westerns. In the 1958 film *The Big Country*, James McKay (Gregory Peck) goes west to marry Patricia Terrill (Carroll Baker), the daughter of powerful rancher Henry Terrill (Charles Bickford). However, he falls out of favor with Patricia, his father and the ranch foreman, Steve Leech (Charlton Heston), when he avoids a confrontation with Buck Hannassey (Chuck Connors), an enemy of the Terrills, refuses to ride a wild horse, and backs down when challenged by Leech because he feels no need to prove himself before his fiancée or anyone else. When he does ride the wild horse, he does it only in the presence of a ranch hand, and when he finally fights Steve, he fights him without anyone else watching, clearly disgusted with their fight as he questions Steve about what the fight proves. McKay finally ends up with Julie Maragon (Jean Simmons), a woman mature enough to understand that James' self-regulation is a sign of character, not cowardice.

In the *Rifleman* episode "The Clarence Bibs Story" (1961), Bibs (Buddy Hackett), a man who mops floors for a living, accidentally kills Pretty Man Longden (X Brands). As a result, he gains respect from his fellow townsmen. At first, Bibs is reluctant to take credit for the killing, but encouraged by two ne'er-do-wells, Wicks (Lee Van Cleef) and Reade (John Milford), Bibs begins to think of himself as a gunfighter. George Tanner (Denver Pyle), Longden's partner, rides into town and asks what happened to Longden. When told his killing was an accident, Tanner accepts the killing and decides to ride on. Before he leaves, he decides to get a beer. In the saloon, a pumped up Bibs decides to show how tough he is by telling the renowned

Nothing proven. Charlton Heston, as Steve Leech (left), and Gregory Peck, as James McKay (right), trade punches in a senseless fight in William Wyler's *The Big Country* (1958, United Artists).

gunfighter, Tanner, to get out of town. Unafraid, but not wanting to get into a needless fight, Tanner, in a dignified manner, finishes his drink and leaves, intending to leave town. This show of self-regulation is not good enough for Bibs, who challenges Tanner to a gunfight. Tanner, still maintaining his dignity while refusing to fight, tells Bibs, "Mr. Bibs ... a word of advice. Sell that gun for what it will bring and go back to your mop. You'll lead a far happier life ... and a fuller one." After Tanner leaves, Bibs challenges McCain, who shoots Bibs' gun out of his holster. When Wicks and Reade chide Bibs for being beaten by McCain, Bibs challenges them and they run away. At this point, Bibs gives up his gun, realizing it is better to be a mop boy than saddled with the reputation of being a gunfighter or dead.

In the 1959 *Gunsmoke* episode "Passive Resistance," cattlemen Joe Kell (Read Morgan) and Hank Voyles (Alfred Ryder) try to force a sheepman, Gideon Seek (Carl Benton Reid), off his land by killing all his sheep. Seek refuses to tell Marshal Matt Dillon (James Arness) why his sheep are dead. Dillon, suspicious of foul play, rides out to Seek's farm to find out what happened. Seek admits the sheep were killed but refuses to tell Dillon who killed them, telling the marshal that he doesn't believe in committing violence against another human being, that the consciences of the men will torment them and that they will be punished in the end.

Later, the two cattlemen burn down Seek's house and wagon because he refuses to leave his farm. Despite these losses, Seek stays to rebuild his house and flock. Seek's determination to stay so infuriates Kell that he drags Seek on the ground, almost killing him. Again, Seek refuses to cooperate with Dillon, repeating that the two men will eventually be punished and he will win in the end.

Voyles gets drunk in the Long Branch to drown his guilty conscience. Kell, unrepentant, tries to drag Voyles out of the saloon so he won't reveal what they did, but Voyles refuses. After Kell leaves, Dillon, who has overheard Voyles and Kell, questions Voyles and gets him to say that Kell dragged Gideon. Dillon confronts Kell, who admits he was involved in the crimes against Seek. Kell draws on Dillon, but Dillon kills him. Dillon tells Chester Goode (Dennis Weaver) that he will make Voyles reimburse Seek for the sheep, house and wagon. Although Seek didn't handle the situation the way Dillon would have, Dillon makes it clear in the introduction of the episode that he believes that Seek's pursuit of justice in his non-violent way marks Seek as someone with a great deal of courage.

Another example of self-regulation is the 1959 *Bronco* episode "The Soft Answer." Bronco Layne (Ty Hardin) is attacked by Indians when a wagon driven by Barnaby Spence (Leo Gordon) comes by. Spence tells the Indians he will give them 25 sheep if they stop attacking Layne, and they leave. Spence then gives Layne a job at his sheep camp. Layne learns that Billy the Kid (Ray Stricklyn), whom Spence hopes to reform, is working for Spence as well. At the sheep camp, Layne meets José and Pedro and learns that Spence is selling sheep to the Indians. While Bronco is there, cattlewoman Kay Ransom (Nancy Gates) and her brother Mike (Mike Road) come by and tell Spence he and his sheep are not welcome, even though Spence says that he owns the land and that sheep and cattle can co-exist. The brother and sister tell Spence he will have to leave since they own the creek the sheep need to keep from dying from thirst and they will not let Spence use the creek.

Arron Running Deer (Robert Colbert), an Indian who works for the Ransoms, warns Bronco that Mike's men are going to raid the sheep camp. Layne and Billy put up a rope that knocks Mike and his men off their horses when they raid the sheep camp, but that setback doesn't stop Mike's men from killing many of the sheep. Spence goes to the Ransom ranch to get money to compensate him for the sheep that were killed. Instead, Mike beats up Spence, who refuses to fight ("the soft answer") because he is a pacifist. (The fact that Leo Gordon plays a gentle pacifist is an interesting choice since Gordon made a career out of playing a heavy in Westerns on television and in film.) Layne then rides in, beats up Mike and takes Spence back to the sheep camp. Kay learns that Mike has been overcharging the Indians for their beef, and she tells him she will charge the Indians a decent price, which will undercut the sale of sheep to the Indians.

On the way back to the sheep camp with the unconscious Spence, Bronco encounters Jackson, Mike's hired gunfighter, and Mike's hired hands. However, they are stopped by Billy from harming Layne and Spence. Spence tells Layne not to exact revenge. Layne accidentally finds a letter written by Abraham Lincoln that says that Spence, who fought in several Civil War battles, should not be court martialed for his newfound pacifistic beliefs, but be allowed to join a medical unit operated by Quakers. Spence from that point on has tried to emulate the kind and pacifistic Quakers, even though he is not sure he can show their brand of courage.

When Mike finds out that Billy the Kid is working for Spence, he wires Pat Garrett to come to arrest him. Mike decides not to wait for Garrett and agrees to meet Spence alone. Layne tricks Mike by arranging to meet him before Spence gets there so he can confront Mike since Layne suspects Mike will hurt Spence. Billy knocks out Layne to keep him from getting hurt by Mike and then confronts and kills Jackson, who has come to kill Spence. Mike and his men try to stampede the sheep with his cattle. Layne and Spence's men manage to turn the stampede, but Mike is trampled, leaving Kay and Spence to come to an accommodation.

In the 1958 *The Rifleman* episode "The Apprentice Sheriff," Dan Willard (Robert Vaughn) is the acting marshal of North Fork. He feels he has to prove himself since he dropped out of West Point due to poor eyesight. When a group of cowboys come into town, Willard feels challenged by their rowdy ways. Lucas McCain (Chuck Connors) has some prudent advice: "You know, Dan, I always thought the best way to enforce the law was a firm hand on a slack rein. That way you got control and no one feels the bit in his mouth." Instead of listening to Lucas' advice, Willard provokes the cowhands into a fight by posting an unnecessary notice that all non-residents need to check their firearms with the sheriff, a rule which results in Willard killing one of the trail hands. Unrepentant, Willard insists on continuing to enforce his ban on firearms, and this leads to a fight with trail boss Keely Thompson (Edward Binns), who feels he has to confront

Willard or lose face with his men. Thompson severely wounds Willard. Although McCain considers the firearms ban unwise, he feels that in order for law to be maintained in North Fork he needs to enforce it. As a result, he fights Thompson, wounding him. When Thompson asks McCain why he didn't kill him, Lucas replies that he showed the same restraint that Thompson showed in not killing Willard. Through Willard's lack of prudence, McCain and Thompson ended up in gunfights they wanted to avoid.

Another example of an experienced lawman teaching a younger man the importance of prudence and self-regulation on the job is found in "License to Kill," a 1958 episode of the *Zane Grey Theatre* TV series. Before Sheriff Tom Baker (Macdonald Carey), with his arm in a cast, can quell a disturbance caused by three cowboys, a stranger, Lane (John Ericson), steps in to stop it, killing one of the cowboys in the process. This killing angers the prudent sheriff, who believes the disturbance could have been handled without any loss of life. Mayor Danforth (Jacques Aubuchon), is impressed by the way the young man handled the disturbance. He decides to give Lane the town marshal's job over the objections of the sheriff because the sheriff is limited by his broken arm and dozens of cowboys are coming to town in a few days. It turns out that Lane is the younger brother of Sheriff Tom, who years earlier forced Lane out of his position as a lawman when he needlessly endangered citizens through his impulsive behavior.

Lane confirms Tom's worst suspicions when he shoots in the leg a young boy who steals a sack of flour instead of simply going to the boy's home and arresting him there peaceably, as Tom suggested. However, with the cowboys coming to town and Tom still physically impaired, the mayor decides to keep Lane on. The cowboys finally arrive. Growder (Peter Whitney) shoots bullets through the ceiling of a tavern, causing Lane to demand that Growder give him his gun and come to jail, even though the bartender has accepted Growder's offer to pay for the damage. When Growder still won't give Lane his gun, Lane shoots a glass out of Growder's hand. Growder then squares off to face Lane, who can't expect any help from the hostile cowboys in the saloon. Tom defuses the situation by stepping between Growder and Lane and offering Growder and the cowboys whiskey. Humiliated, Lane leaves the tavern but later admits that he is too impulsive to be a good lawman. Tom takes this admission as a sign of contrition and suggests that Lane and Tom can perhaps work together as lawmen after all.

In the *Zane Grey Theatre* episode "Thread of Respect" (1959), Italian

Immigrant Gino Pelleti (Danny Thomas) and his son George (Nick Adams) arrive in Yucca City, Arizona, to set up a tailor shop. They are insulted by Jess Newton (James Coburn), who tells them he hates Italians, and one of his friends trips up George. Gino "accidentally" breaks Jess' knife in retaliation. After they set up their tailor shop, George despairs that anyone will come to their shop since some of the townspeople have treated them so rudely. The son wants his father to do something about this treatment and accuses him of being afraid. Dave Radkin (Joe H. Hamilton), who owns the freight company, explains to Gino that the town is fed up with Newton and his followers and will be glad when they leave.

In the saloon, Newton approaches Seth Robson (Denver Pyle), who tells Newton that Gino is a good man, and not the kind of man to be intimidated into leaving town as much as Newton would like Gino to leave. Newton tells him he has a grudge against Italians because an Italian could have saved but did not save his ten-year-old sister when their house was on fire.

Two of Newton's men vandalize Gino's store while he is there. After the men leave, George arrives at the store and asks why Gino didn't stop them and what he is going to do about the vandalism. Gino says he will make them pay for the damage, but George scoffs at him for not doing something immediately, calls him a coward and runs into the street, attacking one of the vandals. Having newfound respect for George, Newton makes the vandal apologize to George for tearing apart the store. Soon thereafter, George is invited to join Newton's "gang" and watches while they engage in their unruly and illegal activities.

When Gino learns about George's association with the Newton gang, he goes to the saloon to try to drag Gino out, telling George that Newton is not much of a man, but someone who basks in the adulation of the younger men he has hang around him and stoops to robbing drunks. When Newton objects to Gino's interference, Gino hits him. Newton challenges Gino to a gunfight, and Gino accepts. In the tailor shop, Robson tries to convince Gino not to go through with the gunfight. Gino tells Robson that ever since his son died in battle in Europe, he has hated violence but insists on facing Newton so that he can keep his son from becoming like Newton. However, he tells Robson, his second, to convince Newton to use dueling pistols and fight according to the dueling code.

At the dueling site the two men walk in opposite directions and fire on the count of ten. Each gun has two bullets. Newton misses with his first bullet and hits Gino in his arm with the second. Gino hits Newton in his leg with his first. Although at this point he has Newton dead to rights, he throws the gun to the ground instead of firing the second shot. When his son tries to congratulate his father, Gino slaps him and says, "Am I any more a man for what I have to do?" It is clear that Gino was never too afraid to fight back and never had to fight Newton to prove he is a man, but only to keep his son from turning into someone like Newton or his followers. He is angry at his son for forcing him to engage in the violence he hates so much. The son comes to understand the motives for his father's actions and father and son hug.

In a 1962 episode of *Bonanza*, "The Crucible," Adam Cartwright's (Pernell Roberts) ability to control his baser impulses is put to a test. After Little Joe (Michael Landon) and Adam get $5000 for selling cattle they drove through the desert to the town of Eastgate, Adam decides to do some hunting and fishing while Little Joe stays in town to watch a murder trial, planning to meet Adam three days later at Signal Rocks. Referring to the trial, Adam tells Little Joe, "A man is responsible for what he does. He loses control of himself, he has to be punished for it. That's the way it is." When Little Joe interjects that he wonders if Adam would feel the same if he were the man on trial for murder, Adam says no one could drive him to murder.

While Adam is on the trail alone, two men force him to disarm and hand them his money, and take away his horse and water, without which he can't survive in the desert wilderness. While wandering around, Adam comes upon a miner's camp and the miner, Peter Kane (Lee Marvin), gives him water, food and rest. He has been prospecting for 20 years without ever striking it rich. Adam asks to borrow his mule and some supplies to meet Little Joe at Signal Rocks and catch the two bandits. Kane asks him why he wouldn't just kill the two men if he caught them instead of taking them in for trial, and Adam responds that it wouldn't be civilized. Kane retorts that in his experience he has found that most men are not particularly civilized and that men can be driven to do anything. Adam claims he is not one of those men.

Kane tells Adam he will let him have the mule and supplies only if Adam helps him for three days, by which time they should reach the main vein of gold. Kane works Adam harder and harder until the three days are up. When Adam prepares to leave, Kane kills the mule, dooming Adam to stay with Kane, and then points the gun at Adam, telling him that he will have to keep digging out the mine without the mule. At night, Adam gets hold of a gun and starts to escape, but it turns out it is a trick (the gun is unloaded) to see if Adam would try to kill Kane while he was sleeping (which Adam does not try to do) and thus prove that Adam isn't civilized.

Little Joe has found Adam's horse and been informed the two men who robbed Adam were killed by irate citizens of Salt Flats when they started shooting up the town and its inhabitants. Little Joe enlists the aid of Hoss (Dan Blocker) and Ben (Lorne Greene) in the search for Adam. Adam hears the gunshots of his brothers and father in the distance and yells at them, but Kane will not let him reach his father and brothers, and the Cartwrights ride away. Adam finally digs to where the main vein should be but finds nothing. Kane informs him that he's known for some time there was no main vein, but he forced Adam to keep on working to see if he would become angry enough to try to kill Kane. Kane digs up some food and water, just enough to keep one of them alive, puts the gun between Adam and him and tells him that the two of them will fight over who gets the gun, water and food. Adam jumps on top of Kane and is choking him but stops when he realizes that killing him will prove that Kane was right, that Adam was not civilized after all. Proving that Adam is not civilized is the only satisfaction that Kane has left since he will never strike it rich. Instead of killing him, Adam magnanimously tries to drag the both of them out of the desert. Ben, Little Joe and Hoss find them, but by then Kane is dead. Adam has proven he is not just civilized, but noble, despite being on the verge of hysteria.

A 1963 *Bonanza*, "The Legacy," examines the role of family upbringing in the character trait of self-regulation and restraining oneself from blind vengeance. Ben Cartwright is shot by an unseen poacher. Hoss, Little Joe and Adam find his lame horse with blood on the saddle by a campsite where three ex-convicts were camped. Hoss, Little Joe and Adam go after the three men thinking they killed their father while Sheriff Roy Coffee (Ray Teal) forms a posse. Before they leave, Coffee warns the boys not to take the law into their own hands if they find the men. After they leave Virginia City, the Cartwright sons learn from a rancher that one of the three men has Ben's rifle and they have scattered in three different directions. Each son follows the trail of one of the men.

Ben is found by a kindly peddler, Jacob J. Dormann (Robert H. Harris), who tends to his wounds. Ben offers to pay Dormann $100 to take him to the Ponderosa. When Dormann suggests that his sons might think Ben is dead and are after the men they think killed him, Ben responds that his sons are too intelligent and decent to seek revenge. He says Adam is too intelligent to act so rashly and Hoss is too slow to anger and too slow to condemn another person to engage in vengeance, although he is not so sure of the quick-tempered Little Joe, whom he doesn't know as well as he knows the other two boys. Despite what he has said about his sons, later he tells

Dormann he is afraid that he wasn't able to raise his boys with the values that would keep them from losing control and taking vengeance on the men they think killed him.

Adam trails his man, Gannon (Philip Pine), to his wife and the general store that he left when he went to prison. Gannon tells Adam he did not kill Ben and that he and the other two men found Ben's horse but ran instead of looking for Ben since they were scared that they would be blamed for Ben's shooting since they were ex-convicts. Adam is unconvinced and tells Gannon to come out onto the street, apparently for a gunfight. However, while waiting for Gannon, Adam thinks it through and decides not to shoot him, but leaves him in the custody of the sheriff.

Hoss tracks his man, Page (James Best), to his farm where he lives with his young son Danny (Rory Stevens). When Page comes in from work in the fields, Hoss tells Page to send his son away. He tells Page he thinks he killed his father just as Page killed his wife, the reason he went to prison. Hoss challenges him to a gunfight but can't go through with it since Danny is watching from the barn door.

Little Joe trails his man to another town where he is knocked out when he asks too many questions. When he regains consciousness, he comes face to face with Billy Chapin (Sandy McPeak), the man he has been trailing, surrounded by Billy's powerful father, Colonel Abel Chapin (Dayton Lummis), and the colonel's hired hands. When Little Joe tells them that Billy killed his father, the colonel, although disgusted with his son, tells Little Joe that he should leave and that if he comes back they will kill him. The colonel tells Billy not to chase after Little Joe once he leaves, but later Billy is able to get Little Joe alone with just the two of them present. Billy is about to kill Little Joe, but Little Joe gets the upper hand. He brings Billy to Billy's father where Billy confesses to be the only one of the three men who shot Ben. The colonel agrees to hold him until Sheriff Coffee can pick him up. The episode ends at the Ponderosa with a proud Ben surrounded by his sons, who did not give in to their baser instincts but instead followed the values their father instilled in them. Dormann is so impressed with Ben and his sons that he won't accept the $100 Ben offered him.

Another example of how refraining from revenge is a sign of self-regulation is demonstrated in the 1959 film *Last Train from Gun Hill*. Marshal Matt Morgan (Kirk Douglas) arrests a young man, Rick Belden (Earl Holliman), responsible for the brutal rape and murder of his Indian wife. When the young man spitefully slanders Morgan's wife, Morgan begins to choke him, but then regains control of himself.

In the 1959 *Lawman* episode "The Gunman," Kurt Monroe (Richard Arlen), who has a reputation as a gunfighter, is waiting in Laramie to meet his fiancée, hoping to start a new life without guns. Troublemakers Chalk Hennessey (Gordon Jones) and Harlin Smith (Hal Baylor) try to provoke Monroe into a fight with Marshal Dan Troop (John Russell). Monroe is reluctant; but as it begins to appear that his fiancée is not going to show up, he succumbs to the flattery and encouragement of the troublemakers and decides to have a showdown with Troop. Troop tries to discourage Monroe from fighting, telling him that a lesson a man has to learn is when to back down, and finally convinces Monroe to do so. Monroe's fiancée arrives, explaining why she was detained, and Monroe is glad he restrained himself.

In the 1960 *Lawman* episode "The Showdown," Blake Carr (James Coburn) is jealous of reformed gunfighter Lance Creedy (John Howard), because he is married to a woman, Mattie Creedy (Roberta Haynes), whom Carr desires. Due to his jealousy, Carr tries to provoke Lance into a fight in front of Troop and others in a saloon, but the gunfighter shows self-regulation by not taking the bait. When Carr, thinking he had humiliated the gunfighter in front of others, asks Troop what he thinks of the gunfighter now, Troop responds that he never thought so highly of a man as he does Lance in this instance. After being repeatedly provoked, Lance reaches the end of his rope and decides to fight it out with Carr; but before he can draw his gun, Mattie convinces him not to fight. Troop shoots Carr to keep him from killing Lance in cold blood.

The idea that truly strong individuals can show their strength through self-regulation is demonstrated in a 1958 *Desilu Playhouse* episode, "Silent Thunder." It begins with a young man, Les Tranier (Earl Holliman), whipping a young Apache, Little Horse (John Drew Barrymore), when Tranier unjustly accuses Little Horse of stealing a horse. When Les runs across him a second time, again falsely accusing Little Horse, this time of butchering a cow that doesn't belong to him, he shoots Little Horse in the hand. Les' father Matt Tranier (Barton MacLane) takes Little Horse home to recover from his wounds, not knowing that Les had whipped Little Horse. While at Matt and Les' ranch, Les repeatedly harasses Little Horse and even convinces someone else to harass Little Horse in town, even though Matt has hired Little Horse to work at the ranch because of his skill in handling horses.

Les becomes upset when Matt gives Little Horse a horse that Les coveted. To make amends with Les, Little Horse offers to give him the horse, but Les refuses. This rebuff humiliates Little Horse, who rides away. Matt catches up with him and gives him a lesson in strength and self-regulation:

"Some strong men don't have to always be using their strength. They know it's there when they need it…. It takes a real man to keep his gun in his holster and his fists in his pockets." However, Les keeps harassing Little Horse, even beating him up when Little Horse refuses Les' demand to break a horse because breaking horses is not Little Horses' specific job. In a final showdown, Les challenges Little Horse to a gunfight. Little Horse, who has been receiving lessons in drawing a gun and shooting from Matt, shoots the gun out of Les' hand before Les can shoot, and then begins to walk away. Incensed by this defeat, Les tells Little Horse to draw again, but Little Horse doesn't move. With his gun at his side ready to shoot, Matt walks slowly up to Les and asks for his gun. Les, chastened by what has happened, gives it to him, and they go back to the ranch.

A 1958 episode of *Zane Grey Theatre*, "To Sit in Judgment," illustrates forgiveness and mercy as well as prudence and self-regulation. Marshal Amos Parney (Robert Ryan) executes Tom MacPherson for killing a man. MacPherson's teenage son Jamie (John Washbrook) vows revenge against Amos. When Amos gets home, his wife Lucy (Betsy Jones-Moreland) questions Amos' motives for hunting down criminals, suspecting that Amos does it not for the sake of justice or the good of the community, but because he simply likes pitting his skill against another man, something that Amos denies. Another MacPherson son, young Rob (Harry Dean Stanton) tries to run Amos down with his horse. Amos draws his gun but doesn't fire it at Rob. Undeterred, Rob swears he will get Amos with his shotgun. When Amos gets back home that night, Lucy says that he showed courage by backing down from Rob. She pleads with Amos to let Rob be and not sit in judgment of him, that he is a victim of poverty and ignorance and that Amos should not take away from him a "chance to turn into a real human being." At that moment, Rob's shotgun blast comes through the window. Amos goes outside to confront Rob and Jamie. He knocks out Rob, but Rob and Jamie get away when Jamie shoots Amos. Lucy and Charlie Spawn (Michael Pate) plead with Amos not to hunt down Rob (who meanwhile has shot another man) and Jamie, but Amos insists on tracking them, believing that Rob will keep on killing. Amos and Charlie find Jamie in his mother's cabin, but Amos shows mercy and forgiveness by not taking him in. Amos persists in tracking Rob. Charlie and Amos find Rob, who draws his gun on Amos. Amos shoots Rob and he falls to the ground, wounded. Amos, in an act of temperance, drops his gun and tries to convince Rob he will not hang if he gives himself up. Rob is not convinced and tries to kill Amos, but Charlie kills Rob.

A pattern that occurs in these films and TV episodes is that men who demonstrate self-regulation tend to be older and those who don't tend to be younger, which is consistent with Jackson, Walton, Harms, Bogg, Wood, Lodi-Smith, Edmonds and Roberts (2008), who found that impulse control increases throughout adulthood. Peterson and Seligman (2004, p. 507) point out the interpersonal benefits of self-regulation:

> People with high self-control make better relationship partners and get along better with other people generally. They exhibit better accommodation, in the sense of adjusting their behavior to get along with their partners, and they also report more satisfying relationships and better adjustment in their relationships [Finkel and Campbell, 2000; Vohs, Ciarocco and Baumeister, 2003].

Ben Cartwright and his three sons all have very good relationships with each other and all are high in self-control. James McKay and Julie Maragon, Lance and Mattie Creedy, and Amos and Lucy Parney are all examples of deep, mature, loving relationships. Matt Morgan obviously loved his wife who was so brutally raped and killed. Lucas McCain has a very close relationship with his son Mark and his good friend, Micah Torrance. Although Barnaby Spence's attempts to curb Billy the Kid's aggressiveness prove to be futile, Billy still has a great deal of respect for Spence because Spence sees something good in him that others don't see. Matt Tranier and Gino Pelleti have very difficult relationships with their sons, as does Tom Baker with his younger brother Lane, but with patience and wisdom Matt and Gino are able to reach an accommodation with their sons, as does Tom with Lane.

Chapter 6

Growing Up and Growing Old

"All I want is to enter my house justified."—Ride the High Country

According to psychologist Erik Erikson (1968), adolescents are in the psychosocial stage of identity achievement vs. identity diffusion. The goal of the adolescent is to form a strong identity, one that is based on his or her own thinking and experiences, reflecting his or her true needs, abilities and actions, and is consistent over time and in different environments. Only by forming a strong identity can adolescents become adults who are independent in their beliefs and actions, or, in other words, true to themselves, and know what and to whom to commit themselves. Committing oneself to a vocation, person or belief regardless of the circumstances is the hallmark of someone who has achieved a strong identity. To find oneself in this way often calls for painful experimentation which takes individuals beyond their "comfort level" as they try out different adult roles to see which one "fits" best. This struggle often calls for courage.

When Bless Keough (Jeffrey Hunter) in *Gun for a Coward* (see Chapter 2) challenges his brother Will (Fred MacMurray) to a fistfight, he is breaking free from Will's overprotectiveness as the means to develop what Erikson would call a strong identity of his own. On the contrary, the 1970 *Gunsmoke* episode "Gentry's Law" involves a parent who so enables his sons not to be responsible for their actions that they don't grow into adults. The Gentry boys, Colt (Peter Jason) and Ben (Robert Pine), come upon a squatter, Floyd Babcock (Don Keefer), butchering one of their cows, something he has done before. To prevent Babcock from doing it again, they pretend they are going to hang him, but they accidentally end up hanging him for real. They bury the body and run away. Marshal Matt Dillon (James Arness) later gets a letter from Babcock's friend Orly Grimes (Shug Fisher), saying that he has found Babcock's grave. When Dillon goes to the Gentry ranch to investigate, Amos (John Payne), father of Colt and Ben, truthfully tells Matt he knows nothing about what happened to Babcock, but adds that he, not the government, is the law on Gentry property.

Dillon then visits Grimes, who says that he saw the Gentry boys in the vicinity of where Babcock was hanged on the day it occurred. When Gentry's sons return to the ranch house, they admit to Amos that they killed Grimes, stressing that it was an accident and reminding the father that he had dealt harshly with poachers before. When Dillon visits the ranch after the sons have gone into hiding, Amos lies that they were in Sedalia at the time of the hanging. Amos' lie disturbs his wife Claire (Louise Latham); this is the first time she has heard her husband lie.

Amos intimidates Grimes into leaving the area so he can't testify against his sons. Dillon tells Amos that he has found out that the Sedalia sheriff hasn't seen the Gentry sons all year. Again, Amos lies by claiming that the boys kept out of the sheriff's sight while visiting their girlfriends there. Claire is becoming more upset by Amos' attempt to cover up for their sons. She believes that Colt and Ben should face the law for what they've done, exclaiming, "Colt and Ben are weak, Amos. They're less than men should be.... They have got to learn to be responsible."

Dillon finds out where the sons are hiding but is shot off his horse by Colt when he gets near their shack. When they return home and tell their parents what Colt did, Claire proclaims, "I will not have cowards and back-shooters for sons." Amos decides to send the boys to Sedalia where he figures they will have a favorable jury. When Matt comes by asking where the boys are, Claire defies her husband by telling him. Matt captures Colt and Ben and is about to take them to Dodge for trial when Amos and his ranch hands ride up to take the boys away from Matt. Matt shoots Amos in the shoulder. Claire rides up and tells Amos she is going with Matt and the boys. When the boys complain about being taken to trial, she tells them to stop whining. Just before he leaves, Matt tells Amos, "I remember a long time ago, you said something about a scrawny calf being better off than a healthy one that's overprotected. I never forgot that. I guess you did." A chastened Amos rides with Matt, Claire, Ben and Colt to Dodge.

Another example of a father enabling his son not to assume adult responsibility is found in the 1958 film *Gunman's Walk*. Lee Hackett (Van Heflin) is a widowed father of two sons. The older boy, Ed (Tab Hunter), is wild, narcissistic, and quick-tempered. Lee, who is proud of having tamed the land through his grit and prowess with a gun, identifies with him and admires his feistiness and unwillingness to back down from any man and his determination to go through anybody or anything to get what he wants, even allowing Ed to call him by his first name. He doesn't realize until the end of the film that Ed's willfulness is largely due to Lee's unwillingness to hold him responsible for whatever he does. Lee has less respect for his younger son Davy (James Darren), who is gentle and restrained and does not want to wear a gun, not understanding him enough to realize that Davy has an inner strength and maturity that Ed lacks.

The film begins with Davy defending Cecily "Clee" Chouard (Kathryn Grant) from the disrespectful amorous advances of Ed, who apparently assumes that she is fair game because her mother was a Sioux Indian. Lee hires Clee's brother Paul to help round up horses. When Lee tells Ed how good Paul is in roping wild horses, Ed becomes determined to rope a wild white mare before Paul does. As they both race after the horse, Ed callously runs Paul off a cliff, killing him. Two Sioux who saw what Ed did charge him with the murder of Paul. At Ed's hearing, a stranger, Jensen Sieverts (Ray Teal), corroborates Ed's lie that Paul accidentally fell from the cliff and Ed is not indicted. Sieverts tells Lee and Ed he doesn't want anything for his testimony but lies and tells Lee that some of his horses might have gotten mixed up with Lee's horses and he would appreciate it if he could cull them from the herd and take them home with him. Ed, of course, knows that the horses will be payment to Sieverts for his lying testimony, something that Lee doesn't realize until later.

The next day, Sieverts culls ten horses from the herd, including the white mare. Since the white mare couldn't be one of Sievert's horses, it dawns on Lee that Sieverts wasn't at the scene of Paul's death. Ed, on the other hand, is angered that Sieverts would take the coveted white mare from him, so he shoots him. Ed is promptly arrested; but while he is in jail, Lee again plots to get Ed out of trouble by telling the wounded Sieverts he will kill him if he reveals what really happened to Paul and brings charges against Ed. Meanwhile, Ed kills an unarmed deputy, the kindly Will Motely (Mickey Shaughnessy), and escapes. Lee finally realizes that he has enabled Ed to be a killer with no qualms or sense of responsibility for his actions. He goes after Ed and tells him, "I'll see you dead before I let you kill another man." Ed decides to fight it out with his father rather than go back to jail, and Lee kills him. Lee, now a broken man, breaks into tears but is consoled by Davy and Clee, whom Davy has asked to marry, contrary to his father's wishes. Despite Davy's distaste for gunplay, by the end of the film he has proven himself to be more of a man with a stronger identity than Ed.

Cattle drives are often the catalyst for the growth and maturation of young men in film and television Westerns. These journeys coincide with the notion of a rite of passage, the test of manhood that an adolescent has to endure in order to be considered an adult in various cultures. In *The Culpepper Cattle Company* (1972), teenager Ben Mockridge (Gary Grimes) delivers laundry for his single mother. He has just purchased his first gun, yearning for adventure as a cowboy. He leaves home to join the Culpepper Cattle Company, which is driving a herd of cattle from Texas to Fort Lewis, Colorado. He is assigned the role of "Little Mary," the cook's assistant. He yearns to do something more and convinces Frank Culpepper (Billy Green Bush) to let him watch the horses at night. While on duty, he is hit over the head and the horses are stolen. Culpepper is going to send him home as a result of his failure to guard the horses, but Mockridge redeems himself by identifying a horse thief, resulting in the cowboys shooting down the horse thieves and getting back their horses. In the melee, Mockridge kills the bartender who was about to shoot the cowboys. As a result of this event, and other signs of "becoming a man" (drinking whiskey and telling tall tales about sexual encounters), Mockridge slowly becomes acculturated into the life of a cowboy.

A turning point comes when Thornton Pierce (John McLiam) extorts $200 from Culpepper for supposedly grazing on his land and takes away the guns of Culpepper and some of his men. The Culpepper crew then comes upon a religious group that wants to settle on some land that Pierce claims is his. Pierce tells Culpepper and his crew and the religious group to leave in an hour. Culpepper decides it is best for business to leave rather than fight with Pierce and takes all his men except for Mockridge. He opts to remain and help the religious group members, who have decided to stay, and tells Culpepper that "some things are more important to a man than cattle." At this point it is clear that Mockridge has truly become his own person with a commitment to his own values. After riding away with Culpepper, four of the cowboys, inspired by Mockridge's example and infuriated that Pierce has treated them so badly and taken away their guns, get guns from the supply wagon and go back to defend the religious community. In the ensuing gunfight, all of Pierce's men and the four cowboys are shot down, leaving only Mockridge, who has mostly watched passively from behind a wagon. The members of the religious group want to pick up and move away without burying the four cowboys who saved them because the ground has been bloodied and God would want them to move. Angered by the group's decision to leave, Mockridge forces them at gunpoint to bury his four friends, then throws his gun away and rides off.

Through bitter experience, Mockridge has developed the strong convictions that will mark him as an adult.

Another film about reaching adulthood during a cattle drive, *Red River* (1948), begins in 1851 when Tom Dunson (John Wayne), his friend Nadine Groot (Walter Brennan) and the woman Dunson loves, Fen (Coleen Gray), are traveling on a wagon train west. Dunson decides to leave the train with a bull and a cow to start a herd in Texas against the wishes of the wagon master and Fen, whom Dunson feels is not strong enough for the trip; he plans to come back for her later. Near the Red River, Dunson and Groot see smoke in the far distance and suspect that the wagons they left have been attacked by the Indians, but they are too far away to do anything about it, especially with Indians in the vicinity. That night, they are attacked by six Indians, whom they kill. One of them is wearing a bracelet that Dunson gave Fen, confirming the fact that her wagon train had been attacked and destroyed. In the morning, Dunson and Groot find the feisty boy, Matthew Garth (Montgomery Clift), who has escaped the wagon train massacre with his cow and take him along as they cross the Red River. They travel through Texas until Dunson finds a place where he wants to raise his herd. He kills a man who tries to clear Dunson off the land since it belongs to Don Diego.

Fourteen years later, Dunson has a huge ranch with a large herd, something he wants to share with Garth, who is now grown up and returned to the ranch after being away during the Civil War years. Unfortunately for Dunson, Garth and Groot, there is no market for cattle in Texas and they decide to take the cattle to Sedalia, Missouri. When Dunson and Garth are branding cattle, including those that don't belong to them, they are challenged by Meeker (Davison Clark) and his hired hand Cherry Valance (John Ireland), who don't like the fact that Dunson is branding their cattle as his own. Dunson placates him by saying he will take them to Missouri, sell them and pay him $2 a head for them when he comes back. The feisty Valance decides to leave Meeker and join Dunson. Dunson comes into his bunkhouse and tells the men that if they sign up for the cattle drive, they have to finish it, but if they don't sign up there will be no hard feelings. After the drive begins, Valance tells Dunson it might be easier to get to Abilene, Kansas, having heard from a girl that the railroad has reached there, than to get to Sedalia. Dunson still insists on going to Sedalia rather than depend on what he considers to be a rumor about Abilene.

While on the drive, Bunk Kenneally (Ivan Perry) accidentally knocks over some pots and pans while trying surreptitiously to get sugar, producing a noise that starts a stampede which results in the death of Dan Latimer (Harry Carey, Jr.) and the loss of three or four hundred head of cattle. Dunson tells Garth to pay Latimer's widow full pay for the drive and to buy her the red shoes she wanted. In the morning, Dunson goes to whip Kenneally, despite his being contrite, for starting the stampede. When Kenneally draws his gun to stop the whipping, Dunson draws his gun, apparently to kill Kenneally. Before Dunson can shoot, Garth wounds Kenneally, apparently saving his life.

As the drive continues, the men, short on food due to losing one of the chuck wagons in the stampede, become sullen. Their morale gets even lower when a wounded man drifts into camp and tells them that approximately 100 border raiders killed everyone else in his cattle drive to Missouri. He also says he has heard that the railroad has reached Abilene. Dunson again refuses to go to Abilene. This prompts three men to tell Dunson that they are quitting. When Dunson refuses to let them go, they draw their guns, but Dunson, Garth and Valance kill them. When Dunson objects to Garth telling him he was wrong to confront the three men, Garth tells him he can give him orders, but not to tell him what to think.

Despite the shooting, three more men leave in the night. Dunson sends Valance and one other man to go after them and increases the pace of the drive to make the men so tired they won't have the energy to run away until Valance comes back with the three men. Dunson becomes meaner and more unreasonable as a result of refusing to sleep in order to keep an eye on anyone wanting to leave. When Valance gets back with two of the men who ran away, having killed the third one, Dunson says he will hang them since they ran away and stole some of the drive's supplies. Garth, backed up by Valance, Buster McGee (Noah Beery, Jr.) and the other men, stops Dunson. They leave Dunson behind as the drive moves on. Dunson vows to Garth that he will kill him.

When Comanches are attacking a wagon train full of "a bunch of gamblers and women," Garth directs the cowboys to save the wagon train. In the attack, Tess Millay (Joanne Dru) is wounded and Garth pulls out the arrow. Tess finds everything else she can about Garth from Groot, apparently attracted to him. She approaches Garth and tells him since they're both scared, they should talk to each other. Garth explains that Dunson was single-minded about the drive in order to reach his goal of Sedalia. Tess surmises that the love Garth and Dunson had for each other all those years is still there. Meanwhile, Dunson gathers men and ammunition to take the herd back. They reach the wagon train nine days behind Garth. While there, Tess shows him Fen's bracelet that Garth gave her.

Tess tells Dunson she couldn't go with Garth because, like Fen, she wasn't strong enough. Dunson said he thought he had a son, but now doesn't. Tess asks Dunson to take her along to Abilene and he agrees.

Garth and the herd finally reach the railroad in Abilene. After Garth sells the cattle, Tess comes to town to warn Garth that Dunson is coming to kill him. The next day, Dunson and his men come to town. As Dunson walks towards Garth, he shoots down Valance before Valance can stop him from reaching Garth. Dunson tries to provoke Garth into fighting by shooting him (creasing his cheek) and hitting him. At first Garth takes the punishment passively, but suddenly to the surprise of Dunson and the delight of Groot, Garth hits back. Dunson and Garth engage in a vicious fistfight until Tess breaks it up with a gunshot, exclaiming they love each other too much to hurt each other. Dunson is so impressed with Tess, he tells Garth to marry the girl and that when they get back to Texas he's going to add an M for Matthew to his Red River brand.

By the time *Red River* begins, Garth has almost a fully developed identity and sense of independence. He has a strong notion of what he wants to do with his life and has shown he could strike out on his own during the Civil War years. (It's not clear what he did during that time, except that it involved the use of his gun, which gave him a "reputation" that even Cherry Valance admires.) However, he still had to achieve one more goal before he became his own man: become fully independent from Dunson. (Although he doesn't let Dunson tell him what to think, he still takes his orders.) He fulfills that final task when he takes the herd away from Dunson to keep him from unnecessarily hanging two men, continuing to run roughshod over his cowboys, and not listening to reason about going to Abilene. Having a lot more temperance and prudence than Dunson, he has to slowly build up to this drastic action.

Several times up to the end, both Dunson and even Valance call Garth "soft." Springer (2005, pp. 119–20) explains the importance of Garth's "softness" in his relationship with Dunson: "But in *Red River* Matt Garth functions as an alternative to Tom Dunson's stern masculine ethos, and he becomes the embodiment of 'feminine' characteristics and values that are most apparent in his more compassionate and humane treatment of the men on the cattle drive." I would argue that Garth is more than only a feminine counterweight to Dunson's excessive masculinity. Garth, certainly by the end of the film, is psychologically androgynous, a mixture of both masculine and feminine traits (Bem, 1974) and thus not only a more complete human being than Dunson but shows the courage to be more authentic than Dunson, who denies the feminine side of his personality in his obsessive quest to take his cattle to Sedalia. Garth has feminine qualities and masculine qualities as well. If he didn't have masculine qualities, he never would have survived the Civil War years, challenged Dunson, helped rescue the wagon train or won the respect of Valance. This would explain the mutual attraction between Garth and the blunt-spoken, assertive, independent and yet very feminine Tess. It would also explain his behavior in the final confrontation with Dunson. To Dunson, Garth's reluctance to fight seems "soft," but it's his attempt at trying to find a reconciliation with Dunson. When that doesn't work, he stops being soft.

Critics have been rather hard on the ending of the film. Typical of these critics is Indick (2008, p. 99):

> The impetus towards a fatal showdown between father and son is built up throughout the entire film. Ending the story with a Hollywood-style happy ending betrays both the dramatic and psychological structure that the film draws upon. Dunston [sic] clearly had to die at the end of *Red River*, preferably at the hands of Matt. By ending the story with reconciliation rather than a fatal confrontation, the underlying feeling is that Matt really is soft, at least according to a philosophy of a man like Dunston [sic], who surely would have killed any man that shot, beat and degraded him in the way that did Matt. Furthermore, we're left with the impression that Dunston [sic] has also softened. No longer a tyrant, he will sit back peacefully and retire, allowing Matt to take control of the ranch. This notion of withdrawal is completely anathema to Dunston's [sic] character.

I agree that the ending is flawed or, as director Howard Hawks would put it, "corny." The reconciliation of Dunson and Garth seems contrived and Dunson's sudden and dramatic transformation, even including Garth in his River D brand, seems far-fetched. (For example, the transformation of Jeremy Rodock in *Tribute to a Bad Man* is more realistic—see below.) However, I find it credible that Dunson would not kill Garth. Throughout most of the film, Dunson has a reason for doing what he does, maybe not a good reason, but a reason based on his moral code. He leaves Fen because he feels that she is not strong enough to go with him. He shoots Don Diego's man because he believes no man should lay claim to land when he lives 400 miles away. He brands Meeker's cattle because he doesn't have the time to separate them from his herd, promising Meeker $2 a head, more money than Meeker could get for his cattle in Texas. He tries to whip Kenneally to set an example, because carelessness on a drive can get someone killed. Finally, he tries to hang Teeler and Laredo to keep anyone else from leaving the drive. As the drive progresses, his reasons become less and less rational and morally defensible until he crosses the line between being tough but fair to being considered "crazy" by the cowboys. By the end of the film, he has completely lost the distinction between the means of being tough and the end of getting the cattle to the railroad. He has no reason to kill Garth, who has successfully delivered the cattle to the railroad and sold the cattle for a check made out to Dunson for $50,000, something he could have found out if he wanted to. It's credible that Dunson would come to his senses if given the chance, which Garth and Tess do, especially considering the strong bond between Garth and him. According to Dan Troop in the *Lawman* television series, a lesson a man has to learn is when to back down, a lesson that that androgynous Garth learns before the hypermasculine Dunson does.

Cowboy (1958) is another film about growing up during a cattle drive. Frank Harris (Jack Lemmon), a Chicago hotel desk clerk, is entranced by cowboy Tom Reece (Glenn Ford) and his trail crew, who take over the hotel once a year. He also falls in love with a hotel guest, Maria Vidal (Anna Kashfi). When Harris learns that Reece plans to take a herd to Maria's father's ranch, he wants to go along to see Maria and become a cowboy. Using money as an inducement, Harris convinces the reluctant Reece to take him along as a partner. To toughen Harris up, Reece treats him harshly. When they reach the Vidal ranch, Harris finds out that Maria is going to marry Don Manuel Arriega (Eugene Iglesias) and he is bitterly disappointed. On the way back to Chicago, Harris becomes mean and callous, treating the men harshly and trying to deprive Reece of some of the proceeds of the cattle sale. Reece points out to Harris that he hasn't become tough, he's become miserable. After Reece saves Harris' life, Harris stops being mean and selfish. On the cattle drive and trip back, Harris learns the lessons that allow him to grow up: when and how to be tough without losing one's humanity, and how to handle disappointment. Unlike *Red River* and *Tribute to a Bad Man* (see below), *Cowboy* depicts the older man teaching the younger man the limits of toughness.

In *The Searchers*, a young male grows up during a long quest, even longer than the trail drive in *Red River* (Kitses, 2004, p. 101):

> At the outset "He who follows," as Scar dubs him, Marty clearly grows in stature over the seven years of the search, quietly emerging as a balancing heroic figure to Ethan, although obviously lacking the latter's heft. Blindsided by the overbearing Ethan with the fact that his mother's scalp hangs from Scar's lance, he maintains his composure and is not dissuaded from entering the camp to rescue Debbie: "*That* don't change it." It is Marty who rescues Debbie, killing Scar in the process. In another comment on Ethan's leadership, it is Marty to whom Mose gives the crucial clue to Scar's whereabouts.

Martin also shows that he is ready to assume an adult role in his evolving attitude towards the formidable Laurie. Even though they have known each other since childhood, it is not until near the end of the film that Martin declares his love for her. He is even willing to fight the ridiculous Charlie McCrory to win her, all the while Laurie showing her approval of Martin (and probably the fact that she enjoys that two men are fighting over her) by her smile.

In *Tribute to a Bad Man* (1956), young Steve Miller (Don Dubbins) finds Jeremy Rodock (James Cagney) shot by some rustlers. Miller takes out the bullet. Rodock recovers and finds the rustlers, killing one and hanging the other. The son of the rustler he killed, young Lars Peterson (Vic Morrow), vows revenge. He joins forces with McNulty (Stephan McNally), a man that Rodock has evicted from his ranch and viciously beaten for suspecting that he made a pass at Rodock's love interest, Jocasta Constantine (Irene Papas), who is living on the ranch and, like Miller, becoming disenchanted with Rodock's harsh ways. Miller tries to convince Jocasta, whom he loves, to come along with him, but she refuses. McNulty and Peterson try to get back at Rodock by stealing his valuable horses. Rodock catches McNulty, Peterson and their partner, Barjak (James Griffith), making them walk to jail through sand, rock and cactus. Barjak passes out, McNulty begs for mercy, but the proud Peterson keeps on walking. Rodock has a change of heart, taking Peterson back to his mother and compensating Peterson and her for killing the father. When Rodock gets back to the ranch, he finds that Miller and Jocasta are leaving together. More understanding and forgiving than before, Rodock allows them to leave. Jocasta, seeing the changes in Rodock, decides to stay. Miller leaves the ranch by himself, having grown from the experience and, as with Matthew Garth and Tom Dunson, and Ethan Edwards and Martin Pawley, teaching an older man how to be more humane and forgiving in the process.

According to psychologist Erik Erikson (1982), the last of his stages of psychosocial development, ego integrity vs. despair, occurs in late adulthood. As individuals come closer to their deaths, they find the need to establish integrity, a feeling of wholeness and comfort with oneself that comes from understanding the meaningfulness of their entire life. Individuals who achieve integrity are able to accept the failures and disappointments in their lives because everything that has happened to them, their good experiences and bad experiences, their disappointments and achievements, and their successes and failures, all fit together in a meaningful whole. When Gil Westrum in *Ride the High Country* comes back to help Steve Judd and tells the dying Judd he will bring the gold to the rightful owners, he not only is doing it out of a sense of loyalty to his friend but realizes that he needs to carry the gold to the legitimate owners in order to "enter his house justified," that is, maintain his sense of integrity and a meaningful life.

In the film *Monte Walsh*, (1970), the lead character, played by Lee Marvin, faces much the same dilemma that Gil Westrum and Steve Judd face. As the West is tamed and comes into the modern era, there is less need for the skills of cowboys like Walsh. A solution to Walsh's financial problems comes in the form of the owner of a Wild West show. Walsh refuses the offer of a job in the show because the role he would play would be a caricature of the cowboy he was; he tells the owner he's not about to "spit" on the life he's led. By refusing to enact a false version of his life, he has maintained his integrity in spite of his worsening circumstances.

Many critics (for example, Cawelti, 1999) have pointed out that Westerns, because of the violence and time period in which they are set, are mainly the domain of males. Since the plots revolve around the hero's need to use violence to maintain his honor, independence, sense of justice and loyalty to others, women have been marginalized in the Western. In the simplest dichotomy, women are either the schoolmarm or dance hall girl–prostitute, often, but not always with a heart of gold. The schoolmarm is a threat to the hero, because she is a civilizing influence that will help bring about the end of the relevance of the hero and the diminishment of his individualism, physical courage and masculine strength. The dance hall girl–prostitute, on the other hand, appeals to the dark, uncivilized qualities of the hero (despite that this type of female is often being portrayed with a heart of gold), and therefore must change or be killed or marginalized with the advance of civilization.

However, Blake Lucas (1998, p. 301) disagrees with the idea that women are unimportant in Westerns. He states,

> [T]he myth that the traditional heroine of a Western is a passive and pallid figure has inevitably led to the belief that her role must be subverted. But scorn of the more familiar types of Western women presents to us the depressing possibility that the classic Western—a genre without equal in its 1946–1964 golden age—may come to be undervalued and rejected as a model, and that along with this many Western heroines who have never been truly appreciated and celebrated will be forgotten. It's time to see the Western in a different light—not as a masculine genre but as one supremely balanced in its male-female aspect and one of the finest places for women characters in all of cinema.

As Philip Indick (2008, pp. 68–69) points out, women are not always passive or unimportant in Westerns. The frontierswoman is quite different from this passive portrayal of women in Westerns:

> [T]the frontierswoman represents a mediating force between the schoolmarm and whore. Unlike the other two types, which are essentially stereotypes, the frontierswoman is a real woman. Neither as debased as the whore nor as hopelessly virginal and pure as the schoolmarm, the frontierswoman is gritty but wholesome, honest but also sexual, and earthy but still refined.

Indick goes on to point out Jean Arthur as Calamity Jane in *The Plainsman* (1936), Phoebe Titus in *Arizona* (1940) and Marian Starrett in *Shane* (1953), and Barbara Stanwyck as Vance Jeffords in *The Furies* (1950), Sierra Nevada Jones in *Cattle Queen of Montana* (1954) and Jessica Drummond in *Forty Guns* (1957) as examples. This portrayal of women means that the frontierswoman can show great courage even if she never draws a gun or commits acts of violence. Hallie Stoddard (Vera Miles) in *The Man Who Shot Liberty Valance* is such a woman. As an older woman, Hallie reveals her love for Tom Doniphon (John Wayne), the man she rejected for Ransom Stoddard (James Stewart), by putting a flower on Doniphon's coffin. In this scene, Hallie displays the kind of courage needed to achieve integrity, the acceptance of one's losses and the wisdom and strength that this acceptance can bring. The strength and wisdom of Hallie come from "a desire that can't be reduced to the love of a man, a desire that inhabits her feelings for Tom and Ranse but ultimately exceeds both of them" (McGee, 2007, p. 138). Lucas (1998, p. 320) goes on to explain further the strength and wisdom that Hallie embodies:

> What is so admirable about Hallie is not her sadness, but that she bears the choice she made with such grace and dignity.... Finally though, Hallie is firmly of her world, the prairie flower blossoming through the seasons. "It used to be a wilderness ... now it's a garden." The line evokes the course of her life, but goes far beyond this, resonating with an empathy for the West rare in any character—for what was in the past, for what it has become, for what it may still be someday. Hallie's hard-earned wisdom is the essence of integrity, an understanding of the meaning of one's whole life, from beginning to the end.

The primary task of the psychosocial stage of integrity vs. despair is being able to face one's death with a calm resignation born of acceptance. Only then does death lose its sting (Erikson, 1982). In the 1976 film *The Shootist*, J.B. Books (John Wayne), a famous gunfighter and sometime lawman, arrives in Carson City, Nevada, in 1901 just as the death of Queen Victoria is announced. The first person he visits, Dr. E.W. Hosteteler (James Stewart), confirms a diagnosis made ten days prior by a Colorado doctor: Books has cancer. Hosteteler adds that it is inoperable and that Books has a short time to live ("Two months, six weeks, less, there's no way to tell"). He later gives Books laudanum for the pain, adding that the pain will get worse to the point that the laudanum will do him no good. He humanely comments that it is no way to die.

Books has lived by a very simple code: "I won't be wronged, I won't be insulted, and I won't be laid a hand on. I don't do these things to other people and I require the same from them." He demonstrates the first part of this code ("I won't be wronged, I won't be insulted") by forcing out at gunpoint Dobkins (Richard Lenz), a newspaperman who wants to write his life story in lurid and undignified terms ("Have you lived so long with death, you're used to it, the death of others, the prospect of your own?") and Marshal Thibodo (Harry Morgan) when he harasses Books. He later rebuffs an old lover, Serepta (Sheree North), who wants to capitalize on Books' death by marrying him and then collaborating with Dobkins on Books' life story, fabricating the events of his life as needed.

However, he demonstrates the second part of his code ("I don't do these things to other people") by apologizing to Mrs. Rogers (Lauren Bacall), the woman at whose boarding house he is staying, for playing a joke on her by introducing himself to the unworldly woman as William Hickok, and by being polite to her son Gillom (Ron Howard) after Gillom objects to Books ordering him about. By living by his code to the end, he maintains his sense of dignity and integrity, which comes only when individuals can say they have lived according to their values and no one else's to the end.

In order to enjoy life as much as possible before his imminent demise, Books asks Mrs. Rogers for a ride in the country, during which he tells her he "had a hell of a good time" in his life, which, according to Robert Butler (1968), would make it easier for him to face his death. Although Books rebuffs Mrs. Rogers when she tries to encourage him to unburden himself to a minister before he dies, he does admit to her that he is a "dying man scared of the dark," an admission that is difficult for a proud man like Books to make, but one, according to Kubler-Ross (1968), that is needed to help someone face death.

To avoid a very painful death, Books challenges three men interested in testing themselves to a gunfight: Jack Pulford (Hugh O'Brian), Mike McSweeney (Richard Boone) and Jay Cobb (Bill McKinney). They meet him on the morning of his 58th birthday. Although shot several times, Books kills all three, only to have a bartender shoot him in the back. Gillom picks up Books' gun and kills the bartender. The dying Books smiles when Gillom disgustedly throws the gun away, pleased that Gillom, who has glamorized gunfighting up to this point, now understands the horrific nature of taking another person's life, a difficult lesson he has learned from Mr. J.B. Books.

According to Robert Butler (1968), in old age, especially if one is close to dying, people engage in a life review, going over the details of their life from earliest childhood to the present to find as much satisfaction and meaning as possible to make it easier to face their death. One outcome of the life review is the desire of older people to leave a legacy, something that endures even though their physical existence has ended. A legacy can be tangible, such as a building or painting, or it can be intangible or even spiritual, such as wisdom or love passed on to the living. On their way to the gold fields in *Ride the High Country*, Steve Judd (Joel McCrea) reviews the events of his life to Gil Westrum (Randolph Scott), discussing his early days as a wild kid, his maturation and the principles he developed along the way. He also passes along what he has learned about living a life of integrity to young Heck Longtree (Ron Starr), a legacy that convinces Longtree to make the transformation from a wild and immature boy, much like Judd when he was younger, into a mature and responsible adult.

Another example of someone who has gone through the life review and, as a result, wants to leave a legacy is found in the 1975 *Gunsmoke* episode "I Have Promises to Keep." The Reverend Byrne (David Wayne) has come to Nescatunga to build a church, a school and a clinic for Comanches. But Dunbar (Kenneth Swofford), the lumber yard owner, expresses the sentiment of the town by refusing to sell him any lumber to build anything for the Comanches, who just a few years before had fought and killed some of the townspeople. At this point, Festus (Ken Curtis), staying temporarily in town, uses his badge to cajole Dunbar into selling the reverend his lumber.

Haggen decides to help the Reverend Byrne build his church despite Byrne's abrasive and overbearing personality. When they go back to town to get more lumber, Dunbar at gunpoint refuses to sell it to them. The Reverend Atkins (Tom Lacy), pandering to the prejudices of the town, tries to excuse the behavior of the townspeople in a conversation with the Reverend Byrne, citing the past conflicts with the Comanches. However, the Reverend Byrne will have none of it, facing down Dunbar and getting the lumber.

Back at their camp, the Reverend Byrne tells Haggen that he was a minister back east. His flock was rich and comfortable. When the reverend's wife died, he realized he was nothing more than a "spiritual bedwarmer," soothing his congregation without really challenging them. When he did begin to challenge them, he was forced into retirement. At that point, he decided he wanted to do something significant to benefit the lives of other people. What he doesn't tell Festus is that he has little time left to do it because of his heart problem.

At night the townspeople, led by Dunbar, burn the unfinished church down. That Sunday, Haggen breaks in on the congregation in church and confronts the townspeople for burning the church, telling them the story that the Reverend Byrne has told him. He tells the Reverend Atkins that he in particular needs to instruct his congregation on what is right and wrong. Back at the campsite, Byrne is about to give up building the church, but Haggen convinces him to continue with the lumber they have. While they are working, the reverend bends over grabbing his chest, and Haggen understands how ill the man is and why he was so abrupt and impatient in his determination to get the church built.

Haggen goes to the Comanche camp and tries to convince the chief to get his people to come to a church service in the unfinished building. The chief refuses, saying that his people need to cling to their old ways as much as possible. Before he leaves, Festus reminds the chief that it is the custom of the Comanches to receive a gift from a visitor who comes in peace, so Festus gives him his mule. Festus hopes the Comanches will repay the gift of the mule by coming to the church service—which they do. In his sermon, instead of trying to proselytize the Comanches, the Reverend Byrne tries to show them the commonalities between Christianity and their religion. While playing the organ, he dies. The chief says he was a strange but good man, and he leaves behind Festus' mule. After the Comanches leave, some of the townspeople, including the Reverend Atkins, come to finish building the church. Atkins admits the error of his ways. Haggen later stands over Byrne's grave and, referring to his work and death, asks "Was it worth it?" and answers, "You bet." The Reverend Byrne has left behind his legacies, both tangible in the form of the church and spiritual, in the form of a greater tolerance between the whites and Comanches.

Chapter 7

Being Authentic

"It sometimes takes great courage to tell the truth, more courage than to fight. You're an honorable man, Frank Ryan."—"Warbonnet" from *Bonanza*

Sometimes courage involves simply telling the truth or presenting oneself in a genuine way, to oneself or to others, what Peterson and Seligman (2004) call authenticity. Being authentic is a high reward–high risk strategy. If one has the courage to pursue it, it could result in the beginning of a new and exciting life, but often only if a person is willing to accept some dire consequences. In the 1958 *Bronco* episode "The Long Ride Back," Bronco Layne (Ty Hardin) is falsely accused by Jacob Stint (Mort Mills) of revealing the escape plans of Confederate soldiers from Elmira Prison during the Civil War, information which resulted in the death of Freedom McNally. This "fake news" makes Tom McNally (Paul Fix), Freedom's father, hate Layne. Stint later admits to McNally that it was Freedom, not Layne, who revealed the escape plans to the Yankees. However, instead of telling Stint's admission to Layne and the townspeople who have ostracized him, McNally pays Stint $5,000 not to tell the truth. When Layne tracks down Stint and brings him back to town to tell the truth, McNally gets up the courage to reveal the true story about his son to the town before Layne or Stint can. In the gunfight between Layne and Stint, McNally tries to kill Stint before he can kill a helpless Layne, but Stint is instead killed by Layne after Stint kills McNally.

A complicated *Cheyenne* episode, "Incident at Indian Springs" (1957), involves redemption, justice and telling the truth. Schoolteacher Jim Ellis (Dan Barton) claims a reward for killing outlaw Roy Curran, from Sheriff

Cheyenne Bodie (Clint Walker). After the other three Curran brothers attack the schoolhouse with Jim and the schoolchildren inside, Jim admits to Bodie and the townspeople that Bodie was the one who really killed Roy, who died when he came to Jim's house for shelter since Jim was his half-brother. After Roy died at their house, Jim's wife, Lynne (Bonnie Bolding), convinced him to ask for the reward. Jim explains to Bodie that he became a schoolteacher to make up for the violence of his half-brothers. After they find out about the truth, all of the townspeople except Bodie abandon Jim, despite the possibility of the Curran gang seeking revenge against Jim. Although Jim tried to deprive him of the reward that was rightfully his, Bodie decides he is morally obligated to help Jim because he is the one who really killed Roy. Lynne tries to convince her husband to run away from the Curran brothers, but Jim says he has to stay. Even though he is frightened, he knows that sooner or later the Currans will catch up with him and he cannot stand living on the run. Bodie and Jim hole up in Jim's cabin when Kenny Powell, one of Ellis' students, comes to help. Soon after, the three Currans and two other gang members attack them. Jim is reluctant to go against his anti-violence beliefs and help defend the cabin against the five killers but reluctantly kills one of his half-brothers to keep him from killing Bodie. When Hub Powell (Carlyle Mitchell), the father of Kenny, finds out that Kenny has gone to help Jim and Bodie, he rounds up the townspeople, and they redeem themselves by subduing the rest of the gang. The townspeople admit they were initially wrong to refuse to help Jim. Jim tells Kenny that he was wrong to lie about killing Roy and that killing is still wrong and he did it only to save Bodie.

In the 1958 film *Cattle Empire*, John Cord (Joel McCrea) comes back to the town where he received a five-year prison sentence for being responsible for his men tearing apart the town and, in the process, shooting some of its inhabitants at the end of a trail drive. He is beaten up badly by a mob before being rescued by Ralph Hamilton (Don Haggerty), a man he blinded while Cord's trail crew wrecked the town. Ralph asks Cord to be the trail boss of a herd made up of his cattle and those of his neighbors because he is convinced that Cord is the only man who can do it, and Cord has too much pride as a cattleman to sabotage the effort.

Cord turns down the offer, but then Garth (Richard Shannon), a rival of Hamilton and his neighbors, offers Cord a job leading his cattle to market. Cord accepts Garth's offer and then goes back to accept Hamilton's offer, figuring to undercut Hamilton's herd while secretly working for Garth. Cord starts out with the Hamilton herd, treating the men roughly (many of them beat him up when he came to town). He sneaks away from the Hamilton herd to let Garth know that he is taking the Hamilton herd to Dismal River, where the herd will be destroyed.

The men in the Hamilton cattle drive, except for Ralph Hamilton, begin to expect treachery from Cord and decide to take their cattle away from the drive, but Cord stops them from doing it. Cord has had a change of heart and goes to Garth to tell him he won't destroy the Hamilton herd but correctly advises Garth to take the herd to Horse Thief Creek instead of Dismal River. Garth thinks Cord is trying to trick him and takes his herd to Dismal River, where they are lost.

The Hamilton cattlemen reach their destination near the town of Fort Benson and threaten to wreck the town. At this point, Hamilton has the courage to tell the truth about what happened five years before. To discredit Cord at that time, Hamilton had Garth hit Cord over the head and then turned Cord's crew loose on the town, ruining Cord's plan of giving the men liquor in camp instead of letting them go into town for it. Later, in town, Hamilton provoked Cord into a fight by taunting him for losing control of his men. In the ensuing fight, Cord's blow blinded Hamilton.

Ralph's confession stops the men from going into town. Instead, they fight Garth and his men, who are trying to take over the Hamilton herd. Garth and his men are defeated by Cord and his men as Cord wounds Garth. Cord rides off after turning over the herd to Douglas Hamilton (Bing Russell), Ralph's younger brother.

Sometimes not being authentic involves the relationships people choose. As mentioned in Chapter 2, the films of Budd Boetticher often involve the self-transformation and self-realization of secondary characters. In *The Tall T* (1957), Pat Brennan (Randolph Scott) ends up riding in a stagecoach with Doretta Mims (Maureen O'Sullivan) and her obnoxious husband Willard (John Hubbard), who has married her for her father's money. Doretta has accepted the marriage because she has a low opinion of herself. When the Mimses and Brennan are held prisoners by Frank Usher (Richard Boone), Chink (Henry Silva) and Billy Jack (Skip Homeier) for a ransom from Doretta's father, the weak-willed Willard betrays his wife, but is killed by Usher for his efforts. At this point, Doretta begins to break down, but Brennan persuades her to help him overcome the kidnappers, an outcome which Brennan is able to achieve with the help of Doretta. Doretta is able to fully accept how cowardly she was to marry a man who was only interested in her money and, as a result of helping Brennan and accepting the truth, has a higher opinion of herself.

Self-realization on a greater scale occurs in Boetticher's *Decision at Sundown* (1957). Bart Allison (Randolph Scott) and his friend Sam (Noah

Beery, Jr.) ride into the town of Sundown just as Tate Kimbrough (John Carroll) is about to marry Lucy Summerton (Karen Steele). When the preacher asks if anyone in the church has objections, Allison says he does, asking Kimbrough if he knew a Mary in Sabine Pass and adding that he is going to kill Kimbrough, apparently for reasons connected to Kimbrough's relationship with Mary. The sheriff, Swede Hansen (Andrew Duggan), and his gunmen, like virtually everyone else in town, are controlled by Kimbrough. They chase after Allison and Sam, both of whom hide in the livery stable, which, in turn, is surrounded by the sheriff and his men. Kimbrough tries to resume the wedding, but Lucy runs away.

During the standoff, Sam tells Allison that he is surprised to find out that Allison wants to kill Kimbrough because of his dead wife, Mary. Meanwhile, Kimbrough goes to the Summerton home to convince Lucy to marry him there, but she is hesitant because of the doubts she has concerning Kimbrough's relationship with Mary. To get a clearer picture of the relationship between Mary and Kimbrough, Lucy goes to the livery stable, where Allison explains to Lucy that Mary was his wife when Kimbrough had an affair with her. Lucy responds that only a woman who is willing to go with another man can be taken away from her husband. Lucy's rebuke angers Allison, who tells Lucy to leave. Sam says that Lucy had a point and that Kimbrough was not the only man Mary was with while he was gone. Sam's comment angers Allison enough to knock Sam down and tell him to leave. Sam says he will leave only temporarily to eat at the restaurant.

While at the restaurant, Sam tells the town doctor, John Storrow (John Archer), that Mary was wild and not about to settle down with any man, despite being married. A week after Allison came back from the Civil War, Mary killed herself rather than have Allison learn about the string of men in her life while he was gone. Sam decides to go back to the livery stable to tell Allison about Mary and convince him to leave town without killing Kimbrough but realizes that it will be difficult: "You can't convince a man about something he doesn't want to know about." On the way to the livery stable, he is gunned down by one of the sheriff's men, who, in turn, is gunned down by Allison.

Back in the saloon, Doc Storrow forces the townspeople to face the fact that their inaction is what allowed Kimbrough to take over the town and Sam to be killed. Charley Summerton (John Litel), the father of Lucy, confesses that by encouraging Lucy to carry through Kimbrough's wishes to marry her, Summerton lost his self-respect. Kimbrough walks in and tells Storrow to stop stirring up trouble; but as soon as he leaves, rancher

Frustrated in love. Tate Kimbrough, played by John Carroll (center), begs Lucy Summerton, played by Karen Steele (left), to marry him after Bart Allison (Randolph Scott, not pictured) has upset his wedding plans. Lucy's father Charles, played by John Litel (right), looks on in Budd Boetticher's *Decision at Sundown* (1957, Columbia Pictures).

Morley Chase (Ray Teal), urged on by Storrow, decides that in order to gain his self-respect he needs to help Allison. Chase and his ranch hands disarm all of the sheriff's men, leaving the sheriff to face Allison alone. Allison kills Swede but is wounded in the hand. The doctor pleads with Allison to stop his foolish quest for vengeance, and at the same time Ruby James (Valerie French), Kimbrough's saloon girlfriend before he decided to marry Lucy, tries to convince Kimbrough not to confront Allison. Despite the pleas of Storrow and Ruby, both men go out into the street to face each other, but before either can shoot, Ruby shoots Kimbrough in the shoulder to stop the fight. Kimbrough leaves town with Ruby, now that he realizes that he has lost the town and Ruby is better for a man like him than is Lucy. Allison goes to the saloon, gets drunk and rides out of town, a broken man, now that he realizes that his quest for vengeance has been meaningless and needlessly caused the death of his best friend and others.

Robert Nott (2004, pp. 202–03) describes Allison's mental state at the end of the film:

[I]t is Scott who makes *Decision at Sundown* as memorable as it is. As a man pushed so far over the brink that he cannot accept that his wife may have been the equivalent of the town whore (making you wonder what kind of husband *he* was), he plays his part with all six cylinders going, reaching for emotions that he rarely conveyed in other films.... His final moments, drunk and disillusioned at the bar, are handled with a sense of understated, bitter resignation.... Whereas the Scott characters in the other Ranown films sometimes carry a badge of hope with them, here Allison realizes his quest is insignificant and has only brought about death (although, arguably, he helped clean up the town by usurping Kimbrough's power).

Another example of realizing the unexpected consequences for acting vengeful is the 1958 film *The Bravados*. Jim Douglas (Gregory Peck) rides 100 miles to Rio Arriba to see the hanging of four men. A man who says he is the hangman, Mr. Sims (Joe DeRita), arrives for the hanging the next day. Douglas tells the sheriff (Herbert Rudley) that he has been tracking the four men about to be hanged for six months and that he wants to look at them. He looks intently at each one of them: Bill Zachary (Stephen Boyd), Ed Taylor (Albert Salmi), Lujan (Henry Silva) and Alfonso Parral (Lee Van Cleef). He then leaves. Later he tells an old flame, Josepha Velarde (Joan Collins), that he is after the men because they raped and killed his wife. While everyone in the town except the sheriff is in the church, "Mr. Sims," who is really an accomplice of the four men and has left the real Mr. Sims dead on the trail, stabs the sheriff, who, in turn, shoots "Mr. Sims." However, the four men manage to escape and leave town, taking Emma Steinmetz (Kathleen Gallant) as a hostage.

A posse is formed with the deputy sheriff, Primo (Ken Scott), the nominal leader, but Douglas is really in charge. Douglas peels off from the posse to capture Parral, who begs for his life, claiming that he had nothing to do with the death of Douglas' wife. The enraged Douglas doesn't believe him and kills him. Next Douglas catches up with Taylor, who unsuccessfully tries to shoot him. As Taylor runs away, Douglas runs him down, ropes him, hangs him up by his heels and kills him.

Luhan, Zachary, and Emma come upon a miner's cabin. Zachary kills the miner, John Butler (Gene Evans), when he flees from the cabin, and Luhan runs to grab the miner's money. Douglas catches up with Zachary and kills him. He goes to Luhan's house where he finds Luhan's wife, Angela (Alicia del Lago), and child. Before Douglas can kill Luhan as he is coming back to his house, Angela knocks him unconscious. When Douglas regains consciousness, Luhan proves to Douglas that he and the three other men did not kill Douglas' wife by producing the money that Luhan took from John Butler, which only Butler could have stolen from Douglas' wife after he raped and killed her.

Seeking revenge. Jim Douglass, played by Gregory Peck (far left), glowers at the men he believes raped and killed his wife: (from left to right behind bars) Bill Zachary (Stephen Boyd), Ed Taylor (Albert Salmi), Alfonso Parral (Lee Van Cleef) and Lujan (Henry Silva) in Henry King's *The Bravados* (1958, 20th Century–Fox).

A chastened Douglas comes back to Rio Arriba and goes straight to the church, asking help from the priest (Andrew Duggan). Douglas knows he has done a great wrong by exacting his revenge on the wrong men despite the fact that he killed men who were going to be hanged for another crime. Even if they had been the men who raped and killed his wife, he realizes he still would be wrong in setting himself up as their judge, jury and executioner. The priest says that the fact that Douglas has accepted responsibility for what he has done puts him ahead of other men in that situation, but Douglas says this rationalization doesn't help him feel better. Hopefully, through prayer and the love of Josepha and his little girl, he can continue the healing process begun when he accepted responsibility for what he had done.

In the film classic *The Ox-Bow Incident*, the self-realization of the participants revolves around a hanging. Gil Carter (Henry Fonda) and Art Croft (Harry Morgan) ride into town looking for Carter's girl, Rose Mapen, who has left town for good. Croft and a despondent Carter are about to leave when someone comes into town declaring that a man named Kincaid has been killed and his cattle stolen. Townspeople form a posse and they start talking about lynching the murderers. Storekeeper Arthur Davies (Harry Davenport) objects. Carter goes to see Judge Daniel Tyler (Matt Briggs) about stopping a lynching from occurring, but the judge isn't able to control the posse. Davies is almost able to convince the men in the posse to let the sheriff, who is at the Kincaid ranch, take care of the capture of the assailants, but the posse finds out that three men were spotted driving cattle near where Kincaid was shot. Major Tetley (Frank Conroy), a man with a dubious Civil War record, and Jeff Darnley (Marc Lawrence), a good friend of Kincaid, convince the posse to go after the three men. The incompetent and vengeful deputy, Butch Mapes (Dick Rich), illegally deputizes the posse and the men take off after the supposed killers. Carter and Croft aren't happy about being a part of the posse but go along because if they don't they might end up being suspects.

The posse captures Donald Martin (Dana Andrews), Alva "Dad" Hardwicke (Francis Ford) and Juan Martinez (Anthony Quinn) because they are in possession of Kincaid's cattle. Martin claims he paid cash for the cattle but can't produce a bill of sale. A majority of the mob decides to hang the three men on circumstantial evidence. When Davies objects, Mapes shuts him up. However, Martin convinces the lynch mob to wait until dawn to hang them so he can write a letter to his wife. Tetley gets the posse to abide by a majority decision about whether or not to hang the three men at dawn. A minority of seven men—Carter, Croft, Gerald Tetley (William Eythe) defying his authoritarian father, Sparks (Leigh Whipper), Davies and two others—vote against the hanging. (It is interesting in this era when Mexicans and African-Americans often played stereotypical and unflattering roles, that arguably the two most admirable men with the most integrity in the whole film are the religious African-American Sparks, the first to step up and vote against the hanging, and the Mexican-American Martinez, who speaks 11 languages and faces his death with great dignity.) The majority goes ahead with the hanging, although Gerald refuses to participate, further defying his father, who considers him a coward.

After the hanging, the sheriff runs into the posse and tells them not only that Kincaid is alive from his gunshot wound and will survive, but also that he caught the real culprits. Martin, Martinez and Hardwicke were innocent and telling the truth. When the major gets back to his house, he locks his son out. After years of being harassed by his father as a weakling

William Wellman's *The Oxbow Incident* (1943, 20th Century–Fox). Shown are the reluctant Gil Carter (Henry Fonda; center foreground with gun), the authoritarian Major Tetley (Frank Conroy; at right, pointing), and the vindictive Jeff Darnley (Marc Lawrence; at right, with fur collar). The three hatless men tied up and accused of murder and robbery are the defiant Juan Martinez (Anthony Quinn; at left, with tilted head), the distraught Donald Martin (Dana Andrews; at right, staring at Tetley and Darnley), and the bewildered "Dad Hardwicke" (Francis Ford; with gray hair barely visible at center back).

and a coward, Gerald finally rebels and tells his father what he really thinks of him: a man who loved every minute of the farce of a "trial" and a hanging and that only power and cruelty mean anything to him. Gerald admits that he was too cowardly to stop his father from hanging the three men, but that his father is also a coward, afraid of his own weakness being exposed. Unable to live with the lies he has told himself over the years, the major shoots himself.

The ashamed and despondent posse members gather at the saloon where Carter reads the letter that Martin wrote to his wife:

> [Mr. Davies] is a good man and done everything he can for me. I suppose there are some other good men here, too, only they don't seem to realize what they're doing. They're the ones I feel sorry for because it will be over for me in a little while, but they will have to go on remembering for the rest of their lives.

The men who hanged Martinez, Martin, and Hardwicke have paid a heavy price for what they have learned about themselves and each other. Carter and Croft ride out of town to give the letter to Martin's widow and help look after her children.

Sometimes being truthful about oneself is necessitated by the need to help others to act authentically. In the 1956 film *Tension at Table Rock*, gunfighter Wes Tancred (Richard Egan) was falsely accused of shooting a man in the back. As a result, he has changed his name and run away from his reputation. In Table Rock he befriends Sheriff Fred Miller (Cameron Mitchell), who is haunted by a savage beating he took as a sheriff in a different town. As a result, Miller almost allows a trail boss, Hampton (John Dehner), to intimidate him into allowing one of his trail hands, Lerner (James Anderson), to go free, even though Lerner committed cold-blooded murder. However, Tancred stands up during the trial and identifies Lerner as the killer and challenges Miller to do the same. When Miller asks Tancred what he knows about having the courage to tell the truth, Tancred responds in the packed courtroom that he knows plenty about not having the courage to tell the truth since he's been running away from himself by taking an assumed name, thus admitting he is Wes Tancred. As a result, Miller gets the courage to identify Lerner as a killer and to stand with Tancred against Hampton and his trail crew, forcing the cattlemen to ride out of town.

As difficult as it might be, telling the truth about oneself can lead to not only a more authentic life, but also one that is more rewarding. In the 1971 episode of *Bonanza*, "Warbonnet," Little Joe Cartwright (Michael Landon) collapses from dehydration while wandering in the desert. A young Paiute, Swift Eagle (Patrick Adiarte), takes his gun and leaves him. But Swift Eagle's grandfather, Red Cloud (Chief Dan George), makes him go back to help him and return his gun, since returning the gun is the honorable thing to do.

Red Cloud and Swift Eagle take Joe to the town of Mills, where Joe can catch a stagecoach back to Virginia City. When Joe gets there, hotel proprietor Frank Ryan (Forrest Tucker) stakes him money so he can contact his family and get cleaned up. Red Cloud and Swift Eagle come into Ryan's saloon where Red Cloud tries to take an Indian warbonnet hanging on the wall. Some saloon men rough up the two Paiutes until Joe stops them. The sheriff puts the two Indians in jail until they can be picked up by the agent from the reservation. Red Cloud tells Joe the warbonnet had been taken from him in a dishonorable manner. Red Cloud's story directly contradicts Ryan's story that he took it from Red Cloud in battle.

Ryan tells Teresa (Linda Cristal), a former girlfriend, that he would like to get closer to her once again, but she has lost respect for him because he has lied about how he got the war bonnet and his other army exploits as well as refusing to marry her because she is a Mexican. Thanks to Ben (Lorne Greene) and Hoss Cartwright (Dan Blocker), the two Paiutes are released to Joe's custody until they can be delivered to the reservation. Red Cloud challenges Ryan to a fight, Ryan armed with a cavalry sword and Red Cloud with a lance, the winner getting the warbonnet. Joe tries to talk the old and outmatched Red Cloud out of the fight, but he refuses.

Ryan doesn't want to fight Red Cloud since he is an old man, but he realizes it would look bad if he backed down. Ryan goes to Red Cloud in the middle of the night with the warbonnet and tells him if he leaves immediately, he can take it. Red Cloud refuses, realizing that if he leaves town like that, it will look as if he stole the warbonnet and ran away. He insists that his honor demands that he fight for it. The next day, Red Cloud comes into town with his lance, and Ryan goes to face him with his sword with the whole town watching. As Ryan approaches Red Cloud, he stops and breaks his sword, refusing to kill the old man. He gives the warbonnet to Red Cloud, admitting in front of the entire town that he stole it from Red Cloud when Red Cloud was imprisoned by the army and that all of his army stories were lies. Ryan adds that unlike Red Cloud, he has no honor. Red Cloud responds, "It sometimes takes great courage to tell the truth, more courage than to fight. You're an honorable man, Frank Ryan."

Back in the saloon, Ryan rejects his prejudiced white girl friend, Mae (Linda Gaye Scott), and goes off with Teresa. He tells Teresa he wants to live according to who he is rather than who he has pretended to be. Joe tells Teresa she has herself a heck of a man.

Sometimes no matter how much people try to deny who they are, the truth has a tendency to smack them in the face. In the 1992 film *Unforgiven*, two cowboys in the town of Big Whiskey carve up the face of a prostitute, Delilah Fitzgerald (Anna Levine), because she giggled at the size of the penis of one of them. The sheriff, Little Bill Daggett (Gene Hackman) decides that their punishment should be the cowboys delivering five ponies to her. Angered by the fact that Delilah has been devastated both personally and professionally by her wounds, the prostitutes, led by Strawberry Alice (Frances Fisher), offer a $1,000 reward to anyone who will kill the cowboys.

The young Schofield Kid (Jaimz Woolvett) goes to enlist the aid of William Munny (Clint Eastwood), who has a past as a murderer and bandit, in collecting the reward. Munny is reluctant because he has reformed

7. Being Authentic

Showing who's boss. Little Bill Daggett, played by Gene Hackman (left), lets William Munny, played by Clint Eastwood (right), know who is in charge in his town in Eastwood's *Unforgiven* (1992, Warner Brothers).

and is now trying to make it as a farmer and widower with two children. Munny finally accepts the offer because his farm is failing and he needs to support his children. They enlist the help of Ned Logan (Morgan Freeman), an old friend of Munny.

Meanwhile, English Bob (Richard Harris), accompanied by his biographer W.W. Beauchamp (Saul Rubinek), arrives in Big Whiskey to collect the reward. However, he is disarmed by Daggett and his deputies, beaten and shipped out of town. Impressed by Daggett, Beauchamp decides to write about him instead of English Bob.

Munny, Logan and the Kid (who, it turns out, is near-sighted) arrive in town. Munny is beaten by Daggett, but is nursed back to health by Logan and the Kid. When Munny recovers, Munny, Logan and the Kid confront the guilty cowboys, and the Kid kills one of them. At this point, the Kid realizes he is not cut out to be a desperado. Munny, however, decides to stay when he finds out Logan has been killed by Bill and his men, while the Kid goes to Kansas to deliver the reward money to Logan's wife and Munny's children. Munny exacts his revenge by killing Daggett and several of his deputies. He tells the remaining townspeople that he will exact more revenge on them if they don't bury Logan or if they hurt any of the prostitutes. Although the postscript suggests that Munny took his children to San Francisco and did well in dry goods, Munny, by the end of the film, realizes that being a killer is a part of his personality that cannot be entirely denied.

Although Munny has tried hard to deny his vicious impulses, he has always known these tendencies were lurking in him. Another character who achieves self-realization is the near-sighted adolescent, "The Schofield Kid," who realizes that killing is not for him after being confronted with its horrible reality.

Sometimes being authentic can be as true for an animal as for a human, and authenticity can bind the two together. In the 1968 *Gunsmoke* episode "Lobo," cattleman Branch Nelson (David Brian) and his men are out after a wolf that has been killing his cattle. Nelson comes upon him, but the wolf gets away when Nelson's horse gets spooked and throws Nelson. Later the wolf stampedes Nelson's cattle, killing one of Nelson's men. Nelson goes to town to offer a bounty so a professional hunter will be enticed to kill the wolf.

In the Long Branch in Dodge, Luke Brazo (Morgan Woodward) confronts hunters Badger (Sheldon Allman) and Catlin (Sandy Kenyon), accusing them of cruelly poisoning coyotes for money. Brazo attacks them, but before he can seriously hurt them, Matt Dillon (James Arness) stops him and puts him in jail. Dillon and Brazo are old friends, so Brazo asks Dillon to help him track and kill the wolf so he can die a dignified death. While they are camping out on the trail of the wolf, Brazo complains about how settlers and cattlemen are polluting the land and ruining the way it was.

The next day, hunters Guffy (Ken Swofford) and Riney (Eddie Firestone) wound the wolf, but he gets away. Brazo and Dillon trap the wolf, and Brazo reluctantly kills him so the wolf, his "old friend," can die a decent death and have a decent burial where "vultures, human or otherwise, can't get at him." Then he will go off and "find me a place where there ain't no such thing as time," that is, a wild place where he can be free as he once was and where he can live the authentic life he craves.

However, when Brazo is burying the wolf, he is jumped and shot by Badger and Catlin. When Brazo recovers, he follows Badger and Catlin to town where they have taken the wolf for the bounty. When Brazo sees the wolf hung up in the town square amidst a cheering crowd, he charges in to cut down the wolf, killing two men in the process. He is captured and taken to jail by Festus (Ken Curtis) to keep him from being beaten to death by the townspeople. Desperate to be free, Brazo threatens to choke to death

Louie Pheeters (James Nusser), who is sleeping off a drunk in the next cell, unless Festus lets him go. Brazo gets Festus' gun and locks him up. Filled with anger and thoughts of revenge, Brazo goes on a rampage, burning buildings and stampeding cattle in a desperate attempt to turn back the clock to when the land was wild. Dillon goes after Brazo as he heads for the mountains where he can be free, "where there ain't no such thing as time." Brazo refuses to let Dillon take him back because he can't be put in a cage or strung up like the wolf. Brazo is killed by Dillon, going down fighting like the wolf did. Before dying, he asks Dillon to bury him where they can't find him, which Dillon does. Brazo, like the wolf, has been true to himself in death as well as in life.

Sometimes being authentic is accepting the bad memories along with the good and the divisions within oneself before being able to reconcile them. In the 1963 *Wagon Train* episode "The Fort Pierce Story," Chris Hale's (John McIntire) wagon train pulls into Fort Pierce and its members encounter Captain Paul Winters' (Ronald Reagan) wife Nancy (Ann Blyth). She is thrilled to see the wagon train because she is very lonely as the only woman on the post and frightened because her husband is out on patrol. When he comes back, the post's commander, Colonel Wayne Lathrop (John Doucette), is upset because Paul comforts his wife instead of coming to him to report directly and that Paul wants to leave the colonel as soon as he can to go back to her. The colonel believes that Nancy is distracting Paul from his duties and "suggests" to Paul that she should leave with the wagon train so he will no longer be distracted.

When Hale asks Paul about the Winters' baby, he finds out the baby died two months ago. Nancy later tells Paul she can't forget the death of her child and has tried to forget it by overindulging in alcohol. Hale tries to convince the colonel to send soldiers along with the wagon train, but the colonel refuses since he has been ordered to defend only the fort. Hale angrily tells him that following orders is not a good enough reason to allow 300 people to be in danger when the Indians are massing to attack the wagon train. That night at a party the colonel throws for the officers and Chris Hale, Nancy is upset upon learning that the wagon train, including a young couple, the Fowlers, and their baby, will not be protected. She gets drunk and embarrasses her husband.

Paul tells Hale it's his fault that Nancy is drinking because it was his insistence that he go out on patrol when the baby was sick and didn't think, despite Nancy's entreaties, that the baby was sick enough for the post doctor to examine before he left. When he came back, the baby was dead.

Scout Copper Smith (Robert Fuller) informs Hale that he received reliable information that a large Indian war party is forming ahead on the wagon train's trail. Paul goes to meet with the colonel. The colonel now not just "suggests" but orders Paul to have Nancy leave alone with the wagon train, even though he still refuses to order an escort for the wagon train despite Smith's latest information. Paul tries to convince the colonel to let Nancy stay, to no avail.

Nancy tells Paul that she won't make any more drunken scenes because she is ready to live with the bad memories as well as the good ones and that after holding the Fowlers' baby, she is ready to try for another baby. Paul tells her she has to leave on the wagon train and refuses to listen to her when she protests. After the wagon train leaves the next morning with Nancy on it, Paul agonizes over his decision to let Nancy go and tells the colonel that isolating himself from people and denying their feelings won't make him a better soldier and that serving people, like his wife and those on the wagon train, takes precedence over blindly obeying orders. Paul informs the colonel that he is going after his wife, even though the colonel tells him that it is an act of desertion. After Paul leaves, the colonel takes out a photograph of a young woman, apparently somebody he felt he had to give up in order to serve the army.

The wagon train circles to prepare for an Indian attack as Smith goes back to the fort to get help. At the fort, the colonel sends out Sergeant Wick (Robert Wilke) and a patrol to "follow the wagon train and bring back Captain Winters." Smith is chased by three Indians but manages to fight them off with the help of Paul. When Sergeant Wick's patrol catches up with Smith and Paul, Paul convinces Wick and his patrol to obey the colonel's orders literally by following the wagon train and then bringing Paul in. When Paul, Smith and Wick's patrol reach the wagon train, it is besieged and badly outnumbered, but the soldiers chase off the Indians. Paul meets up with Nancy and tells her he wants her to come back with him when he has to face a court martial.

When Paul gives his report, the colonel claims there is no court martial, that Sergeant Wick must have "misunderstood my orders" or his orders "weren't worded properly." The colonel has gracefully backed down despite what he said about the primary importance of obeying orders. When Paul says he still plans to have his wife stay with him, the colonel replies that each man has to serve the army in his own way. In one of their previous conversations, the colonel told Paul that Paul is a divided man, divided between the army and his wife, and Paul responded that most men are divided. What Paul has done by going after his wife is to accept divided loyalties as a first step in bridging that gap and not denying a part of himself, just as his wife has learned to accept her bad memories as well as her good ones as the only way of again living her life fully and authentically. Even the colonel, in accepting Paul's way of serving the army, has become more in touch with the divisions within himself and more authentic.

Sometimes being authentic can be very lonely. *High Noon* (1952) begins with the marriage of Hadleyville's Marshal Will Kane (Gary Cooper) and Amy Fowler (Grace Kelly) as three of Frank Miller's gang, Jack Colby (Lee Van Cleef), Jim Pierce (Robert Wilke) and Ben Miller (Sheb Wooley), ride into town. After the ceremony, Will turns in his badge and is about to leave (the new marshal is coming into town the next day). News arrives that Frank Miller has been pardoned and Ben, Colby and Pierce are waiting for him at the train station. Since Frank is expected to arrive at noon on the train and the wedding party expects him and his gang to take revenge on Hadleyville, especially Will, for sending him to prison, the wedding party and the town's leading citizen, Mayor Jonas Henderson (Thomas Mitchell), hustle Will and Amy out of town. However, after riding their buggy out onto the prairie a ways, Will realizes that he is helpless without his gun out in the open and has to turn back because he has never run before and the gang will make trouble for the town. ("I've got to go back. That's the whole thing.") Will expects the townspeople to help him if he goes back. Amy wants to keep running and tells Will she will leave him on the noon train if he stays.

In Hadleyville, Will finds Judge Percy Mettrick (Otto Kruger), the man who convicted Frank, leaving town to escape Miller's gang. He considers Will a fool for staying, doubting the townspeople will help him. At the hotel, Deputy Marshal Harvey Pell (Lloyd Bridges) is having breakfast with his lover Helen Ramirez (Katy Jurado), a businesswoman who is a silent partner in a store. Having heard about the Miller gang coming into town, he goes to see Will, telling him that he will help him against the gang if Will backs him for the position of permanent marshal. When Will refuses to "buy" his help, Pell throws down his deputy's badge and walks out. When Pell tells Helen about his confrontation with Will, who was formerly Helen's lover before Pell, she is so disgusted that she breaks up with him. Since Helen was also the lover of the vengeful Frank and Will is Frank's archenemy, she decides to sell her business and leave town.

Will sees Amy, who has decided to wait for the train away from the station where Colby, Pierce and Ben are waiting for the train, at the hotel. As they engage in conversation, both Amy and Will find out neither has changed their minds. Will goes upstairs to warn Helen about Frank, but she tells him she already knows. After Will leaves the hotel, the smarmy hotel clerk (Howland Chamberlain), obviously antagonistic towards Will, explains that Helen was the lover of both Frank and then Will. The clerk adds that he doesn't like Will because when Will cleaned up the town, he lost business and that some others in the town feel the same way.

When Ben Miller comes into the saloon, he receives a hearty welcome from the barkeep and other patrons. As Ben is leaving the saloon, Will is entering. They look at each other, but Ben only smiles and moves on. As Will enters the saloon, Will hears the barkeep, Gillis (Larry J. Blake), betting on Will being killed, which so infuriates Will that he slugs him. Will is chastened and apologizes when the barkeep tells him that he was wrong in hitting him since he has a badge and a gun and the barkeep doesn't. Will has come to the saloon to get deputies to support him, but nobody volunteers, either because they are friends of Frank or because, when they helped Will clean up the town the first time, there were six deputies and now he has none.

Will then goes to the home of Sam Fuller (Henry Morgan), who hides in his house while his wife, obviously lying, tells Will he is not home. The one-eyed drunk, Jimmy (William Newell), tells Will he will help him, but Will gently refuses. In her hotel room, Helen tells Harvey that she is leaving because when Will is killed, the town will die. Will goes to the church to get help. First some men volunteer, but others dissent. The mayor, a calculating politician, convinces them not to help Will because if they do, people "up North" will hear about shooting and killing in the streets and won't invest in the town. He adds that if Will leaves, there won't be any trouble that day and the new marshal can handle anything that occurs when he arrives, a solution that, according to the mayor, is best for the town and best for Will.

Will then goes to the home of the ex-marshal, Martin Howe (Lon Chaney, Jr.), to get help. The old and disillusioned Howe won't help him, telling Will that with his busted knuckles and arthritis he is no good to Will and would be more a handicap than a help. Amy goes up to Helen's room and asks Helen if she is the reason why Will is not leaving and, if so, to convince him to leave. Helen tells Amy she is not the reason why Will is leaving and that if Amy doesn't know the reason, "I cannot explain it to you." Helen, however, doesn't understand why Amy is leaving. Amy explains that when her father and 19-year-old brother were killed by guns, she was so disgusted with violence that she became a Quaker. Helen's attitude softens towards Amy and she invites Amy to wait with her until the train comes, but adds that if Will were her man, she would stay.

Squirming out of the fight. Herb Baker, played by James Millican (right), struggles to find the right excuse to back out of helping Will Kane, played by Gary Cooper (left), in Stanley Kramer's *High Noon* (1952, United Artists).

When Will goes to the stable, apparently thinking of leaving, Pell follows him there and Will admits he is scared and thought about leaving but has decided to stay. A fistfight ensues; Will wins. Will's last hope for help is dashed when Herb Baker (James Millican) refuses to help. The 14-year-old stable boy offers Will his help, but Will refuses. Will writes his last Will and Testament and leaves it in his office.

Frank arrives on the train and the four gunmen go to find Will. When Will kills Ben, Amy gets off the train to find Ben dead and then goes into the marshal's office. Will, holed up in a barn, kills Colby. When Frank and Pierce set the barn on fire, Will rides a horse out of the barn. When Pierce seeks cover outside the marshal's office, Amy shoots him in the back. Frank grabs Amy, using her as a shield, and tells Will he will let Amy go if he comes out into the street. Will comes into the street, Amy gets free from Frank, and Will shoots Frank dead.

The gunplay is over and the citizens come out of hiding. The stable boy brings Will and Amy their buggy, Will gently puts his hand on the shoulder of the stable boy, and with disgust throws his badge on the ground before Amy and he drive away.

Will is a conflicted figure. At first, he runs away with his bride when he finds out about Frank and his gang coming to Hadleyville. Even though he says he needs to turn around and go back to Hadleyville out of being true to his personal code ("They're making me run. I've never run from anybody before."), he tries to make Amy, and himself, feel better by looking at the situation in a positive way. But as far as Martin Howe and Judge Mettrick are concerned, a naïve way:

> Despite the fact that Amy believes trouble is inevitable, at this point it does not seem likely that Will expects or would even desire to face the Miller gang on his own. Furthermore, as we learn later in the film, he has never faced Miller on his own before, since in his earlier encounter he was backed up by a group of professional deputies along with volunteers from the community. Initially, Will does not expect to confront Frank Miller without community support; and it is at least arguable that, were the community completely united behind Will, the Miller gang would think twice about seeking vengeance or engaging in any other acts of violence [McGee, 2007, p. 118].

When towards the end of the film it appears that he will have to face the Miller gang alone, his illusions about the town shattered, and realizing he is likely in a situation over his head, he has a moment of weakness when go goes to the barn, admitting to Pell that he is scared and thinking about running. Partly because he doesn't like Pell telling him to leave, but mostly because he wants to remain true to himself, he beats up Pell and stays. However, despite his commitment to stay, from that point on his fear continues to grow. When he at last faces the Miller gang, "Kane is down to the bare essence of who he is" (McGee, 2007, p. 127):

> As Miller walks into the camera, there's a cut to the most famous shot in the film. It begins with a close-up of Kane's face, which has been juxtaposed with the face of Miller. As opposed to Miller's cool professionalism as he examines his gun, Kane's face exposes a man clearly on the verge of a nervous breakdown. Then, in the famous crane shot..., the camera tracks back and up as Kane looks around desperately for help that isn't coming, nervously adjusts his gun belt, wipes the sweat from his brow, and finally turns to walk away from the camera toward the encounter.

By the end of the film, Will has demonstrated not only his physical bravery, but also his psychological bravery by overcoming his fears, and even his moral bravery by going against a community that considers him a fool at best and against its interests at worst. (People "up North" won't supposedly invest in a town where violence takes place.)

Will also demonstrates his authenticity, his adherence to his moral code in little ways even before he faces the Miller gang. When he knocks down Gillis the barkeep, he apologizes and tries to pick him up when he realizes he was wrong, as an armed lawman, to hit an unarmed citizen, even one as obnoxious as Gillis. He refuses to "buy" Pell's support by backing him for marshal when he considers that would be wrong. Desperate as he is, he refuses the help of Jimmy the drunk and the stable boy, realizing that even though they might be marginally helpful, they would be no match for the Miller gang. True to his commitment to the law, he refuses to jail Pierce, Colby and Ben while they are waiting for Frank since they hadn't done anything wrong yet; and when Frank shows up, he gets the Miller gang's attention and lets them fire the first shot in order to say he fought them in self-defense.

The townspeople are, of course, either rationalizing "upright" citizens or "friends" of Frank. Most of the citizens give the usual excuses given for not fighting ("I have a wife and kids," "I'm not a lawman"), but the mayor tries a different tack. His claim that Will should leave town because people "up North" won't invest in Hadleyville and that once the new marshal comes to town everything will be worked out with the Miller gang rings hollow. There's no reason to believe that the new marshal will keep the Miller gang from misbehaving, especially since they probably have grudges against other people in the town who helped send Frank to prison. That the Miller gang has some unsavory plans for the town is hinted at when at the end of the film on the gang's way to the showdown with Will the reckless and immature Ben impulsively breaks a store window to grab a woman's hat. Pierce chastises him ("Can't you wait?"), implying that although Pierce doesn't like this impulsive behavior now, later he expects the gang will have its way with the town. Although the mayor may really believe what he is saying, it ends up sounding just as another excuse for cowardice.

There is possibly another unspoken reason the townspeople won't help Will and Amy: they're outsiders, both literally and figuratively. At the beginning of the film, even before news of the Miller gang in town reaches the wedding party, Will and Amy are apparently preparing to leave town (their buggy is already packed when they decide to hurriedly run away). Even if they stayed in town, Will, who never went to church and was the love interest of Helen, an outsider because of her Mexican heritage and ownership of the saloon, and Amy, the Quaker, would be considered outsiders by the "good people" of Hadleyville, even though the wedding party was full of good cheer. The "good people" of Hadleyville might have felt differently about helping them if Will and Amy were more integrated into the community.

The most credible excuse for not helping Will comes from the bitter ex-marshal, Martin Howe. Will can see for himself that Howe has the busted knuckles and arthritis that would keep him from helping Will and even get him killed worrying about Howe. Howe also shows great insight when he says, "It figures. It's all happened too sudden. People have to talk themselves into law and order before they do anything about it, maybe because down deep they don't care. They just don't care." Although this is not the most charitable explanation for the town's cowardice, at least it leaves open the possibility that if they had more time to think about it, they would act.

Besides Will, the most thoughtful and authentic characters in the film are the two women. Because of gender roles at the time, they aren't expected to take up a gun to face the Miller gang and therefore don't have to wrestle with this particular dilemma. When Amy kills Pierce, she shoots him in the back out of sight while he is loading his empty guns. (This brings up an interesting possibility that the townspeople didn't consider, shooting at the Miller gang from well-concealed positions when the gang started shooting.) Throughout the film, Helen acts authentically. She gives sound, credible reasons for her decisions. She is a realist about the consequences of Will facing the Miller gang. Helen is leaving not because she is a coward, but because as a capable businesswoman she has to look after herself. She realizes that when Will dies, the town will die, having no illusions about the ability of the town to tame the Miller gang. When she tells Amy that if Will were her man she would stay, it is believable.

Helen's love relationships are problematic. It would seem that coupling with Pell, whom she openly disdains as a "boy" and her relationship with the very difficult Frank, would seem poor choices for such a perceptive woman. However, Helen and Will seem to have developed a deep intimacy, which begs the question: Why did they break up? In some ways they seem better suited than Will and Amy. As a worldly outsider himself and someone with great empathy, Will probably comes closest to understanding how a Mexican woman feels living in a town where she is so disdained that she can only own a saloon openly and needs to have a silent partner to own the more respectable store. One explanation why they broke up, unflattering to Will, is that he wasn't willing to cross the racial divide to marry or have a long-term relationship with a Mexican woman.

Amy grows more than anyone else in the film. At first, she is overwhelmed by the sudden change from a happy bride to possible widowhood and falls back on her pacifistic beliefs, which in the past have given her comfort. However, these abstract beliefs don't seem adequate for this real-life dilemma. As it turns out, Amy has more courage than Helen, and maybe Amy herself, give her credit for. She has the courage to wrestle with her deeply held beliefs even though it brings back the horrible memories of the death of her father and brother and to accept that at least in this case, she needs to go against them, risking her life to kill another human being.

Foster (1994, p. 77) explains that her pacifistic beliefs bonds her to Helen and even Will:

> Helen Ramirez, in particular, ridicules the masculine domain of senseless brutality. As a non-white figure, she apparently has the privileged subject position of being able to see and know the foolishness of the violence of patriarchal western culture. When Harvey (Lloyd Bridges), Ramirez's boyfriend, makes fun of the Kane initial flight from town, away from the oncoming violence, Helen regards him with a look of revulsion which turns into a grave laugh. Kane himself makes an utterance that establishes a strong undercurrent against hero worship and expectations of men: "If you think I like this, you're crazy," he says to Amy, even as he is compelled into turning around to return to town to fight his enemy.

What separates Will from Harvey is that Will understands the difference between senseless violence demanded by some masculine code of honor and doing the right thing. This is shown very clearly when Will apologizes to Gillis for knocking him down. The characters that John Wayne typically played in that situation would never have admitted he was wrong or even realized why he would be wrong, believing that the masculine code of honor and doing the right thing are one and the same.

Likewise, when Amy backshoots Pierce, she is breaking the tenet of the masculine code of the West that you don't backshoot someone. However, she realizes by then the difference between senseless violence and doing the right thing.

Chapter 8

The Revisionist Western

> "I don't want to be a hero—I just want the money."—*A Fistful of Dynamite*, aka *Duck, You Sucker*

The concept of courage was expanded and greatly deepened with the onset of the Golden Age of Westerns, which stretched roughly from 1946 to 1964, with its psychological themes. The notion of courage took a much different form starting in the mid- to late-1960s with the advent of the revisionist or post-modern Western. According to Jim Kitses (1998, p. 19), the seeds of revisionism were well planted during the Golden Age as Westerns became more complex:

> Ford, the essence of the classical artist, meditated on revisionism as early as *Fort Apache* (1948), and became increasingly reflective and critical with later works. Is *The Searchers* revisionist? Is *Ride the High Country* the last classical Western? Or is it, like most of Peckinpah and Leone, on the boundary, overlapping and embracing, both recycling and going beyond earlier styles? Boundaries are unstable, and the art and culture always more layered and elusive than the paradigm.

However, Kitses (2004, p. 255) also explains that, at least when it came to the moral and psychological dimensions of the genre, the Western became radically changed in the hands of Sergio Leone:

> "I don't want to be a hero—I just want the money": Rod Steiger's Juan in *A Fistful of Dynamite* speaks for most of Leone's people. There are no cowboys in Leone's West, only bounty hunters, bandits and drifters.

Therefore, in Leone's world, virtue is hard to come by (Kitses, 2004, pp. 255–56):

> But in the land of the blind, the one-eyed man is king. In a landscape peopled by the morally blinkered, a modicum of virtue qualifies for an incipient heroism. Eastwood's

hero is only rarely disinterested in his motives. But where all coexist in the same grey world, actions that suggest a morally positive outcome stand out, even if taken for personal reasons rather than in defence of the community.... Leone's frontier is one where everyone appears corrupt, but where fine distinctions can still be made. The one saving value of Leone's dark West is friendship, the interrogated value—ambiguous, expedient, comically unstable—that runs through films and brightens its principals.

In other words, the ability of courage, such as it is in the revisionist Western, to lead to other virtues was severely compromised.

After the Italian Westerns, a noteworthy departure from the traditional Western was Sam Peckinpah's *The Wild Bunch* (1969). Although not totally unexpected from Peckinpah, given his previous Westerns such as *The Deadly Companions* and *Ride the High Country*, it still broke new ground in the genre with its violence and cynicism. The film begins with six men riding into the Southwestern town of Starbuck dressed in Army fatigues some time during the era of World War I, planning to rob a bank. Unbeknownst to them, Deke Thornton (Robert Ryan), who used to ride with one of the "soldiers," Pike Bishop (William Holden), who are coming into town, is waiting in ambush with Harrigan (Albert Dekker), who leads a motley bunch of bounty hunters and railroad men. However, while in the bank, the robbers spot Harrigan's men and shooting begins. Almost all of the robbers get away by mingling with the townspeople, but one of them is eventually gunned down. The bloodbath leaves a number of townspeople dead or wounded.

One of the gang members is so badly wounded that he asks Pike to kill him, which he does. Back in town, Harrigan tells Thornton to lead the others to capture the remaining members of the gang: Pike, Dutch Engstrom (Ernest Borgnine), Tector Gorch (Ben Johnson), Lyle Gorch (Warren Oates) and Angel (Jaime Sánchez). Otherwise, Thornton will have to go back to prison where he was tortured. Thornton tells Harrigan it isn't necessary to threaten him since he gave him his word he would go after the gang. Pike and his men cross into Mexico where they meet Freddie Sykes (Edmond O'Brien), who outfits them with horses. Unfortunately, when they open the bags they have stolen, they find only washers instead of coins, having been set up by Harrigan.

Pike tells Dutch he only needs to "make one good score" and then can retire, but Dutch is skeptical that can happen. Pike reminisces how Thornton and he had good times robbing together until Thornton was captured in a whorehouse while Pike escaped. Despite what has happened to them, Dutch and Pike agree they wouldn't have it any other way. Tector gets irritated by Freddie and threatens to kill him. Pike steps in, telling

Friendly territory. The Wild Bunch, led by Dutch Engstrom, played by Ernest Borgnine (center left on horseback) and Pike Bishop, played by William Holden (center right on horseback), get some rest and relaxation in a hospitable village in Sam Peckinpah's *The Wild Bunch* (1969, Warner Brothers).

Tector, "When you side with a man, you stay with him. If you can't do that, you're like some animal. You're finished. We're finished. All of us." Thornton and the unsavory louts who make up his posse stop at the border while Pike, Dutch, the Gorches and Angel go to the Angel's village, which has been devastated by Mapache and Huerta's federales. Angel finds out that during the attack, his father was killed and his woman, Teresa, was taken willingly by Mapache as his own. Angel wants revenge, but Pike convinces him to forget it, at least for the moment.

Pike and the rest of his bunch go to Agua Verde where Mapache, the federals and their two German advisors are quartered. When Pike jokes that they are just like the "bandit," General Mapache, Dutch gets indignant, telling Pike that they aren't like Mapache since they don't hang anyone, adding that he hopes the Mexican people rid Mapache and his army from the land. When Angel confronts Teresa, she makes it clear that she wants to be Mapache's woman. He gets so angry that he shoots Teresa while she is in Mapache's lap. This prompts the federales to grab Angel and threaten

8. The Revisionist Western

Pike and the rest of his men. However, the federales relent when they learn that they mean no harm to Mapache and the German advisors suggest Pike and his men could be useful to them. Mapache offers to pay Pike and his men a considerable amount of money if they rob an American train carrying weapons and give them to Mapache. Pike agrees with the plan, but only if Mapache lets Angel go, which he does.

When Pike and his bunch are alone, Angel says that he refuses to rob a train for Mapache, an enemy of his village. Pike gets him to go along by offering him one of the 16 cases of weapons and a box of ammunition, which Angel says he will give to his village to fight Mapache, although Angel will have to give up his share of Mapache's payment for the weapons to the rest of the gang.

Thornton guesses that Pike and his men will hit the train and he plans to stop them but is handicapped by being forced to use Harrigan's "gutter trash" and green U.S. army recruits to guard the train. Pike's men rob the train of the weapons and ammunition, and the unexpected bonus of a machine-gun. They get away into Mexico with Thornton's men chasing them. When Pike and his men meet Mapache's troops outside of Agua Verde, Pike stops them from stealing the weapons without paying for them by threatening to blow them up before the federales can get them. Pike goes to Agua Verde by himself and tells Mapache that as he pays for the weapons piecemeal, he will deliver them to Mapache piecemeal, including the machine-gun as a "gift" to Mapache. When Angel and Dutch come in for the last payment, Mapache reveals that he knows Angel gave a case of weapons to his village. As a result, Mapache takes Angel prisoner and Dutch rides away.

Back at their camp, Pike, Dutch and the Gorches decide not to rescue Angel. Sykes, who is temporarily away from the gang's camp, is shot in the leg by one of Thornton's men, who have been keeping watch on the gang. When Pike tells Dutch that Thornton's men shot Sykes because Thornton gave his word to the railroad he would get the gang, Dutch makes an ethical distinction by stating that it doesn't matter if you give your word, but to whom you give your word. To get Thornton and his men off their backs, Pike and his men ride back to Agua Verde and the supposed protection of Mapache. However, when they get back they see Angel being tortured. Pike tries to buy him back from Mapache, but he refuses. Pike backs off and he and the rest of his bunch, except Dutch, consort with "the muchachas." Afterwards, the four of them decide to get Angel. When they ask for Angel, Mapache slits his throat, prompting them to kill Mapache. This leads to a standoff, broken when Pike kills one of the Germans. A bloodbath ensues with Pike, Dutch and the Gorches along with numerous federales and townspeople being killed.

Thornton and his men ride into Agua Verde and Thornton's "gutter trash" strip the dead bodies of their possessions and claim the bodies of Pike, Dutch and the Gorches for the bounties. Thornton refuses to join in, only taking Pike's gun. Pike's men ride away while Thornton sits outside of the town. Sykes, who has joined the Mexicans opposed to the federals, finds Thornton and tells him they have killed the rest of his men. Thornton accepts Sykes' offer to join them.

With all the shooting in the film, physical courage isn't in short supply. When it comes to morality, it is a different, more complex story, which according to Bandy and Stoehr (2012) makes it an example of the genre's revisionism. They point out that in the scene where Dutch states that their bunch is different from Mapache because they don't hang anybody, Dutch could be deceiving himself into believing that he is morally superior because there are other ways that the bunch have killed or been responsible for killing people. Bandy and Stoehr (p. 231) also explain why Pike has no reason to claim the moral high ground:

> Pike, despite his emphasis on an ethos that will ensure the survival of the group as a group, seems willing to define the band's ultimate purpose as one of sheer greed, which makes his adherence to their code morally questionable at best when both ends and means are considered. Angel (Jaime Sánchez), their Mexican comrade, asks Pike hypothetically whether Pike would ever sell guns to men who had killed his own family—hence putting into question the rightness of their new mission of stealing guns to sell to Mapache, who is an enemy of Angel's people. The bunch's leader replies, "Ten thousand dollars cuts an awful lot of family ties." Pike appears fully greed-driven when he responds in this way, and therefore so does his old-fashioned principle of gang unity.

Bandy and Stoehr (pp. 232–33) argue that Dutch is the film's moral center, such as it is, but the bunch's courage, including Dutch's, doesn't always achieve moral ends:

> Despite being an outlaw and a killer, Dutch is the one member of the group whose loyalty seems to be defined by more than monetary gain. His obvious personal affection for Pike and his compassion for Angel (after the latter has been abducted by Mapache) are clear evidence of this.
>
> But Dutch's commitment is to a band of ruthless outlaws, therefore bringing into serious question the values in play here—values that are far from those of the traditionally heroic westerner. While one might initially think that Peckinpah celebrates the westerner whose freedom requires liberation from the constraints and impositions of an ordered society and a growing civilization, such an interpretation would be a mistake. We must never forget that these are the brutal killers of innocents—ruthless egoists whose ethos is driven by greed and whose courage should not be admired uncritically. The audience is provoked to ask, "Courage and unity and honor—but for the sake of *what*?"

8. The Revisionist Western

Kitses (2004, p. 222) sees Angel (an interesting choice of name) as the film's moral center, but demonstrates a psychological dimension to Pike that helps us to understand, if not excuse his moral shortcomings:

> "Angel dreams of love, while Mapache eats the mango." Like Elsa of *Ride the High Country*, Angel is the spiritual centre, the innocent vision, the imperiled values of the world of *The Wild Bunch*. Angel's complete loyalty to himself and "family ties," his killing of Teresa in the lion's den, his commitment to "my people, my village, Mexico," these can only describe a world of action for Bishop that his own life touched and departed from. The idea is sustained by another aspect of Pike's past, his love for the woman he hoped to marry blasted by her husband out of malice rather than jealousy, Bishop himself still limping from that wound of long ago. The quiet moment Pike shares with a prostitute before the final battle extends this delicate network of meaning, the scene carrying a bitter sense of what could have been and suggesting a capacity for love untapped. The scene also recalls Pike's escape from the bordello, the wounded Thornton left behind. In this light, Bishop's decision to return for Angel is classic Peckinpah action, the movement of a man into his past, a reassertion of identity, an honouring of the most important contracts, with one's self, God's law.

There's another quality that Bishop has that is in very short supply in revisionist films: forgiveness. (*God Forgives, I Don't* is the title of a revisionist Western.). Even though Thornton tried to kill him in Starbuck and doggedly chases the gang into Mexico, Pike forgives him because he understands that a man like Thornton needs to continue chasing the bunch because he gave his word, even if it is to a reprehensible man like Harrigan. This ability to forgive someone else because you understand their perspective, is key to forgiveness (Rizkalla, Wertheim and Hodgson, 2008).

I would argue that Deke Thornton, and not Angel, is the film's moral center. After all, Angel is involved in the bloodbath in Starbuck, a bloodbath that Thornton tells Harrigan should have been avoided by telling the townspeople about the ambush. It is also morally dubious to believe that Angel's killing of Teresa is somehow commendable, even if it is in "the lion's den." It would have shown more courage for Angel to restrain himself and accept Teresa's rejection of him rather than overreact (to put it mildly) by killing her. Deke, on the other hand, has not only been physically separated from the bunch the whole film, but morally separated as well. He is someone with the courage to want to stop the bloodbath in Starbuck by telling the townspeople beforehand. He demonstrates integrity by keeping his word, even to someone like Harrigan, and has a more morally defensible reason for chasing the gang, keeping out of the hellhole of a prison he was in, than the reason why the bunch attacked the bank in Starbuck and makes a deal with Mapache: greed. It is also perfectly consistent with Deke's moral character that he would throw in with Mexicans who are on a higher moral plane than Mapache and Huerta's federales.

Going to rescue Angel is a perfect climax. Despite their greed, killings and at times dubious loyalty to each other, the bunch, even the bullying and racist Gorches, have the courage to accept the life they have chosen and the consequences of it. They realize that their path can only lead to their violent destruction so they might as well go out in a blaze of glory trying to save their comrade. Bandy and Stoehr (2012, p. 233) put it this way:

> [T]he battle that concludes the film must be viewed as utterly nihilistic, despite the fact that the wild bunch is responding vengefully to Mapache's horrifying murder of Angel before their very eyes. Their vengeance against Mapache, knowing that they will surely die, is far from an ennobling final stand. By refusing to question the moral implications of their decision to sell guns to Mapache, and thereby ignoring Angel's protests, these men have reduced themselves to killers who sell killing machines to other killers with no regard for distinctions between killers and victims. If anything, their final stand is merely a reach for retribution that comes too late, given the situation that has resulted from their purely economic alliance with Mapache.

In other words, despite any admirable qualities they, particularly Bishop and Dutch, have, they have gone too far down the road to perdition to make any redemption possible. Deke and Sykes come the closest to being able to redeem themselves, and even that is problematical.

After *The Wild Bunch*, Westerns have ranged from those that are totally revisionist (e.g., *High Plains Drifter*, 1973) to those which are partly revisionist and partly traditional (e.g., *Pale Rider*, 1985, and the remake of *3:10 to Yuma*, 2007) to the generally traditional (e.g., *Broken Trail*, 2006, see Chapter 4).

High Plains Drifter is cynically, unmercifully and persistently revisionist. Kitses (2004, p. 288) puts its succinctly and well:

> Avenging the murdered sheriff of Lago, the mysterious Stranger punishes the three killers, their capitalist employers and the townspeople who ignored his cries for help. He makes the town's dwarf, Mordecai, its mayor, rapes one woman and forces himself on another, and has the town painted red to welcome the paroled killers, whom he kills before leaving.

High Plains Drifter has all the elements of the revisionist Western: townspeople who are total cowards, living in a town run by evil and greedy capitalists. At least in *High Noon*'s Hadleyville there was Will and Amy Kane. The Stranger is nothing but pure vengeance, whose courage, if you want to call it that, amounts to nothing more than retribution. It is difficult to even call him authentic because, unlike Pike and Dutch, we don't know nearly enough about him to know how true he is to himself.

An approximate remake of *Shane*, *Pale Rider* begins with a gang from a mining company attacking a camp of independent miners and chasing them out of Carbon Canyon, California. One miner, Hull Barret (Michael Moriarty), tries to fight back, but is knocked down as the marauders tear down the miners' tents and shacks and kill the dog of 15-year-old Megan Wheeler (Sydney Penny). After the raiders leave, Megan buries her dog and asks God for a miracle. Soon Barret rides into town for supplies even though the mining company's thugs beat him up the last time he was there. Clarence Blankenship (Richard Hamilton) at the general store gives Barret goods on credit (even though Barret and the miners are deeply in debt to him) because Blankenship hates Coy LaHood (Richard Dysart), the owner of the mining company.

After Barret leaves the general store, the mining company thugs begin to beat him up. The Preacher (Clint Eastwood) suddenly comes to Barret's defense and beats up the thugs, while Barret lies under the wagon. Barret invites the Preacher to stay with him, his "fiancée" Sarah Wheeler (Carrie Snodgrass) and Sarah's daughter Megan. As the Preacher rides into camp on a white horse, Megan is reading a passage from the Bible about a rider on a pale horse, whose name was Death, and that Hell followed him. At their cabin, Sarah talks about leaving the mining camp, but Megan and Barret want to stay. Hull tells the Preacher that although he is looking after Sarah and Megan, he isn't "living in sin." He would like to marry Sarah, but she is distrustful of men since her husband abandoned her.

Barret tells the Preacher that he believes that if he could just split a huge rock, he could find gold under it. The Preacher takes a sledgehammer and begins to pound on it and Barret joins in (a scene obviously inspired by *Shane*'s tree stump scene). Josh LaHood (Christopher Penn), the son of the mine owner, and one of his huge thugs, Club (Richard Kiel), confront the Preacher and Barret. Suddenly Club grabs a sledgehammer and splits a big piece of the rock off. He then attacks the Preacher, but the Preacher easily disables the much bigger man. As Josh and Club ride off, Barret, the Preacher, and other men in the camp proceed to finish breaking down the rock, under which Barret finds a gold nugget.

Coy LaHood arrives by train after trying to get the law and politicians to clear the independent miners out of Carbon Canyon. He becomes very upset that the Preacher has stopped the company men from chasing the "tin pans" out of Carbon Canyon, disrupting his plan to tear apart the Canyon with his hydraulic hoses for gold as he is doing in other canyons. The Preacher, Barret, Sarah and Megan go into town to use the gold to pay off Barret's debts. Coy invites the Preacher into his office and tries to bribe him to forsake the miners, but the Preacher refuses. An angry Coy tells the Preacher that he and the "tin pans" have 24 hours to leave the

Striking it rich. A jubilant Hull Barret (left), played by Michael Moriarity, shows a gold nugget to his love interest, Sarah Wheeler, played by Carrie Snodgrass (right), and her daughter Megan, played by Sydney Penny in Clint Eastwood's *Pale Rider* (1985, Warner Brothers).

Canyon. The Preacher counters that the miners might leave for $1000 a claim. Coy, not wanting to spend even more money on hired guns, agrees to that offer.

After the Preacher has returned, the miners argue over whether or not to take Coy's offer. The Preacher tells them if they don't, Coy will call in Stockburn (John Russell), a "marshal," and his six "deputies," for whom "killing is a way of life," to chase them out. Hull convinces the miners to stay to preserve their dignity and because their claims might be worth more than $1000. Later that evening, Megan tells the Preacher that she loves him and wants to make love to him, but he gently refuses and asks that she trust him that it's best for her. Megan angrily responds that it must be her mother that he loves.

In town, the Preacher tells the LaHoods that the miners decided to stay and then he apparently leaves camp for good. LaHood dams up the creek running through the miners' property so they will find it difficult to mine for gold. Sarah is very angry at Barret for not accepting LaHood's offer now that it appears the miners can't work their claims and the Preacher is apparently gone. The other miners are also discouraged but, urged on by Barret, decide to stick it out one more day. A miner, Spider, finds a huge gold rock and decides to go to town with his sons to buy all the goods he couldn't buy before and show the rock off to Coy. After Spider leaves, Barret asks Sarah if there's a chance the two of them could be together on a long-term basis and she says yes. Megan goes to the LaHood mining operation where Josh greets her and then proceeds to try to rape her in front of the jeering men. Club is about to stop it but the Preacher appears and stops it himself, shooting a gun out of Josh's hand and shooting his hand, then taking Megan away.

A drunken Spider taunts LaHood while in town. Stockburn and his "deputies" hired by Coy go out to confront Spider and goad him into drawing his gun as a pretext for then riddling him with bullets. Stockburn tells Spider's sons to tell the Preacher to meet him in town.

When the Preacher brings Megan back to her mother, Barret shows him Spider's body and gives the Preacher Stockburn's message. The Preacher tells the miners to continue sticking together. When the Preacher is alone with Sarah, despite her pleas to the contrary, he tells her he needs to face Stockburn to settle an old score. Sarah admits her feelings for the Preacher, kisses him gently to see what it's like before he leaves for good, and is about to leave him when the Preacher beckons her back.

In the morning, Barret insists on joining the Preacher and the two of them blow up LaHood's mining company's operation. While there, the Preacher tricks Barret, stranding him at the mining company. The Preacher goes to town by himself, kills four of LaHood's thugs, Stockburn's six deputies, and an astonished Stockburn, who recognizes him as the man he thought was dead. Barret prevents Coy from backshooting the Preacher. Megan rides into town to beg the Preacher to stay, thanking him and telling him that she and everyone loves him, but he rides off.

Despite the differences between *Shane* and *Pale Rider* (California instead of Wyoming, "tin pans" vs. a mining company instead of homesteaders vs. ranchers, a 15-year-old lovestruck girl replacing a younger boy), there are a number of similarities that stamp the latter as a remake of the former. Hull Barret is a stand-in for Joe Starrett (even the last names are similar), the Preacher is a stand-in for Shane, Sarah is a stand-in for Marian Starrett, Stockburn is a stand-in for Wilson, and even Spider is a stand-in for Stonewall. *Pale Rider*'s plot follows the trajectory of the earlier film although with some twists, the Preacher bedding Sarah and the Preacher tricking rather than knocking out Barret to keep him from the final showdown, to name a few.

However, there are some critical differences between the films due to the revisionist tendencies of the latter. First of all, although the Rykers are evil, at least they are not raping the land the way LaHood's mining company is. Previous films, such as the interesting *The Last Hunt* (1956), decried the disappearance of the buffalo and wild game, but generally weren't as environmentally conscious as *Pale Rider*. Kitses (2004) points out the contrast between the "tin pans" whose methods are less destructive to the environment than the methods of the LaHoods, whose explosive discharges of water completely tear down the hillsides.

Secondly, the film is more sexualized than earlier Westerns. Megan doesn't just "love" the Preacher, she wants to "make love" to him whereas in *Shane*, Joey's attraction to the gunfighter is strictly hero worship. Marian apparently has feelings for Shane, but since she doesn't act on them, it's not clear exactly what they are. Are they purely lust? Or is she infatuated with a "knight in shining armor"? Or does Shane represent the freedom she craves from her humdrum life? It's clear, however, that Sarah's attraction to the Preacher is sexual, enhanced by his physical power. Her curiosity about what it would be like to make love to the Preacher leads her to give him a chaste kiss, but he entices her into something much more physical than that. A weakness of the film is that it completely avoids the consequences of this lovemaking. The next day, Barret doesn't mention anything about it, either because he is oblivious to it or wants to pretend he is oblivious. This will always be something between Barret and Sarah, whether Barret realizes something happened or not. Kitses (2004, p. 305) explains the complications of this night together:

> [I]n Sarah's encounter we are to understand that she is given the opportunity to find out what a real (or unreal) man is like. Hopefully, memories of this will not diminish the intimacy she shares with Hull, and what that good man does not know will not evidently hurt him (even if, as seems likely, the god will leave his seed behind.)

Perhaps Barret will be able to forgive Sarah for this encounter, even if "the god will leave his seed behind." However, if Sarah had the courage and prudence to restrain herself, she might find that the intimacy she developed in a long-term relationship with Barret would be more gratifying than the one-night stand with the Preacher, as exciting and "magical" as that might be. In any case, by having sex with Sarah, the Preacher doesn't prove to be as good a friend to Barret as Shane is to Joe Starrett. (At least the Preacher shows enough restraint not to have sex with an underage but willing Megan.)

The most important of the revisionist influences in the film is the otherworldliness of the Preacher. He shows up when Megan prays to God for a miracle and rides a "pale horse." Stockburn could swear he was dead. His powers seem almost supernatural. He seems more of an ideal than a flesh-and-blood man. As a result, he can't help but diminish poor Barret in the eyes of Sarah, Megan and the mining community, according to Kitses (2004, p. 302):

> How can Hull win? He is being measured against a mythical standard, a superhero's masculinity.... Eastwood has described his hero variously as a supernatural being from a higher plane, an archangel, and one of the Four Horsemen of the Apocalypse.

Barret even comes off second best to Joe Starrett, who didn't hide under a wagon in a brawl with the villains but stood back to back with Shane in the fight at Grafton's and has to be knocked out unfairly with a gun butt before Shane can subdue him before the final showdown with Wilson and the Rykers. Still, Barret persists and doesn't give up even to the point of seeming reckless. Who truly has more courage or is more estimable, the ordinary man with ordinary powers fighting against overwhelming odds or the man with virtually superhuman powers? In fact, despite his incredible feats and well-meaning platitudes, the Preacher is so unreal and mythical, he is beyond courage, and therefore beyond redemption or growth. He is not going to end up running a dry goods store like William Munny. Moving on at the end of the film is not going to be as bothersome or courageous for the Preacher as it is for Shane.

A minor but interesting comparison of characters in the two films is between Chris Calloway in *Shane* and Club in *Pale Rider*. Both men are at first antagonistic to their films' heroes but redeem themselves by helping out the heroes in the final showdown. However, Chris Calloway makes it clear why he is helping out Shane whereas the inarticulate Club does not.

James Mangold's 2007 *3:10 to Yuma*, a remake of Delmer Daves 1957 film (see Chapter 3), has elements of both revisionist and traditional Westerns. It is one of those remakes that works, and in some ways even improves on the original. It begins with marauders burning down Dan Evans' (Christian Bale) barn in Arizona. As they ride away, Dan tells his 14-year-old son William (Logan Lerman) that he will take care of the situation, but the son is skeptical, obviously without much respect for his father. Dan's wife Alice is angry because Dan didn't tell her the marauders were trying to chase him off his land because he owes their boss, Glen Hollander (Lennie Loftin), money that he needed to pay for water for his ranch and medicine for his younger son Mark, and he hasn't kept up the payments.

Dan, William and Mark go out to round up the cattle scattered by the raid as Ben Wade (Russell Crowe) and his men are on their way to rob the stagecoach. Just as it seems that the stagecoach guards have successfully fought off Wade's men, Wade stampedes the Evans cattle in front of the stagecoach, causing it to overturn and allowing the gang to capture it. Gang member Charlie Prince (Ben Foster) callously kills a wounded and helpless guard. Wade kills a guard and the gang member that the guard was using as a shield, justifying it by saying that Tommy was careless and didn't follow the gang's rule by not checking to see if all the guards were dead or disabled, thus being indirectly responsible for his own death. However, Wade spares the life of a wounded Pinkerton man he recognizes, Byron McElroy (Peter Fonda), whom Dan, William and Mark help after Wade lets Dan have his cattle back, but only after he "borrows" three of Evans' horses.

The gang rides into Bisbee and Prince tells the unsuspecting citizens that the stage has been robbed, prompting a posse led by the marshal and railroad man Grayson Butterfield (Dallas Roberts), to leave town to mistakenly chase the gang. Charlie and the gang leave Bisbee to go across the border while Wade stays to romance and bed down the barmaid. Meanwhile, the marshal, Butterfield and the posse meet Evans and his sons out of town. Based on what Dan tells the posse, they realize that the gang was in Bisbee. When they get back to town, Dr. Potts (Alan Tudyk) takes the bullet out of McElroy. Dan then confronts Hollander, complaining about his men burning down his barn and damming the creek that would water his cattle. The callous Hollander says it was in his rights to dam the creek on his lands and that Dan needs to get off the land in a week so Hollander can recover what Dan owes him. When Dan pathetically offers Hollander his Civil War medal, the one he received when losing part of his leg, Hollander replies, "Sometimes a man has to be big enough to see how small he is." An angry Dan grabs a gun to confront Hollander again, but instead runs into Wade, who pays Dan for cattle he lost and time spent by Dan and his boys during the holdup. While they are talking, the marshal and his men capture Wade. Dan joins the posse for the $200 that he will get for transporting Wade to Yuma prison, money he needs to save his ranch. Before the posse can get Wade in the stagecoach, Prince rides into town and shoots two townspeople, letting everyone know he knows that they have captured Wade.

The coach with Wade goes to Evans' ranch with Prince watching them the whole way. The stagecoach, acting as a decoy, goes on without Wade. McElroy, Wade, Tucker (Kevin Durand), Doc Potter and Dan's family stay at the ranch. During supper with Dan's family, Wade flirts with Alice, who is flattered by his attention. Alice tries to stop Dan from going, making it plain that Wade and his gang are too much for him, but Dan says he needs to do it for them to survive. Dan, Butterfield, McElroy, Potter and Tucker leave to take Wade to Contention to catch the 3:10 to Yuma. William sneaks off to try to join the posse. While the posse is camped out, Wade tells Dan that he should have stayed home protecting his family. When Dan replies that he doesn't like a man like Wade on the loose, Wade responds that it's man's nature to take what he wants. When Wade claims that Dan could have provided for his wife better, Dan loses his temper and threatens him. Instead of getting angry about being threatened, Wade says he likes this side of Dan, since he is getting under Dan's skin and is starting to act more like Wade.

Wade uses a fork to kill the obnoxious, taunting Tucker, prompting McElroy to beat up Wade. Wade's gang attacks the "decoy stagecoach" only to see that Wade is not on it. However, before killing everyone on the stage, Prince finds out from a guard that Wade is being taken to Contention to catch the 3:10 to Yuma. Prince forces the gang to ride 80 miles in a short time to save Wade.

Back on the trail, Wade tells Dan he doesn't like his sensitive conscience, but has nothing but contempt for the rigid, hypocritical, Bible-toting McElroy, who's killed Apache children along with the men. Wade jumps McElroy and takes his shotgun, pushing McElroy off a cliff to his death and disarming the rest of the posse. Just when it seems that Wade will get away, William appears for the first time, sneaking up on Wade and making him give up his weapon. The posse takes him into custody again. Later, as Wade talks to William, it becomes apparent that William respects Wade more than he does Dan and that William has more in common with Wade than Dan would like. The men are attacked by Apaches, who wound Dan. In the fight, Wade takes Dan's gun, knocks out Dan and takes the horses. Dan convinces Butterfield and Potter to go after Wade in order to get the reward.

When Wade comes across a railroad gang, one of them, Walter Boles (Forrest Fyre), recognizes Wade and they recapture him. Potter, Butterfield, Dan and William catch up with the captured Wade just as he is being tortured by the railroad man Boles, whose brother was killed by Wade. The four men forcibly take Wade away, Potter getting killed in the process. The group reaches Contention and Dan and Butterfield put Wade up in a hotel while William watches for the train and Wade's gang. In the hotel room, Dan refuses to accept a $1,000 bribe to let him go, telling Wade that it would be hard to explain how Wade got away and Dan suddenly got richer. Butterfield brings the town marshal and two of his men to guard

Wade. Wade's gang rides into town. Prince offers $200 to anyone who kills one of Wade's captors. The townspeople flock around Prince to get the $200, which causes the marshal and his two men to leave the hotel and lay down their weapons. Immediately they are brutally slain by Prince and the gang.

Back in the hotel room, William, who had previously hero-worshipped Wade, becomes disillusioned with him when he convinces him that he is nothing more than a rotten, brutal killer with no ethics. With the marshal and his two men dead, Butterfield tells Dan to let Wade go and he will still pay him the $200. When Dan insists on taking Wade to the train station, William begs him to let Wade go, but Dan says he owes it to Potter and McElroy to see it through. Dan tells Butterfield to see that William gets back safely to the ranch, to keep Hollander from taking over the ranch and to let his family have the water from the dammed-up creek, and to give Alice $1,000. Butterfield agrees to the demands. Dan tells William to remember him as the man who walked Ben Wade to the train station when no one else would. Wade reveals that, when he was eight, his mother abandoned him. Dan in turn tells Wade that he got his Civil War medal when his foot was shot off by somebody in his own unit when it was in retreat.

As they make their way to the train station, gang members and townspeople after the reward let loose a hail of bullets, trying to kill Dan. When they are in a relatively safe spot, Dan explains to Wade that he came to Arizona and fought to stay there on his ranch because his younger son Mark needed a drier climate due to his tuberculosis, not because he was stubborn. As Dan and Wade get closer to the train, William sneaks up on the gang and lets loose a herd of cattle from their pens, which get in the way of the men trying to kill Dan. Wade and Dan reach the train, but Prince kills Dan. Wade, angry that Dan has been killed, kills Prince and the rest of the gang. William points the gun at Wade but doesn't kill him. Wade gets on the train and is held prisoner but is not worried about getting away again.

The remake of *3:10 to Yuma* is an interesting combination of elements of the traditional and revisionist Westerns, although not as successful in that regard as *The Wild Bunch*. Its brutal and graphic violence is much more reminiscent of revisionist rather than traditional Westerns. More importantly, the theme of the corporate takeover of the West is something quite common to revisionist Westerns. The railroad, as it is in so many revisionist Westerns, is a clearly evil force bent on taking over as much land as it can, even to the point of destroying the lives of ranchers like the Evanses, who are too small to resist. As Hollander tells Dan, "Sometimes a man has to be big enough to see how small he is." The railroad workers who capture Wade are oppressive and racist bosses who maltreat the Chinese working under them. To include the railroad more in the story, Butterfield is a railroad man, whereas in the 1957 version he is a stagecoach owner, a curious change in the story considering that the real John W. Butterfield was indeed an owner of an Arizona territory stagecoach line, not a railroad. Also, the lawmen in the film, as is true in so many revisionist Westerns, are less than stellar representatives of the judicial system. Although McElroy has a great deal of grit and courage, something that even Wade admires, he is a hypocritical racist who kills children. He is also a Pinkerton, which in revisionist Westerns are tools of the corporate state stamping out individuality in the West.

The two individuals who reflect the values of the traditional Western are Dan and William. As Wade points out, Dan hasn't provided very well for his family. However, from beginning to end, out of love for his family he has the courage to never stop trying. He moves his family to Arizona for the sake of his son, confronts Hollander in Bisbee, volunteers to take Wade to Contention for the money that will save his ranch, and against extreme odds takes Wade to the train station not only to save his ranch, but to leave a legacy for his sons. Dan also has the courage to restrain himself when confronted by the marauders in the beginning of the film and Wade during the holdup, even though this diminishes him in the eyes of William. Dan also displays the courage to be authentic when he admits to Wade that he won his medal while his unit was retreating, shot by one of the men from his unit.

William also grows during the experience. At first, he is too immature to realize how shallow Wade is and doesn't have the empathy to understand his father and how courageous he is. However, by the end of the film he has a deeper understanding of his father's worth and has mustered the courage to grow up. As his father says, William has the best parts of him, demonstrated not only by his courage to do what he must do to support his family, but the courage to restrain himself from killing Wade at the end, showing the temperance his father would have shown.

Where the film becomes problematical is the ending. As mentioned in Chapter 3, I disagreed with critics who found the ending of the 1957 film unconvincing, arguing that Wade's vanity motivated him to "pay back" Dan for saving his life by jumping on the train to Yuma, a prison from which the vastly confident Wade felt he could escape. Likewise, in the 2007 version Dan is one of four people (the others are Butterfield, Potter and William) who saved Wade's life. Another possible reason why the 2007

Wade might have jumped on the train was to make sure Dan's family received everything that Butterfield agreed to give them. This is not totally convincing. First of all, although Butterfield seemed to be decent enough, there's doubt that he could carry through his promise to Dan if the evil and all-powerful railroad really wanted Dan's ranch.

Secondly, Wade, by his own admission, is ruthless and without a conscience. Despite this, however, Wade opens up to Dan by revealing how he had been abandoned as a child, showing a vulnerability he hasn't shown before, which is reciprocated by Dan admitting he received his medal for less than heroic conduct. This implies that the two men had developed a bond that could explain Wade's behavior at the end. Another possible factor for Wade's actions is that Wade admired and even envied Dan because he not only had as much courage as Wade but had something else Wade could not develop: a deep affection for others. Therefore, it was possibly this admiration (as well as admiration for William) that leads Wade to help the father and son.

But why did Wade kill Prince *and* the rest of the gang as well? (In the 1957 film, Dan shoots Prince, who in this version is nowhere as psychopathic as the 2007 version.) It could be that Wade wanted revenge for Prince killing a man he had bonded with. Or it could be that only by killing Prince and the rest of the gang could he stop them from stopping him from getting on the train. He could also be doing it to protect William, who would be vulnerable to Prince and the rest of the gang once he hopped on the train.

However, in the final analysis, by making the 2007 Ben Wade so much more evil and brutal than the 1957 Ben Wade, the filmmakers have made it even more difficult to explain why Wade would jump on the train at the end and kill his cohorts in crime instead of killing Dan and William. The fact that the 2007 Wade is much less capable of redemption and growth than the 1957 Wade makes the ending of the 2007 film less believable than the ending of the 1957 film.

Chapter 9

Lonesome Dove

"By God, it's been quite a party."—*Lonesome Dove*

In 1989, after decades of decline of the television and film Western, *Lonesome Dove* premiered. Based on the Pulitzer Prize–winning Larry McMurtry novel, the miniseries boasted a stellar cast (Robert Duvall, Tommie Lee Jones, Angelica Huston, etc.), wonderful cinematography, a compelling musical score and an excellent screenplay with crisp dialogue. It was generally a big hit with both the critics and viewing audience, according to Gary Yoggy (1995, p. 588):

> While earning almost universal critical acclaim, *Lonesome Dove* was also a huge commercial success by nearly every criterion. It scored the biggest miniseries ratings triumph in five television seasons and made money for the network from its first airing alone, a rare phenomenon for a miniseries. *Lonesome Dove* scored a four-night rating of 26.1 with a 39 percent share of the audience. The first two-hour segment was the most watched program of the week (January 30–February 5), drawing over 44 million viewers, a 28.5 rating and a 42 percent share. Part four ranked first for the following week (February 6–February 12) with comparable figures: 41.5 million viewers, 27.3 rating and a 41 percent share. Parts two and three ranked eighth and fourth for the week respectively, with only slightly less impressive figures.

In particular critics tended to emphasize how traditional and yet at the same time how new and refreshing it was. Richard Zoglin (February 6, 1989, p. 78) of *Time Magazine* was typical:

> *Lonesome Dove* is surprisingly nonrevisionist in its picture of the West. The good guys still perform stunning heroics with six-shooters, and Indians are faceless villains who whoop when they ride. Yet in its everyday details—the dust and the spit, the casual conversations about whoring, the pain of a man getting a mesquite thorn removed from his thumb—this may be the most vividly rendered old West in TV history.

Martha Bayles echoed other critics in her *Wall Street Journal* review (February 3, 1989):

> The miniseries pulls off the rare feat of updating a myth without also outdating it. As a uniquely American image of honor, the Western hero still packs an emotional wallop—when he is done right. And in *Lonesome Dove*, he definitely is done right.

More than its success with viewers and reviewers, it encapsulates the role in the Western genre of courage and the virtues it leads to.

Augustus McRae (Robert Duvall) and Woodrow Call (Tommy Lee Jones), ex–Texas Rangers, are the proprietors of a cattle company with very little business. An old friend from their Texas Ranger days, Jake Spoon (Robert Urich), rides into their town of Lonesome Dove and tells them of the wonderful country and opportunities for cattle ranching in Montana. Jake is being pursued by a Fort Smith sheriff, July Johnson (Chris Cooper), for the accidental murder of the town mayor.

Soon after Spoon rides in, Spoon, McRae and Call, along with their ranch hands, Joshua Deets (Danny Glover), Dish Boggett (D.J. Sweeney) and Newt Dobbs (Ricky Schroeder), go down into Mexico to steal horses. En route back to Texas, they encounter Pedro Flores (John Quijada) and steal the herd he stole in Texas.

Inspired by Spoon's stories about the Montana cattle market, McRae and Call decide to drive cattle to Montana along with Deets, Pea Eye Parker (Timothy Scott), Newt, Dish and the other ranch hands. Spoon and his lover, prostitute Lorena "Laurie" Wood (Diane Lane), follow while Spoon assures Laurie that they will leave the cattle drive eventually in order to go to San Francisco.

On a trip to San Antonio to get a cook for the cattle drive, McRae tells Call about Clara Allen (Angelica Huston), the love of his life, and his regrets about letting her go. He also confronts Call about his refusal to recognize Dobbs as his son because his mother was a prostitute whom he deserted because of her profession.

Spoon leaves Laurie in order to gamble in San Antonio. McRae comes to console her, telling her not to pin her hopes on Spoon or any one person or one thing, but to enjoy the little things of life: a glass of buttermilk, good whiskey, a soft bed, or McRae himself. He confesses that he went on the cattle drive only to see Clara, who is now raising horses with her husband near Ogallala, Nebraska.

Laurie and McRae encounter the vicious half-breed renegade Blue Duck (Frederick Forrest), who is chased away by McRae. McRae sends Dobbs to guard Laurie, but Blue Duck comes back, knocks Dobbs out and steals Laurie, intending to sell her to the Comancheros. Blue Duck decides to give the Comancheros Laurie and horses if they promise to kill McRae. The Comancheros chase McRae, but he gets away. McRae runs across July Johnson, his deputy Roscoe Brown (Barry Corbin), July's stepson Joe Boot (Adam Faraizl) and Janey (Nina Siemaszko). July has stopped chasing Spoon and is now looking for his runaway wife, Ellie (Glenne Headly), who has fallen in with some buffalo hunters. Leaving the others behind, McRae and Johnson find the Comanchero camp. McRae kills all of them and liberates Laurie; but while they are gone, Blue Duck kills Brown, Boot and Janey. Johnson blames himself for not being there to protect them.

In Fort Worth, Spoon falls in with some bank robbers. After they leave Fort Worth, gang leader Dan Suggs (Gavan O'Herlihy) decides they should steal horses. When Spoon objects, Suggs intimidates him into going along. The gang kills two of the men leading horses and wounds another who gets away (Spoon doesn't participate in the shooting). The man who got away alerts Call and McRae, and the two of them with Parker, Dobbs and Deets track down and capture the gang, but not before Suggs kills two farmers in cold blood. When McRae and Call catch up to the gang, Jake tells them he didn't have anything to do with the killings. However, according to the moral code of Call and McRae, anyone who joins a gang is responsible for what the gang does, whether or not that individual pulls the trigger. McRae and Call hang the entire gang, including Spoon.

Johnson's wife Ellie and two buffalo hunters arrive at Clara's ranch, where Ellie has a baby. After she leaves, Johnson reaches Clara's, where she tells him Ellie left the baby with her and went away. Johnson goes to Ogallala to see Ellie, but she leaves the next day with the two buffalo hunters. Johnson accepts a job at Clara's ranch to help replace her incapacitated husband, and later he finds out that Ellie and the two buffalo hunters were killed by Indians.

McRae, Call, their drovers and the herd arrive in Ogallala. In town, an army scout starts beating Dobbs. Call retaliates by beating the scout almost to death. McRae explains to Dobbs that Call beat the scout because Dobbs is Call's son. At Clara's ranch, Clara declares to McRae her love for him but says that if McRae stays with her, it will hurt Laurie. Clara also couldn't marry him since he isn't honest enough for her. Clara asks Laurie to stay with her when McRae leaves with the trail crew. Just before he leaves, McRae tells Laurie he will come back to her, but won't marry her, giving her an opportunity to see if other men are right for her. When the trail crew reaches Montana, McRae explains to Dobbs that Call won't admit he's Dobbs' father because it would be admitting to others and even to himself that he made a mistake by conceiving Dobbs and walking away from his mother.

On a scouting mission, McRae and Parker are attacked by Indians. McRae gets two arrows in the leg and Parker a bullet in the shoulder. Parker goes back to the herd to get help. An old man finds McRae and takes him to Miles City where a doctor removes his leg. The doctor tells McRae that the other leg also has to come off or McRae will die. McRae refuses. After Parker reaches the herd, Call tracks McRae to Miles City. Despite Call's pleas, McRae still refuses to have his leg removed. He explains to Call that his pride won't let him live without legs. McRae asks that he be buried in Texas by the creek where he used to sit with Clara. He asks Call to buy McRae's half of the herd and give the money to Laurie and to tell Dobbs that he is his son. McRae's last words: "By God, it's been quite a party."

Call picks out a valley in Montana to build his ranch. He tells Parker, Jasper Fant (Barry Tubbs) and Dobbs to drive 100 cattle to a nearby fort and sell them at a fair price to both parties with Dobbs in charge. Fant doesn't like that Dobbs is put in charge and beats him up, but Dobbs keeps getting up until he can't get up any more. In the middle of the fight, Parker is about to stop it, but Call signals him not to, apparently because stopping the fight would keep Dobbs from assuming the responsibility of a leader and maintaining the respect of the other men. When Dobbs is finally able to get up, he tells Fant to mount his horse and get back to work. The fact that Dobbs keeps getting up after being knocked down, that he insists in being still in charge after the fight, but isn't vindictive towards Fant, shows he has grown up a great deal.

In the spring, Call tells Dobbs he's the range boss and gives him his horse and his father's watch. Although Dobbs is upset that Call did not come out and say that Dobbs was his son, in Call's eyes his actions have acknowledged Dobbs as his son. Call takes off on a long and arduous journey to bring McRae's body to Lonesome Dove despite the fact that the people along his trip think he is crazy for doing it. When a reporter in Lonesome Dove asks Call about his having a vision, he responds that it was a "hell of a vision."

Lonesome Dove illustrates well the role that courage plays in the other virtues, mainly in the character of Call. He redeems himself at the end of the story by tacitly admitting that Dobbs is his son. By turning over his ranch, horse and father's watch to Dobbs and almost beating the army scout to death in order to save Dobbs, Call demonstrates his authenticity and love for Dobbs, love a man like Woodrow finds difficult to express, even if he does it in his own way. Deets risks his life to pick up an Indian baby who is in danger and dies protecting the baby. Because of McRae's tenderness towards her, Laurie finds the courage to love again after being brutalized by Blue Duck.

When they hang Jake despite the fact that he rode with them and they are saddened by it, McRae and Call show the sense of justice that has marked their lives, admittedly a rough sense of justice, but one they have followed consistently. In a subtler way, Call demonstrates his fairness when he tells Dobbs to negotiate a price for their horses that is fair not only to them but to the army. Call also shows temperance and self-regulation when he doesn't stop Fant from beating up Dobbs, even though he previously beat the army scout almost to death when he attacked Dobbs. Call realizes that although the army scout could have hurt or even killed Dobbs, Fant wasn't going to hurt him that badly, and that if Dobbs was going to be the ranch boss he would have the respect of the men only if he fought his own battles. Clara also demonstrates her prudence by not agreeing to marry McRae because she knows the marriage wouldn't work for either of them.

The fistfight with Fant is only one example of the many ways that Dobbs has the courage to overcome obstacles to grow up and become his own man. McRae's last words, "By God, it's been quite a party," show he has the integrity to face his own death that comes only from having lived a satisfying and meaningful life. McRae shows his authenticity when he decides he would rather die than live a life he doesn't want (without legs). That Call says that his life has had a hell of a vision indicates that he also will be ready to face death when his time comes. Call's determination to bring McRae's body back to Lonesome Dove when others consider him foolish for doing so shows his moral courage.

Conclusion

Echoing thinkers going back to Aristotle, Winston Churchill, someone who had an intimate knowledge of courage (physical, moral or psychological) based on his considerable knowledge of history and firsthand experience, once said, "Courage is rightly esteemed the first of human qualities ... because it is the quality that guarantees all others" (Mansfield, 1996, p. 94). The poet Maya Angelou expressed much the same thought when she stated, "Courage is the most important of all the virtues, because without courage you cannot practice any other virtue consistently" (McGregor, 2014, May 28). What makes courage such an important, meaningful and appealing part of Westerns is not just that it comes "wrapped up in more than one way" but that it is often instrumental, and perhaps even necessary, for the other virtues to be fulfilled. Without courage, Gil Westrum in *Ride the High Country* would not have come loyally to the aid of his friend Steve Judd and thus redeemed himself. Without courage, in *High Noon* Amy Kane couldn't have expressed her love for Will Kane by coming to his aid, despite her deeply held pacifistic beliefs. Without courage, Howie Kemp in *The Naked Spur* could not have let his $5,000 reward float downstream with the body of Ben Vandergroat as a necessary step in letting go of his tormented past and accepting the risk of getting hurt again by starting out with Lina Patch. Without courage, Matt Morgan in *Last Train from Gun Hill* would not have the restraint to stop himself from killing the man who brutally raped and murdered his wife. Without courage, Ben Mockridge in *The Culpepper Cattle Company* couldn't have faced the challenges he needed to confront in order to grow up. Without courage, Hallie Stoddard in *The Man Who Shot Liberty Valance* couldn't have accepted the disappointments as well as the joys of her life in order to find meaning in it as she neared the end of it. Without courage, Wes Tancred in *Tension at Table Rock* couldn't have been truly authentic by announcing his reviled true name in a crowded courtroom. Without courage, Jim Douglass in *The Bravados* couldn't have accepted the responsibility for killing out of pure vengeance the three men he mistakenly thought raped and killed his wife. Without courage, Woodrow Call in *Lonesome Dove* could not have acknowledged (albeit in his own way) Newt Dobbs as his son, even though it was painful that by acknowledging that Dobbs' was his son, he also implicitly acknowledged that the mother of his son was a prostitute from whom he walked away, and without courage he would not have undertaken to bring Gus McRae's body hundreds of miles to Lonesome Dove to be buried despite the hardships the journey entailed and the ridicule from those who considered the effort crazy.

However, Indick (2008) states that although the Western is still alive, it will never achieve its former importance in popular culture due to modern-day audiences' perception of the classical Westerns as sexist, racist and imperialist, and their lack of tolerance for the films' slow pacing. Nevertheless, Indick (2008, p. 195) goes on to conclude:

> New Westerns are being made for the screen as well as television. They are much different from the old Westerns, and they will not revive the genre to any of its former grandeur. Yet they are keeping the genre alive, just barely, and modernizing it for future generations. The old motifs of Western expansionism, alcoholism, violence and racism are giving way to stories about gay cowboys (*Brokeback Mountain*) and independent single mothers (*The Missing*). Nevertheless, the archetypal themes that the Western represents—independence, isolationism and individualism—remain the primary forces behind the genre. The frontier still holds a mythic significance for Americans. It is still the place where the American character is reborn. The longing for a land where the individual is free to determine his own goals, pursue his own definition of happiness, and live according to his own code of honor, is as strong today as it was a century ago. The Western still stands as the principal American mythology.

I would take it one step further. The Western will survive, no matter the era, as long as it embodies how all the various forms of courage can lead to all of the virtues because nothing could be more essential to how people should live their lives and who they are. By demonstrating courage to realize the other virtues, those virtues are made deeper and more meaningful, whether it's Gil Westrum's loyalty to his friend Steve Judd, Amy Kane's love for her husband, or dozens of other examples from Westerns of how courage can ennoble the human spirit.

According to Major Thorn in *They Came to Cordura*, his fellow travelers all needed courage to overcome the "crippled child" in them in order to be brave and noble. It is probably an overstatement to say that all of us have a "crippled child" within us, but as long as human beings are vulnerable, they will need courage to overcome their vulnerabilities to express the virtues that represent the best of their capabilities. The appeal of Westerns, at least the best of them, is their ability to boil down to moments of truth the choices of whether or not to summon up the courage to express what is best in us, whether it's Will Kane's decision in the barn whether or not to ride away from the Miller gang, Amy Kane in the marshal's office deciding whether or not to take up a gun in her husband's defense, Gil Westrum deciding whether or not to come to the aid of Steve Judd, or Wes Tancred deciding whether or not to help his friend by revealing his infamous true identity in a crowded courtroom. The choices we make in the modern world may not be as dramatic, life-threatening or clear-cut as these, but they are choices at one time or another we all have to make, choices that will form our character, for good or ill. That is why the relevance and meaning of Westerns will never die.

Filmography

Films

Arizona (1940). Director: Wesley Ruggles; Story: Clarence Budington Kelland; Screenplay: Claude Binyon; Producer: Wesley Ruggles; Music: Victor Young. *Cast*—Jean Arthur (Phoebe Titus); William Holden (Peter Muncie); Warren William (Jefferson Carteret); Porter Hall (Lazarus Ward); Edgar Buchanan (Judge Bogardus); Paul Harvey (Solomon Warner); George Chandler (Haley); Byron Foulger (Pete Kitchen); Regis Toomey (Grant Oury).

The Badlanders (1958). Director: Delmer Daves; Novel: W.R. Burnett; Screenplay: Richard Collins; Producer: Aaron Rosenberg; Music: Joseph Cacciola, Louis De Francesco, Philp Green and Alexander Laszlo. *Cast*—Alan Ladd (Peter Van Hoek); Ernest Borgnine (John McBain); Katy Jurado (Anita); Claire Kelly (Ada Winton); Kent Smith (Cyril Lounsberry); Nehemiah Persoff (Vincente); Robert Emhardt (Sample); Anthony Caruso (Comanche); Adam Williams (Leslie); Ford Rainey (Warden).

The Ballad of Gregorio Cortez (1982). Director: Robert M. Young; Book: Americo Paredes; Screenplay: Victor Villasenor and Robert M. Young; Producers: Moctesuma Esparza and Michael Hausman; Music: W. Michael Lewis and Edward James Olmos. *Cast*—Gregorio Cortez (Edward James Olmos); James Gammon (Sheriff Frank Fly); Tom Bower (Boone Choate); Bruce McGill (Reporter Blakely); Brion James (Captain Rogers); Alan Vint (Mike Trimmell); Timothy Scott (Sheriff Morris); Pepe Serna (Romaldo Cortez); Michael McGuire (Sheriff Glover); Barry Corbin (B.R. Abernathy); Rosanna DeSoto (Carlota Munoz); Ned Beatty (Lynch Mob Leader); Jack Kehoe (Prosecutor Pierson).

Bend of the River (1952). Director: Anthony Mann; Novel: Bill Gulick; Screenplay: Borden Chase; Producers: Aaron Rosenberg and Frank Cleaver; Music: Hans J. Salter. *Cast*—James Stewart (Glyn McLyntock); Arthur Kennedy (Emerson Cole); Julie Adams (Laura Baile); Rock Hudson (Trey Wilson); Lori Nelson (Margie Baile); Jay C. Flippen (Jeremy Baile); Chubby Johnson (Captain Mello); Howard Petrie (Tom Hendricks); Stepin Fetchit (Adam); Henry Morgan (Shorty); Frances Bavier (Mrs. Prentiss); Royal Dano (Long Tom).

The Big Country (1958). Director: William Wyler; Novel: Donald Hamilton; Adaptation: Jessamyn West and Robert Wyler; Screenplay: James R. Webb, Sy Bartlett and Robert Wilder; Producers: Gregory Peck, Robert Wyler and William Wyler; Music; Jerome Moross. *Cast*—Gregory Peck (James McKay); Jean Simmons (Julie Maragon); Carroll Baker (Patricia Terrill); Charlton Heston (Steve Leech); Burl Ives (Rufus Hannessey); Charles Bickford (Major Henry Terrill); Alfonso Bedoya (Ramon Gutierrez); Chuck Connors (Buck Hannassey); Chuck Hayward (Rafe Hannassey): Buff Brady (Dude Hannassey); Jim Burk (Cracker Hannassey).

The Bravados (1958). Director: Henry King; Novel: Frank O'Rouke; Screenplay: Philip Yordan; Producer: Herbert B. Swope, Jr.; Music: Lionel Newman, Hugo Friedhofer and Alfred Newman. *Cast*—Gregory Peck (Jim Douglass); Joan Collins (Josefa Velarde); Stephen Boyd (Bill Zachary); Albert Salmi (Ed Taylor); Henry Silva (Lujan); Kathleen Gallant (Emma Steinmetz); Barry Coe (Tom); George Voskovec (Gus Steinmetz); Herbert Rudley (Sheriff Sanchez); Lee Van Cleef (Alfonso Parral); Andrew Duggan (Padre); Ken Scott (Deputy Sheriff—Primo); Gene Evans (John Butler); Joe DeRita (Mr. Simms).

Broken Arrow (1950). Director: Delmar Daves; Novel: Elliott Arnold; Screenplay: Albert Maltz; Producer: Julian Blaustein; Music: Hugo Friedhofer. *Cast*—James Stewart (Tom Jeffords); Jeff Chandler (Cochise); Debra Paget (Sonseeahray); Basil Ruysdael (General Oliver Howard); Will Geer (Ben Slade); Joyce MacKenzie (Terry); Arthur Hunnicutt (Milt Duffield); Jay Silverheels (Geronimo).

Broken Lance (1954). Director: Edward Dmytryk; Story: Philip Yordan; Screenplay: Richard Murphy; Producers: Sol C. Siegel and Darryl F. Zanuck (uncredited); Music: Leigh Harline. *Cast*—Spencer Tracy (Matt Devereaux); Robert Wagner (Joe Devereaux); Jean Peters (Barbara); Richard Widmark (Ben Devereaux); Katy Jurado (Senora Devereaux); Hugh O'Brian (Mike Devereaux); Eduard Franz (Two Moons); Earl Holliman (Denny Devereaux); E.G. Marshall (Horace, the Governor); Carl Benton Reid (Clem Lawton); Philip Ober (Van Cleve); Robert Burton (Mac Andrews).

Buchanan Rides Alone (1958). Director: Budd Boetticher; Novel: Jonas Ward; Screenplay: Charles Lang and Burt Kennedy (uncredited); Producers: Harry Joe Brown and Randolph Scott; Music: Mischa Bakaleinikoff. *Cast*—Randolph

Scott (Buchanan); Craig Stevens (Abe Carbo); Barry Kelley (Lew Agry); Tol Avery (Simon Agry); Peter Whitney (Amos Agry); Manuel Rojas (Juan de la Vega); L.Q. Jones (Pecos Hill); Robert Anderson (Waldo Peck); Joe De Santis (Esteban Gomez); William Leslie (Roy Agry); Jennifer Holden (K.T.).

Buck and the Preacher (1972). Directors: Sidney Poitier and Joseph Sargent; Story: Ernest Kinoy and Drake Walker; Screenplay: Ernest Kinoy; Producers: Joel Glickman, Herb Wallerstein, Harry Belafonte (uncredited) and Sidney Poitier (uncredited); Music: Benny Carter. *Cast*—Sidney Poitier (Buck); Harry Belafonte (The Preacher); Ruby Dee (Ruth); Cameron Mitchell (Deshay); Denny Miller (Floyd); Nita Talbot (Madam Esther); John Kelly (Sheriff); Tony Brubaker (Headman).

The Burning Hills (1956). Director: Stuart Heisler; Novel: Louis L'Amour; Screenplay: Irving Wallace; Producer: Richard Whorf; Music: David Buttolph. *Cast*—Tab Hunter (Trace Jordan); Natalie Wood (Maria-Christina Colton); Skip Homeier (Jack Sutton); Eduard Franz (Jacob Lantz); Earl Holliman (Mort Bayliss); Claude Akins (Ben Hindeman); Ray Teal (Joe Sutton); Frank Puglia (Tio Perico); Hal Baylor (Braun); Tyler MacDuff (Wes Parker).

Cattle Empire (1958). Director: Charles Marquis Warren; Story: Daniel B. Ullman; Screenplay: Eric Norden, Endre Bohem and Charles Marquis Warren; Producer: Robert Stabler; Music: Paul Sawtell and Bert Shefter. *Cast*—Joel McCrea (John Cord); Gloria Talbott (Sandy Jeffrey); Don Haggerty (Ralph Hamilton); Bing Russell (Douglas Hamilton); Richard Shannon (Garth); Paul Brinegar (Tom Jefferson Jeffrey); Charles H. Gray (Tom Powis); Hal K. Dawson (George Washington Jeffrey).

Cattle Queen of Montana (1954). Director: Allan Dwan; Story: Thomas Blackburn; Screenplay; Robert Blees and Howard Estabrook; Producer: Benedict Bogeaus; Music: Louis Forbes, Howard Jackson and William Lava. *Cast*—Barbara Stanwyck (Sierra Nevada Jones); Ronald Reagan (Farrell); Gene Evans (Tom McCord); Lance Fuller (Colorados); Anthony Caruso (Natchakoa); Jack Elam (Yost); Yvette Dugay (Starfire); Morris Andrum (J.I. "Pop" Jones); Myron Healey (Hank); Chubby Johnson (Nat Collins).

Cheyenne Autumn (1964). Director: John Ford; Novel: Howard Fast (uncredited); Screenplay: James R. Webb; Producers: Bernard Smith and John Ford (uncredited); Music: Alex North. *Cast*—Richard Widmark (Capt. Thomas Archer); Carroll Baker (Deborah Wright); Karl Malden (Capt. Wessels); Sal Mineo (Red Shirt); Dolores Del Rio (Spanish Woman); Ricardo Montalban (Little Wolf); Gilbert Roland (Dull Knife); Arthur Kennedy (Doc Holliday); James Stewart (Wyatt Earp); Edward G. Robinson (Secretary of the Interior Carl Schurz); Elizabeth Allen (Guinevere Plantagenet); John Carradine (Major Jeff Blair); Victor Jory (Tall Tree).

Cowboy (1958). Director: Delmer Daves; Book: Frank Harris; Screenplay: Edmund H. North and Dalton Trumbo; Producer: Julian Blaustein; Music: George Duning. *Cast*—Glenn Ford (Tom Reese); Jack Lemmon (Frank Harris); Anna Kashfi (Maria); Brian Donlevy (Doc Bender); Dick York (Charlie); Richard Jaeckel (Paul Curtis); Victor Manuel Mendoza (Paco Mendoza); King Donovan (Joe Capper); Donald Randolph (Senor Vidal); Eugene Iglesias (Don Manuel Arriega).

The Culpepper Cattle Company (1972). Director: Dick Richards; Story: Dick Richards; Screenplay: Eric Bercovici and Gregory Prentiss; Producers: Jerry Bruckheimer and Paul Helmrick; Music: Jerry Goldsmith and Tom Scott. *Cast*—Gary Grimes (Ben Mockridge); Billy Green Bush (Frank Culpepper); Luke Askew (Luke); Bo Hopkins (Dixie Brick); Geoffrey Lewis (Russ); Wayne Sutherlin (Missoula); John McLiam (Thorton Pierce); Matt Clark (Pete); Charles Martin Smith (Tim Slater); Larry Finley (Mr. Slater); Jan Burrell (Mrs. Mockridge).

Dances with Wolves (1990). Director: Kevin Costner; Novel and Screenplay: Michael Blake; Producers: Bonnie Arnold, Kevin Costner, Jake Eberts and Jim Wilson; Music: John Barry. *Cast*—Kevin Costner (Lt. Dunbar); Mary McDonnell (Stands With a Fist); Graham Greene (Kicking Bird); Rodney A. Grant (Wind in His Hair); Floyd "Red Crow" Westerman (Ten Bears); Tantoo Cardinal (Black Shawl); Robert Pastorelli (Simmons); Charles Rocket (Lt. Elgin); Maury Chaykin (Major Fambrough).

The Deadly Companions (1961). Director: Sam Peckinpah; Novel and Screenplay: A.S. Fleischman; Producer: Charles B. Fitzsimmons; Music: Martin Skiles. *Cast*—Brian Keith (Yellowleg); Maureen O'Hara (Kit Tildon); Steve Cochran (Billy Keplinger); Chill Wills (Turk); Strother Martin (Parson); Will Wright (Dr. Acton).

Decision at Sundown (1957). Director: Budd Boetticher; Story: Vernon L. Fluherty; Screenplay: Charles Lang, Jr. Producers: Harry Joe Brown and Randolph Scott; Music: Heinz Roemheld. *Cast*—Randolph Scott (Bart Allison); John Carroll (Tate Kimbrough); Karen Steele (Lucy Summerton); Valerie French (Ruby James); Noah Beery, Jr. (Sam); John Archer (Doc Sorrow); Andrew Duggan (Sheriff Swede Hanson); John Litel (Charles Summerton); Ray Teal (Morley Chase); James Westerfield (Otis); Richard Deacon (Zaron).

Devil's Doorway (1950). Director: Anthony Mann; Screenplay: Guy Trosper; Producer: Nicholas Nayfack; Music: Daniele Amfitheatrof. *Cast*—Robert Taylor (Lance Poole); Paula Raymond (Orrie Masters); Louis Calhern (Verne Coolan); Edgar Buchanan (Zeke Carmody); James Mitchell (Red Rock); Spring Byington (Mrs. Masters); Bruce Cowling (Lt. Grimes); Marshall Thompson (Rod MacDougall); Rhys Williams (Scottie MacDougall); James Millican (Ike Stapleton); Fritz Leiber (Mr. Poole); Chief John Big Tree (Thundercloud).

The Far Country (1954). Director: Anthony Mann; Story and Screenplay: Borden Chase; Producer: Aaron Rosenberg; Music: Henry Mancini (uncredited), Hans J. Salter (uncredited), Frank Skinner (uncredited) and Herman Stein (uncredited). *Cast*—James Stewart (Jeff Webster); Corinne Calvet (Renee Vallon); Walter Brennan (Ben Tatum); Ruth Roman (Ronda Castle); John McIntire (Mr. Gannon); J.C. Flippen (Rube); Harry Morgan (Ketchum); Steve Brodie (Ives); Royal Dano (Luke); Gregg Barton (Rounds); Connie Gilchrist (Hominy); Jack Elam (Frank Newberry).

The Fastest Gun Alive (1956). Director: Russell Rouse; Story: Frank D. Gilroy; Screenplay: Frank D. Gilroy and Russell Rouse; Producer: Clarence Greene; Music: Andre Previn. *Cast*—Glenn Ford (George Temple aka George Kelby, Jr.); Jeanne Crain (Dora Temple); Broderick Crawford (Vinnie Harold); Russ Tamblyn (Eric Doolittle); Allyn Joslyn (Harvey Maxwell); Leif Erickson (Lou Glover); John Dehner (Taylor Swope); Noah Beery, Jr. (Dink Wells); J.M. Kerrigan (Keith McGovern); Rhys Williams (Brian Tibbs); Virginia Gregg (Rose Tibbs); Chubby Johnson (Frank Stringer); John Doucette (Ben Buddy).

A Fistful of Dynamite (also known as *Duck, You Sucker*) (1971). Director: Sergio Leone; Story: Sergio Leone and Sergio Donati; Screenplay: Luciano Vincenzoni, Sergio Donati and Sergio Leone; Producers: Claudio Mancini, Fulvio Morsella and Ugo Tucci; Music: Ennio Morricone. *Cast*—Rod Steiger (Juan Miranda); James Coburn (John H. Mallory); Romolo Valli (Dr. Villega); Maria Monti (Adelita, coach passenger); Rik Battaglia (Santerna); Franco Graziosi (Governor Huerta); Antoine Saint-John (Gutierez/Col. Gunther Reza); Vivienne Chandler (Coleen, John's girlfriend); David Warbeck (Nolan, John's friend).

Forty Guns (1957). Director, Producer and Screenplay: Sam Fuller; Music: Harry Sukman. *Cast*—Barbara Stanwyck (Jessica Drummond); Barry Sullivan (Griff Bonell); Robert Dix (Chico Bonell); Dean Jagger (Sheriff Ned Logan); Eve Brent (Louvenia Spanger); Hank Worden (Marshall John Chisum); Jidge Carroll (Barney Cashman); Paul Dubov (Judge Macy); Ziva Rodann (Rio).

From Hell to Texas (1958). Director: Henry Hathaway; Book: Charles O. Locke; Screenplay: Robert Buckner and Wendell Mayes; Producer: Robert Buckner; Music: Daniele Amfitheatrof. *Cast*—Don Murray (Tod Lohman); Diane Varsi (Juanita Bradley); Chill Wills (Amos Bradley); Dennis Hopper (Tom Boyd); R.G. Armstrong (Hunter Boyd); Jay C. Flippen (Jake Leffertfinger); Margo (Mrs. Bradley); John Larch (Hal Carmody); Ken Scott (Otis Boyd); Rodolfo Acosta (Bayliss).

The Furies (1950). Director: Anthony Mann; Novel: Niven Busch; Screenplay: Charles Schnee; Producer: Hal B. Wallis; Music: Franz Waxman. *Cast*—Barbara Stanwyck (Vance Jeffords); Wendell Corey (Rip Darrow); Walter Huston

(T.C. Jeffords); Judith Anderson (Flo Burnett); Gilbert Roland (Juan Herrera); Thomas Gomez (El Tigre); Beulah Bondi (Mrs. Anaheim); Albert Dekker (Mr. Reynolds); John Bromfield (Clay Jeffords); Wallace Ford (Scotty Hyslip); Blanche Yurka (Herrera's mother); Louis Jean Heydt (Bailey).

Gun for a Coward (1957). Director: Abner Biberman; Screenplay: R. Wright Campbell; Producer: William Alland; Music: Irving Gertz (uncredited), Frank Skinner (uncredited) and Henry Russell (uncredited). Cast—Fred MacMurray (Will Keough); Jeffrey Hunter (Bless Keough); Janice Rule (Aud Niven); Chill Wills (Loving); Dean Stockwell (Hade Keough); Josephine Hutchinson (Mrs. Keough); Betty Lynn (Claire); Iron Eyes Cody (Chief); John Larch (Stringer); Paul Birch (Andy Niven); Bob Steele (Durkee).

Gunman's Walk (1958). Director: Phil Karlson; Story: Ric Hardman; Screenplay: Frank Nugent; Producer: Fred Kolmar; Music: George Duning. Cast—Van Heflin (Lee Hackett); Tab Hunter (Ed Hackett); Kathryn Grant (Clee Chouard); James Darren (Davy Hackett); Mickey Shaughnessy (Deputy Sheriff Will Motely); Robert F. Simon (Sheriff Harry Brill); Edward Platt (Purcell Avery); Ray Teal (Jensen Sieverts); Paul Birch (Bob Selkirk); Michael Granger (Curly); Will Wright (Judge); Bert Convy (Paul Chouard).

The Hanging Tree (1959). Director: Delmer Daves, Karl Malden (uncredited) and Vincent Sherman (uncredited); Novel: Dorothy M. Johnson; Screenplay: Wendell Mayes and Halsted Welles; Producers: Martin Jurow and Richard Shepherd; Music: Max Steiner. Cast—Gary Cooper (Dr. Joseph Frail); Maria Schell (Elizabeth Mahler); Karl Malden (Frenchy Plante); George C. Scott (George Grubb); Karl Swenson (Tom Flaunce); Virginia Gregg (Edna Plaunce); John Dierkes (Society Red); King Donovan (Wonder); Ben Piazza (Rune).

High Noon (1952). Director: Fred Zinnemann; Story: John W. Cunningham; Screenplay: Carl Foreman; Producers: Carl Foreman (uncredited) and Stanley Kramer (uncredited); Music: Dimitri Tiomkin. Cast—Gary Cooper (Marshal Will Kane); Thomas Mitchell (Mayor Jonas Henderson); Lloyd Bridges (Deputy Marshal Harvey Pell); Katy Jurado (Helen Ramirez); Grace Kelly (Amy Kane); Otto Kruger (Judge Percy Mettrick); Lon Chaney (Martin Howe); Harry Morgan (Sam Fuller); Eve McVeagh (Mildred Fuller); Ian McDonald (Frank Miller); Sheb Wooley (Ben Miller); Lee Van Cleef (Jack Colby); Robert Wilke (Jim Pierce); Larry J. Blake (Gillis, saloonkeeper); James Millican (Deputy Sheriff Herb Baker); Lucien Prival (Joe, Ramirez Hotel barman).

High Plains Drifter (1973). Director: Clint Eastwood; Screenplay: Ernest Tidyman and Dean Riesner (uncredited); Producers: Robert Daley and Jennings Lang; Music: Dee Barton. Cast—Clint Eastwood (The Stranger); Verna Bloom (Sarah Belding); Marianna Hill (Callie Travers); Mitchell Ryan (Dave

Drake); Jack Ging (Morgan Allen); Stefan Gierasch (Mayor Jason Hobart); Ted Hartley (Lewis Belding); Billy Curtis (Mordecai); Geoffrey Lewis (Stacey Bridges); Walter Barnes (Sheriff Sam Shaw); Paul Brinegar (Lutie Naylor); Richard Bull (Asa Goodwin).

The Last Hunt (1956). Director: Richard Brooks: Novel: Milton Lott; Screenplay: Richard Brooks; Producer: Dore Schary; Music: Daniele Amfitheatrof. Cast—Stewart Granger (Sandy McKenzie); Robert Taylor (Charlie Gilson); Lloyd Nolan (Woodfoot); Debra Paget (Indian girl); Russ Tamblyn (Jimmy O'Brien); Constance Ford (Peg); Joe De Santis (Ed Black).

Last Train from Gun Hill (1959). Director; John Sturges; Story: Les Crutchfield; Screenplay: James Poe; Producers: Paul Nathan, Hal B. Wallis and Kirk Douglas; Music: Dimitri Tiomkin. Cast—Kirk Douglas (Marshal Matt Morgan); Anthony Quinn (Craig Belden); Carolyn Jones (Linda); Earl Holliman (Rick Belden); Brad Dexter (Beero); Brian Hutton (Lee Smithers); Ziva Rodann (Catherine Morgan); Bing Russell (Skag); Val Avery (Steve the bartender); Walter Sande (Sheriff Bartlett).

Little Big Man (1970). Director: Arthur Penn; Novel: Thomas Berger; Screenplay: Calder Willingham; Producers: Gene Lasko and Stuart Millar; Music: John Paul Hammond. Cast—Dustin Hoffman (Jack Crabb); Faye Dunaway (Mrs. Pendrake); Chief Dan George (Old Lodge Skins); Martin Balsam (Mr. Merriweather); Richard Mulligan (General George Armstrong Custer); Jeff Corey (Wild Bill Hickok); Aimee Eccles (Sunshine); Kelly Jean Peters (Olga Crabb); Carole Androsky (Caroline Crabb); Robert Little Star (Little Horse); Cal Bellini (Younger Bear).

The Magnificent Seven (1960). Director: John Sturges; Screenplay: William Roberts, Walter Newman (uncredited), Walter Bernstein (uncredited), Shinobu Hashimoto (uncredited), Hideo Oguni (uncredited) and Akira Kurosawa (uncredited); Producers: John Sturges, Lou Morheim and Walter Mirisch; Music: Elmer Bernstein. Cast—Yul Brynner (Chris Adams); Eli Wallach (Calvera); Steve McQueen (Vin Tanner); Horst Buchholz (Chico); Charles Bronson (Bernardo O'Reilly); Robert Vaughn (Lee); Brad Dexter (Harry Luck); James Coburn (Britt); Vladimir Solokov (Old man in Ixcatlan); Rosenda Monteros (Petra); Jorge Martinez De Hoyos (Hilario); John Alonso (Miguel); Pepe Hern (Tomas); Whit Bissell (Chamlee, the undertaker); Val Avery (Henry, traveling corset salesman); Bing Russell (Robert, Henry's friend).

A Man Called Horse (1970). Director: Elliot Silverstein; Story: Dorothy M. Johnson and Gregory Crosby; Screenplay: Jack DeWitt; Producers: Frank Brill and Sandy Howard; Music: Leonard Rosenman. Cast—Richard Harris (John Morgan); Judith Anderson (Buffalo Cow Head); Jean Gascon (Batise); Manu Tupou (Yellow Hand); Corinna Tsopei (Running Deer); James Gammon (Ed);

William Jordan (Bent); Eddie Little Sky (Black Eagle); Michael Baseleon (Longfoot); Iron Eyes Cody (Medicine Man).

Man of the West (1958). Director: Anthony Mann; Novel: William C. Brown; Screenplay: Reginald Rose; Producer: Walter Mirisch; Music: Leigh Harline. Cast—Gary Cooper (Link Jones); Julie London (Billie Ellis); Lee J. Cobb (Dock Tobin); Arthur O'Connell (Sam Beasley); Jack Lord (Coaley); John Dehner (Claude Tobin); Royal Dano (Trout); Robert Wilke (Ponch).

The Man Who Shot Liberty Valance (1962). Director: John Ford; Story: Dorothy M. Johnson; Screenplay: James Warner Bellah and Willis Goldbeck; Producers: Willis Goldbeck and John Ford (uncredited); Music: Cyril J. Mockridge. Cast—John Wayne (Tom Doniphon); James Stewart (Ransom Stoddard); Vera Miles (Hallie Stoddard); Lee Marvin (Liberty Valance); Edmond O'Brien (Dutton Peabody); Link Appleyard (Andy Devine); Ken Murray (Doc Willoughby); John Carradine (Maj. Cassius Starbuckle); Jeanette Nolan (Nora Ericson); John Qualen (Peter Ericson); Carleton Young (Maxwell Scott); Woody Strode (Pompey); Denver Pyle (Amos Carruthers); Strother Martin (Floyd); Lee Van Cleef (Reese).

Monte Walsh (1970). Director: William A. Fraker; Novel: Jack Schaefer; Screenplay: Lukas Heller and David Zelag Goodman; Producers: Hal Landers and Bobby Roberts; Music: John Barry. Cast—Lee Marvin (Monte Walsh); Jeanne Moreau (Martine Bernard); Jack Palance (Chet Rollins); Mitchell Ryan (Shorty Austin); Jim Davis (Cal Brennan); G.D. Spradlin (Hal Henderson); John Hudkins (Sonny Jacobs); Michael Conrad (Dally Johnson); Bo Hopkins (Jumpin' Joe Joslin); John McLiam (Fightin' Joe Hooker); Allyn Ann McLerie (Mary Eagle); Matt Clark (Rufus Brady); Billy Green Bush (Powder Kent); Charles Tyner (Doctor).

My Darling Clementine (1946). Director: John Ford; Book: Stuart N. Lake; Story: Sam Hellman; Screenplay: Samuel G. Engel and Winston Miller; Producer: Samuel G. Engel; Music: Cyril J. Mockridge. Cast—Henry Fonda (Wyatt Earp); Linda Darnell (Chihuahua); Victor Mature (John "Doc" Holliday); Cathy Downs (Clementine Carter); Walter Brennan (N.H. "Old Man" Clanton); Tim Holt (Virgil Earp); Ward Bond (Morgan Earp); Don Gardner (James Earp); Alan Mowbray (Granville Thorndyke); John Ireland (Billy Clanton); Grant Withers (Ike Clanton); Roy Roberts (Mayor of Tombstone); Jane Darwell (Kate Nelson); Russell Simpson (Deacon John Simpson).

The Naked Spur (1952). Director: Anthony Mann; Screenplay: Sam Rolfe and Harold Jack Bloom; Producer: William Wright; Music: Bronislau Kaper. Cast—James Stewart (Howard Kemp); Janet Leigh (Lina Patch); Robert Ryan (Ben Vandergroat); Ralph Meeker (Roy Anderson); Millard Mitchell (Jesse Tate).

Night Passage (1957). Director: James Nielson; Story: Norman A. Fox; Screenplay: Borden Chase; Producer; Aaron Rosenberg: Music: Dimitri Tiomkin. *Cast*—James Stewart (Grant McLaine); Audie Murphy (The Utica Kid); Dan Duryea (Whitey Harbin); Dianne Foster (Charlott Drew); Elaine Stewart (Verna Kimball); Brandon DeWilde (Joey Adams); Jay C. Flippen (Ben Kimball); Herbert Anderson (Will Renner); Robert Wilke (Concho); Hugh Beaumont (Jeff Kurth); Jack Elam (Shotgun).

The Outlaw Josey Wales (1976). Director: Clint Eastwood; Book: Forrest Carter; Screenplay: Philip Kaufman and Sonia Chernus; Producer: Robert Daley, James Fargo and John G. Wilson; Music: Jerry Fielding. *Cast*—Clint Eastwood (Josey Wales); Chief Dan George (Lone Watie); Sandra Locke (Laura Lee); Bill McKinney (Terrill); John Vernon (Fletcher); Paula Trueman (Grandma Sarah); Sam Bottoms (Jamie); Geraldine Kearns (Little Moonlight); Woodrow Parfrey (Carpetbagger); Joyce Jameson (Rose); Sheb Wooley (Travis Cobb); Royal Dano (Ten Spot); Matt Clark (Kelly); Will Sampson (Ten Bears).

The Ox-Bow Incident (1943). Director: William Wellman; Novel: Walter Van Tilburg Clark; Screenplay: Lamar Trotti; Producers: Lamar Trotti and William Goetz; Music: Cyril J. Mockridge. *Cast*—Henry Fonda (Gil Carter); Dana Andrews (Donald Martin); Mary Beth Hughes (Rose Mapen); Anthony Quinn (Juan Martinez); William Eythe (Gerald Tetley); Harry Morgan (Art Croft); Jane Darwell (Ma Grier); Matt Briggs (Judge Daniel Tyler); Harry Davenport (Arthur Davies); Frank Conroy (Major Tetley); Marc Lawrence (Jeff Farnley); Dick Rich (Deputy Butch Mapes); Francis Ford (Alva "Dad" Hardwicke); Leigh Whipper (Sparks).

Pale Rider (1985). Director: Clint Eastwood; Screenplay: Michael Butler and Dennis Shryack; Producers: Clint Eastwood, Fritz Manes and David Valdes; Music: Lennie Niehaus. *Cast*—Clint Eastwood (Preacher); Carrie Snodgrass (Sarah Wheeler); Michael Moriarty (Hull Barret); Chris Penn (Josh LaHood); Richard Dysart (Coy LaHood); Sydney Penny (Morgan Wheeler); Richard Kiel (Club); Doug McRath (Spider Conway); John Russell (Stockburn).

The Plainsman (1936). Director: Cecil B. DeMille; Writers: Waldemar Young, Harold Lamb and Lynn Riggs; Producers: Cecil B. DeMille, William LeBaron (uncredited) and William H. Pine (uncredited); Music: George Antheil. *Cast*— Gary Cooper (Wild Bill Hickok); Jean Arthur (Calamity Jane); James Ellison (Buffalo Bill Cody); Charles Bickford (James Lattimer); Helen Burgess (Louisa Cody); Porter Hall (Jack McCall); Paul Harvey (Yellow Hand); Victor Varconi (Painted Horse).

Posse from Hell (1961). Director: Herbert Coleman; Novel and Screenplay: Clair Huffaker; Producer: Gordon Kay; Music: Joseph Gershenson. *Cast*— Audie Murphy (Banner Cole); John Saxon (Seymour Kern); Zohra Lampert (Helen Caldwell); Vic Morrow (Crip); Robert Keith (Capt. Jeremiah Brown);

Rodolfo Acosta (Johnny Caddo); Royal Dano (Uncle Billy); Frank Overton (Burt Hogan); James Bell (Benson); Paul Carr (Jock Wiley); Ward Ramsey (Sheriff Isaac Webb); Lee Van Cleef (Leo); Ray Teal (Banker); Forrest Lewis (Dr. Welles); Charles Horvath (Hash).

Red River (1948). Director: Howard Hawks; Story: Borden Chase; Screenplay: Borden Chase and Charles Schnee; Producer: Howard Hawks; Music: Dimitri Tiomkin. *Cast*—John Wayne (Tom Dunson); Montgomery Clift (Matthew Garth); Joanne Dru (Tess Millay); Walter Brennan (Nadine Groot); Coleen Gray (Fen); John Ireland (Cherry Valance); Noah Beery, Jr. (Buster McGee); Harry Carey, Sr. (Mr. Millville); Harry Carey, Jr. (Dan Latimer); Paul Fix (Teeler Yacey).

Reprisal! (1956). Director: George Sherman; Novel: Arthur Gordon; Story: David P. Harmon; Screenplay: David P. Harmon, Raphael Hayes and David Dortort: Producers: Helen Ainsworth, Lewis J. Rachmil and Guy Madison: Music: Mischa Bakaleinikoff. *Cast*—Guy Madison (Frank Madden); Felicia Farr (Catherine Cantrell); Kathryn Grant (Taini); Michael Pate (Bert Shipley); Edward Platt (Neil Shipley); Otto Hulett (Sheriff Jim Dixon); Wayne Mallory (Tom Shipley); Robert Burton (Jeb Cantrell); Ralphy Moody (Matara); Frank DeKova (Charley Washackle).

Ride Lonesome (1959). Director: Budd Boetticher; Screenplay: Burt Kennedy; Producers: Harry Joe Brown, Randolph Scott and Budd Boetticher; Music: Heinz Roemheld. *Cast*—Randolph Scott (Ben Brigade); Karen Steele (Carrie Lane); Pernell Roberts (Sam Boone); James Best (Billy John); James Coburn (Whit); Lee Van Cleef (Frank).

Ride the High Country (1962). Director: Sam Peckinpah; Writers: N.B. Stone, Sam Peckinpah (uncredited) and William Roberts (uncredited); Producer: Richard E. Lyons; Music: George Bassman. *Cast*—Randolph Scott (Gil Westrum); Joel McCrea (Steve Judd); Mariette Hartley (Elsa Knudsen); Ron Starr (Heck Longtree); Edgar Buchanan (Judge Tolliver); R.G. Armstrong (Joshua Knudsen); Jenie Jackson (Kate, the madam); James Drury (Billy Hammond); L.Q. Jones (Sylvus Hammond); John Anderson (Elder Hammond); John Davis Chandler (Jimmy Hammond); Warren Oates (Henry Hammond).

Rio Bravo (1959). Director and Producer: Howard Hawks; Story: B.H. Campbell; Screenplay: Jules Furthman and Leigh Brackett; Music: Dimitri Tiomkin. *Cast*—John Wayne (John T. Chance); Dean Martin (Dude); Ricky Nelson (Colorado Ryan); Angie Dickinson (Feathers); Walter Brennan (Deputy Stumpy); Ward Bond (Pat Wheeler); John Russell (Nathan Burdette); Pedro Gonzalez-Gonzales (Carlos Robante); Estelita Rodriquez (Consuela Robante); Claude Akins (Joe Burdette); Walter Barnes (Charlie, the bartender); Bob Steele (Matt Harris); Bing Russell (Man murdered in cantina).

Run of the Arrow (1957). Director, Producer and Screenplay: Sam Fuller; Music: Victor Young. *Cast*—Rod Steiger (O'Meara); Sara Montiel (Yellow Moccasin); Brian Keith (Captain Clark); Ralph Meeker (Lt. Driscoll); Jay C. Flippen (Walking Coyote); Charles Bronson (Blue Buffalo); Olive Carey (Mrs. O'Meara); H.M. Wynant (Crazy Wolf); Neyle Morrow (Lt. Stockwell); Frank DeKova (Red Cloud); Tim McCoy (Gen. Allen); Stuart Randall (Col. Taylor).

Sargeant Rutledge (1960). Director: John Ford; Novel: James Warner Bellah; Screenplay: James Warner Bellah and Willis Goldbeck; Producers: Patrick Ford and Willis Goldbeck; Music: Howard Jackson. *Cast*—Jeffrey Hunter (Lt. Tom Cantrell); Woody Strode (Sgt. Braxton Rutledge); Constance Towers (Mary Beecher); Billie Burke (Mrs. Cordelia Fosgate); Juano Hernandez (Sgt. Matthew Luke Skidmore); Willis Bouchey (Col. Otis Fosgate); Carleton Young (Capt. Shattuck); Judson Pratt (Lt. Mulqueen).

The Searchers (1956). Director: John Ford; Novel: Alan LeMay; Screenplay: Frank S. Nugent; Producers: Merian C. Cooper and Patrick Ford; Music: Max Steiner. *Cast*—John Wayne (Ethan Edwards); Jeffrey Hunter (Martin Pawley); Vera Miles (Laurie Jorgensen); Ward Bond (the Reverend Captain Samuel Johnson Clayton); Natalie Wood (Debbie Edwards); John Qualen (Lars Jorgensen); Olive Carey (Mrs. Jorgensen); Henry Brandon (War Chief Scar); Ken Curtis (Charlie McCorry); Harry Carey, Jr. (Brad Jorgensen); Hank Worden (Mose Harper); Antonio Moreno (Emilio Gabriel Fernandez y Figueroa); Walter Coy (Aaron Edwards); Dorothy Jordan (Martha Edwards).

7 Men from Now (1956). Director: Budd Boetticher; Story and Screenplay: Burt Kennedy; Producers: Andrew V. McLaglen, Robert E. Morrison and John Wayne (uncredited); Music: Henry Vars. *Cast*—Randolph Scott (Ben Stride); Gail Russell (Annie Greer); Walter Reed (John Greer); Lee Marvin (Bill Masters); Don "Red" Barry (Clete); John Larch (Payte Bodeen); Stuart Whitman (Lt. Collins); John Beradino (Clint); Chuck Roberson (Mason); Steve Mitchell (Fowler).

Shane (1953). Director: George Stevens; Novel: Jack Schaefer; Screenplay: A.B. Guthrie, Jr., and Jack Sher; Producers: George Stevens and Ivan Moffat. Music: Victor Young. *Cast*—Alan Ladd (Shane); Van Heflin (Joe Starrett); Jean Arthur (Marian Starrett); Brandon DeWilde (Joey Starrett); Jack Palance (Jack Wilson); Ben Johnson (Chris Calloway); Emile Meyer (Rufus Stryker); John Dierkes (Morgan Ryker); Elisha Cook, Jr. (Frank "Stonewall" Torrey); Ellen Corby (Mrs. Torrey); Edgar Buchanan (Fred Lewis).

The Shootist (1976). Director: Don Siegel; Novel: Glendon Swarthout; Screenplay: Miles Hood Swarthout and Scott Hale; Producers: M.J. Frankovich and William Self; Music: Elmer Bernstein. *Cast*—John Wayne (J.B. Books); Lauren Bacall (Bond Rogers); Ron Howard (Gillom Rogers); James Stewart (Dr. Hostetler); Richard Boone (Sweeney); Hugh O'Brian (Pulford); Bill McKinney (Cobb); Harry Morgan (Sheriff Thibido); John Carradine (Beckum); Sheree North (Serepta); Rick Lenz (Dobkins); Scatman Crothers (Moses).

Stagecoach (1939). Director: John Ford; Story: Ernest Haycox; Screenplay: Dudley Nichols and Ben Hecht; Producers: Walter Wanger and John Ford (uncredited); Music: Boris Morros, Richard Hageman, W. Frank Harling, Louis Gruenberg, Leo Shuken, John Leipold and Gerard Carbonara (uncredited). *Cast*—Claire Trevor (Dallas Jeffries); John Wayne (Henry aka "The Ringo Kid"); John Carradine (Hatfield); Thomas Mitchell (Dr. Josiah Boone); Andy Devine (Buck Rickabaugh); Donald Meek (Samuel Peacock); Louise Platt (Lucy Mallory); Tim Holt (Lt. Blanchard); George Bancroft (Curley Wilcox); Barton Churchill (Henry Gatewood); Tom Tyler (Luke Plummer).

The Strawberry Roan (1948). Director: John English; Story: Julian Zimet; Screenplay: Dwight Cummins and Dorothy Yost; Producer: Armand Schaefer; Music: Mischa Bakaleinikoff. *Cast*—Gene Autry (Gene Autry); Champion (Champ, the Strawberry Roan); Gloria Henry (Connie Bailey); Jack Holt (Walt Bailey); Dickie Jones (Joe Bailey); Pat Buttram (Hank); Rufe Davis (Chuck); John McGuire (Bud Williams); Eddy Waller (Steve).

The Tall T (1957). Director: Budd Boetticher; Story: Elmore Leonard; Screenplay: Burt Kennedy; Producers: Harry Joe Brown and Randolph Scott; Music: Heinz Roemheld. *Cast*—Randolph Scott (Pat Brennan); Richard Boone (Frank Usher); Maureen O'Sullivan (Doretta Mims); Arthur Hunnicutt (Ed Rintoon); Skip Homeier (Billy Jack); Henry Silva (Chink); John Hubbard (Willard Mims); Robert Burton (Tenvoorde).

Tell Them Willie Boy Is Here (1969). Director: Abraham Polonsky; Book: Harry Lawton; Screenplay: Abraham Polonsky; Producers: Jennings Lang and Philip A. Waxman; Music: Dave Grusin. *Cast*—Robert Redford (Deputy Sheriff Christopher Cooper); Katharine Ross (Lola); Robert Blake (Willie Boy); Susan Clark (Dr. Elizabeth Arnold); Barry Sullivan (Ray Calvert); John Vernon (George Hacker); Charles Aidman (Judge Benby); Charles McGraw (Sheriff Frank Wilson).

Tension at Table Rock (1956). Director: Charles Marquis Warren; Novel: Frank Gruber; Screenplay: Winston Miller; Producer: Sam Wiesenthal; Music: Dimitri Tiomkin. *Cast*—Richard Egan (Wes Tancred); Dorothy Malone (Lorna Miller); Cameron Mitchell (Sheriff Fred Miller); Billy Chapin (Jody Burrows); Royal Dano (Harry Jameson); Edward Andrews (Kirk); John Dehner (Hampton); DeForest Kelley (Jim Breck); Joe De Santis (Ed Burrows); Angie Dickinson (Cathy); Paul Richards (Sam Murdock); John Pickard (Cord); James Anderson (Lerner).

They Came to Cordura (1959). Director: Robert Rossen; Screenplay: Glendon Swarthout; Story: Ivan Moffat and Robert Rossen; Producer: William Goetz; Music: Elie Siegmeister. *Cast*—Gary Cooper (Maj. Thomas Thorn); Rita Hayworth (Adelaide Geary); Van Heflin (Sgt. John Chawk); Tab Hunter (Lt. William Fowler); Richard Conte (Corp. Milo Trubee); Dick York (Pvt. Renziehausen); Michael Callan (Pvt. Andrew Hetherington); Robert Keith (Col. Rogers); Carlos Romero (Arreaga); Edward Platt (Col. DeRose).

3:10 to Yuma (1957). Director: Delmer Daves; Story: Elmore Leonard; Screenplay: Halsted Welles; Producer: David Heilweil; Music: George Duning. *Cast*—Glenn Ford (Ben Wade); Van Heflin (Dan Evans); Felicia Farr (Emmy); Leona Dana (Mrs. Alice Evans); Henry Jones (Alex Potter); Richard Jaeckel (Charlie Prince); Robert Emhardt (Mr. Butterfield); Ford Rainey (Bisbee Marshal).

3:10 to Yuma (2007). Director: James Mangold; Story: Elmore Leonard; Screenplay: Halsted Welles, Michael Brandt and Derek Haas; Producers: Stuart M. Besser, Dixie J. Capp, Aaron Downing, Ryan Kavanaugh, Cathy Conrad and Lynwood Spinks; Music: Marco Beltrami. *Cast*—Russell Crowe (Ben Wade); Christian Bale (Dan Evans); Ben Foster (Charlie Prince); Logan Lerman (William Evans); Dallas Roberts (Grayson Butterfield); Peter Fonda (Byron McElroy); Vanessa Shaw (Emma Nelson); Alan Tudyk (Doc Potter); Luce Rains (Marshal Weathers); Gretchen Mol (Alice Evans); Lennie Loftin (Glen Hollander); Rio Alexander (Campos); Johnny Whitworth (Darden).

The Tin Star (1957). Director: Anthony Mann; Story: Joel Kane, Dudley Nichols and Barney Slater; Producers: William Perlberg and George Seaton; Music: Elmer Bernstein. *Cast*—Henry Fonda (Morgan Hickman); Anthony Perkins (Sheriff Ben Owens); Betsy Palmer (Nona Mayfield); Michael Ray (Kip Mayfield); Neville Brand (Bart Bogardus); John McIntire (Dr. Joe McCord); Mary Webster (Millie Parker); Lee Van Cleef (Ed McGaffey); James Bell (Judge Thatcher); Howard Petrie (Mayor Harvey King).

Tribute to a Bad Man (1956). Director: Robert Wise; Story: Michael Blankfort and Jack Schaefer; Producer: Sam Zimbalist; Music: Miklos Rozsa. *Cast*—James Cagney (Jeremy Rodock); Don Dubbins (Steve Miller); Stephen McNally (McNulty); Irene Papas (Jocasta Constantine); Vic Morrow (Lars Peterson); James Griffith (Barjak); Onslow Stevens (Hearn); James Bell (L.A. Peterson); Jeanette Nolan (Mrs. Peterson); Chubby Johnson (Baldy); Royal Dano (Abe); Lee Van Cleef (Fat Jones).

The Unforgiven (1960). Director: John Huston; Novel: Alan LeMay; Screenplay: Ben Maddow; Producers: Harold Hecht, James Hill, and Burt Lancaster; Music: Dimitri Tiomkin. *Cast*—Burt Lancaster (Ben Zachary); Audrey Hepburn (Rachel Zachary); Audie Murphy (Cash Zachary); John Saxon (Johnny Portugal); Charles Bickford (Zeb Rawlins); Lillian Gish (Mattilda Zachary); Albert Salmi (Charlie Rawlins); Joseph Wiseman (Abe Kelsey); June Walker (Hagar Rawlins); Kipp Hamilton (Georgia Rawlins); Arnold Merritt (Jude Rawlins); Doug McClure (Andy Zachary); Carlos Rivas (Lost Bird).

Unforgiven (1992). Director: Clint Eastwood; Screenplay: David Webb Peoples; Producers: Clint Eastwood, David Valdes and Julian Ludwig; Music: Lennie Niehaus. *Cast*—Clint Eastwood (William Munny); Gene Hackman (Sheriff "Little Bill" Daggett); Morgan Freeman (Ned Logan); Richard Harris (English Bob); Jaimz Woolvett (The Schofield Kid); Saul Rubinek (W.W. Beauchamp); Frances Fisher (Strawberry Alice); Anna Thomson (Delilah Fitzgerald).

Valdez Is Coming (1970). Director: Edwin Sherin; Novel: Elmore Leonard; Screenplay: Roland Kibbee and David Rayfiel; Producers: Roland Kibbee, Sam Manners, Ira Steiner and Burt Lancaster (uncredited); Music: Charles Gross. *Cast*—Burt Lancaster (Valdez); Susan Clark (Gay Erin); Frank Silvera (Diego); Jon Cypher (Frank Tanner); Richard Jordan (R.L. Davis); Barton Heyman (El Segundo); Hector Elizondo (Mexican rider); Phil Brown (Malson).

White Feather (1955). Director: Robert Webb; Story: John Prebble; Screenplay: Delmer Daves and Leo Townsend; Producer: Robert L. Jacks; Music: Hugo Friedhofer. *Cast*—Robert Wagner (Josh Tanner); John Lund (Col. Lindsay); Debra Paget (Appearing Day); Jeffrey Hunter (Little Dog); Eduard Franz (Chief Broken Hand); Noah Beery, Jr. (Lt. Ferguson); Virginia Leith (Ann Magruder); Emile Meyer (Magruder); Hugh O'Brian (American Horse); Milburn Stone (Commissioner Trenton); Iron Eyes Cody; (Indian Chief).

The Wild Bunch (1969). Director: Sam Peckinpah; Story: Walon Green and Roy N. Sickner; Screenplay: Walon Green and Sam Peckinpah; Producers: Phil Feldman and Roy N. Sickner; Music: Jerry Fielding. *Cast*—William Holden (Pike Bishop); Ernest Borgnine (Dutch Engstrom); Robert Ryan (Deke Thornton); Edmond O'Brien (Freddie Sykes); Ben Johnson (Lyle Gorch); Warren Oates (Tector Gorch); Jaime Sanchez (Angel); Emilio Fernandez (General Mapache); Albert Dekker (Pat Harrigan); Strother Martin (Coffer); L.Q. Jones (T.C. Nash); Bo Hopkins (Clarence "Crazy" Lee Stringfellow); Dub Taylor (the Reverend Wainscoat); Sonia Amelio (Teresa, Angel's girl).

Television Series and Miniseries

The Big Valley, "The Murdered Party" (1965). Director: Virgil W. Vogel; Story: Jack Curtis; Producers: Arthur Gardner, Arnold Laven, and Jules V. Levy;

Music: George Duning. *Cast*—Barbara Stanwyck (Victoria Barkley); Richard Long (Jarrod Barkley); Peter Breck (Nick Barkley); Lee Majors (Heath); Linda Evans (Audra Barkley); Warren Oates (Korby Kyles); Larry D. Mann (Jacob Kyles); Fred Holliday (Emmet Kyles); Paul Potash (Alan Kyles); Walter Woolf King (Judge); Mort Mills (Sheriff Fred Madden); Napolean Whiting (Silas); Jim Boles (Barber); Bill Quinn (George Allison); Charles Wagenheim (Baggage man); Paul Fix (District Attorney Greene).

Bonanza, "The Crucible" (1962). Director: Paul Nickell; Story: John T. Dugan; Producers: David Dortort and James W. Lane; Music: David Rose. *Cast*—Lorne Greene (Ben Cartwright); Pernell Roberts (Adam Cartwright); Dan Blocker (Hoss Cartwright); Michael Landon (Joe Cartwright); Lee Marvin (Peter Kane); Howard Ledig (Frank Preston); Barry Cahill (Jim Gann).

Bonanza, "The Jury" (1962). Director: Christian Nyby; Story: Robert Vincent Wright; Producers: David Dortort and James W. Lane; Music: David Rose. *Cast*—Lorne Greene (Ben Cartwright); Pernell Roberts (Adam Cartwright); Dan Blocker (Hoss Cartwright); Michael Landon (Joe Cartwright); Jack Betts (Jamie Wrenn); Don Haggerty (Bud Murdoch); James Bell (Hjalmer Olson); Ray Teal (Sheriff Roy Coffee); Bobs Watson (Junior).

Bonanza, "The Last Trophy" (1960). Director: Lewis Allen; Story: Bill S. Ballinger; Producer: David Dortort; Music: David Rose. *Cast*—Lorne Greene (Ben Cartwright); Pernell Roberts (Adam Cartwright); Dan Blocker (Hoss Cartwright); Michael Landon (Joe Cartwright); Hazel Court (Lady Beatrice Dunsford); Edward Ashley (Lord Marion Dunsford); Bert Freed (Solomon Belcher); Naomi Stevens (Touma); Ken Mayer (Whitey).

Bonanza, "The Legacy" (1963). Director: Bernard McEveety; Story: Anthony Wilson; Producers: David Dortort and James W. Lane; Music: David Rose. *Cast*—Lorne Greene (Ben Cartwright); Pernell Roberts (Adam Cartwright); Dan Blocker (Hoss Cartwright); Michael Landon (Joe Cartwright); Robert H. Harris (Jacob Dormann); Philip Pine (Gannon); James Best (Page); Sandy McPeak (Billy Chapin); Jeanne Baird (Jeanie); Ray Teal (Sheriff Roy Coffee); Dayton Lummis (Col. Abel Chapin).

Bonanza, "Warbonnet" (1971). Director: Arthur H. Nadel; Story: Robert Biheller and Charles Goldwad; Producers: Richard Collins, David Dortort and John Hawkins; Music: David Rose. *Cast*—Lorne Greene (Ben Cartwright); Dan Blocker (Hoss Cartwright); Michael Landon (Joe Cartwright); Forrest Tucker (Frank Ryan); Chief Dan George (Red Cloud); Linda Cristal (Teresa); Patrick Adiarte (Swift Eagle); Russ Marin (Sheriff); M. Emmet Walsh (Mattheson); John Wheeler (Hill); Lee de Broux (Elias).

Bronco, "The Long Ride Back" (1958). Director: Leslie H. Martinson; Story: James O'Hanlon; Producers: William T. Orr and Arthur W. Silver; Music: John

Neel. *Cast*—Ty Hardin (Bronco Layne); Gerald Mohr (Enrique "Ricky" Cortez); Kathleen Crowley (Redemption McNally); Mort Mills (Jacob Stint); Paul Fix (Tom McNally); Charles Fredericks (Crane).

Bronco, "The Soft Answer" (1959). Director: Leslie Goodwins; Story: Arnold Belgard; Producers: William T. Orr and Arthur W. Silver; Music: Mack David and Jerry Livingston. *Cast*—Ty Hardin (Bronco Layne); Nancy Gates (Kay Ransom); Leo Gordon (Barnaby Spence); Ray Stricklyn (Billy the Kid); Mike Road (Mike Ransom); Joseph Ruskin (Jackson); Robert Colbert (Arron Running Deer); Gregg Barton (Baldy); Spencer Chan (Ah Wing).

Broken Trail (2006). Director: Walter Hill; Story: Alan Geoffrion; Producers: Michael Frislev, Damian Ganczewski, Alan Geoffrion, Walter Hill, Chad Oakes and Ronald Parker; Music: David Mansfield and Van Dyke Parks. *Cast*—Robert Duvall (Prentice Ritter); Thomas Haden Church (Tom Harte); Greta Scacchi (Nola Johns); Chris Mulkey (Big Ears); Rusty Schwimmer (Big Rump Kate); Gwendoline Yo (Sun Foy); Scott Cooper (Gilpin); Valerie Tian (Ging Wa); Olivia Cheng (Ye Fung); Jadyn Wong (Ghee Moon); Donald Fong (Lung Hay); Caroline Chan (Mai Ling); James Russo (Captain Billy Fender).

Cheyenne, "Deadline" (1957). Director: Joseph Kane; Novel: Harlan Ware; Story: John Byrne and Sloan Nibley; Producers: William T. Orr and Arthur W. Silver; Music: William Lava. *Cast*—Clint Walker (Cheyenne Bodie); John Qualen (Charley Dolan); Ann Robinson (Paula Copeland); Mark Roberts (Boyd Copeland); Bruce Cowling (Len Garth); Charlita (Maria); John Truax (Fred Murkle).

Cheyenne, "Decision" (1956). Director: Richard L. Bare; Story: Roy Huggins and Dean Riesner; Producers: Roy Huggins and William T. Orr; Music: William Lava. *Cast*—Clint Walker (Cheyenne Bodie); Richard Denning (Capt. Quinlan); James Garner (Lt. Lee Rogers); Ray Teal (Maj. Heffler); Nancy Hale (Ann Saunders); Clegg Hoyt (Sgt. Beaugard); Terry Frost (Sgt. Short).

Cheyenne, "Home Is the Brave" (1960). Director: Emory Horger; Story: George Waggner and Richard Matheson; Producers: William T. Orr and Arthur W. Silver; Music: Stan Jones and William Lava. *Cast*—Clint Walker (Cheyenne Bodie); Paula Raymond (Ruth Thompson); John Howard (John Thompson); John Archer (Prescott); Donna Martell (Maria Prescott); Brad Johnson (Sheriff Dan Blaisdell); Regis Toomey (Dr. Henry Malcomb); Mickey Simpson (Pete Windsor).

Cheyenne, "Incident at Indian Springs" (1957). Director: Thomas Carr; Story: George F. Slavin; Producers: William T. Orr and Arthur W. Silver; Music: Stan Jones and William Lava. *Cast*—Clint Walker (Cheyenne Bodie); Bonnie Bolding (Lynne Ellis); Dan Barton (Jim Ellis); Carlyle Mitchell (Hub Powell); Christopher Olsen (Kenny Powell); John Cliff (Ed Curran); Robert Anderson (Pete Murdock); Michael Dante (Roy Curran).

Desilu Playhouse, "Silent Thunder" (1958). Director: Ted Post; Story: John McGreevey and James Edwards; Producers: Warren Lewis and Don Sharpe; Music: Johnny Green. *Cast*—John Drew Barrymore (Little Horse); Earl Holliman (Les Tranier); Barton MacLane (Matt Tranier); Wallace Ford (Ringo); Patricia Smith (Leola); Myron Healey (Rusty); Don Beddoe (Clint); Mike Ragan (Clyde).

Gunsmoke, "Gentry's Law" (1970). Director: Vincent McEveety; Story: Jack Miller; Producers: Joseph Dackow and John Mantley; Music: John Carl Parker. *Cast*—James Arness (Matt Dillon); Milburn Stone (Doc); Amanda Blake (Kitty); Ken Curtis (Festus); Buck Taylor (Newly); John Payne (Amos Gentry); Louise Latham (Claire Gentry); Peter Jason (Colt Gentry); Robert Pine (Ben Gentry); Shug Fisher (Orly Grimes); Don Keefer (Floyd Babcock); Darlene Conley (Leelah Case).

Gunsmoke, "The Golden Land" (1973). Director: Gunnar Hellstrom; Story: Hal Sitowitz; Producers: Leonard Katzman and John Mantley; Music: Rex Koury (uncredited). *Cast*—James Arness (Matt Dillon); Milburn Stone (Doc); Ken Curtis (Festus); Amanda Blake (Kitty); Buck Taylor (Newly); Paul Stevens (Moshe Gorofsky); Victor French (Rouse Ruxton); Richard Dreyfuss (Gearshon Gorofsky); Kevin Coughlin (Calvin Ruxton); Joseph Hindy (Laibel Gorofsky); Bettye Ackerman (Zisha Gorofsky); Wayne McLaren (Homer Ruxton); Scott Selles (Semel Gorofsky); Robert Nichols (Willie).

Gunsmoke, "Gone Straight" (1957). Director: Ted Post; Story: John Meston and Les Crutchfield; Producer: Norman MacDonnell; Music: Rex Koury (uncredited). *Cast*—James Arness (Matt Dillon); Dennis Weaver (Chester); Carl Betz (Nate Timble); Marianne Stewart (Mrs. Timble); Joe De Santis (Gunter); Tige Andrews (Mike Postil); Ward Wood (Parker); John Dierkes (Ace).

Gunsmoke, "The Good People" (1966). Director: Robert Totten; Story: James Landis; Producers: Philip Leacock and John Mantley; Music: Rex Koury (uncredited). *Cast*—James Arness (Matt Dillon); Milburn Stone (Doc); Ken Curtis (Festus); Amanda Blake (Kitty); Roger Ewing (Thad); Steve Gravers (Jed Bailey); Glenn Strange (Sam Noonan); Allen Case (Gabe Rucker); Tom Simcox (Seth Rucker); Shug Fisher (Silas Shute); Morgan Woodward (Ben Rucker).

Gunsmoke, "Gunfighter, R.I.P." (1966). Director: Mark Rydell; Story: Hal Sitowitz and Michael Fisher; Producers: Philip Leacock and John Mantley; Music: Ernest Gold. *Cast*—James Arness (Matt Dillon); Milburn Stone (Doc); Amanda Blake (Kitty); Ken Curtis (Festus); Roger Ewing (Thad); Darren McGavin (Joe Bascome); France Nuyen (Ching Lee); H.T. Tsiang (Ching Fa); Glenn Strange (Sam Noonan); Stefan Gierasch (Mark Douglas); Michael Conrad (Paul Douglas); Allen Emerson (Burt).

Gunsmoke, "Hackett" (1970). Director: Vincent McEveety; Story: William Kelley; Producers: Joseph Dackow and John Mantley; Music: Leon Klatzkin. *Cast*—James Arness (Matt Dillon); Milburn Stone (Doc); Amanda Blake (Kitty); Ken Curtis (Festus); Buck Taylor (Newly); Earl Holliman (Will Hackett); Morgan Woodward (Quentin Sargent); Jennifer West (Geneva Sargent); Robert Totten (Tully); Ken Swofford (Bronk); Glenn Strange (Sam Noonan).

Gunsmoke, "I Have Promises to Keep" (1975). Director: Vincent McEveety; Producers: John Mantley and John G. Stephens; Music: Rex Koury (uncredited). *Cast*—James Arness (Matt Dillon); Milburn Stone (Doc); Ken Curtis (Festus); Buck Taylor (Newly); David Wayne (the Reverend Byrne); Tom Lacy (the Reverend Atkins); Ken Swofford (Dunbar); Fran Ryan (Hannah); Ted Jordan (Burke); Ken Renard (Tonkowa).

Gunsmoke, "Lobo" (1968). Director: Bernard McEveety; Story: Jim Byrnes; Producers: Joseph Dackow and John Mantley; Music: Leon Klatzkin. *Cast*—James Arness (Matt Dillon); Milburn Stone (Doc); Ken Curtis (Festus); Amanda Blake (Kitty); Morgan Woodward (Luke Brazo); Sheldon Allman (Badger); Sandy Kenyon (Caitlin); Buck Taylor (Newly); Ken Swofford (Guffy); Eddie Firestone (Guffy); David Brian (Branch Nelson); Glenn Strange (Sam Noonan); James Nusser (Louie Pheeters).

Gunsmoke, "Lynch Town" (1973). Director: Bernard McEveety; Story: Calvin Clements, Sr., Anne Snyder and Joann Carlino; Producers: Leonard Katzman and John Mantley; Music: Rex Koury (uncredited). *Cast*—James Arness (Matt Dillon); Milburn Stone (Doc); Ken Curtis (Festus); Amanda Blake (Kitty); Buck Taylor (Newly); David Wayne (Judge Warfield); Mitch Vogel (Rob Fielder); Warren J. Kemmerling (Sheriff Ridder); Ken Swofford (Jake Fielder); Norman Alden (Tom Hart); Julie Cobb (Minnie Nolen); Nancy Jeris (Kate Geer); Scott Brady (John King).

Gunsmoke, "Passive Resistance" (1959). Director: Ted Post; Story: John Meston; Producer: Norman MacDonnell; Music: Rex Koury (uncredited). *Cast*—James Arness (Matt Dillon); Dennis Weaver (Chester); Milburn Stone (Doc); Amanda Blake (Kitty); Carl Benton Reid (Gideon Seek); Alfred Ryder (Hank Voyles); Read Morgan (Kell); Dabbs Greer (Jonas).

Gunsmoke, "The Squaw" (1975). Director: Gunnar Hellstrom; Story: Jim Byrnes; Producers: John Mantley and John G. Stephens; Music: John Carl Parker. *Cast*—James Arness (Matt Dillon); Milburn Stone (Doc); Ken Curtis (Festus); Buck Taylor (Newly); John Saxon (Gristy Calhoun); Arlene Martel (Quanah); Tom Reese (Charlie Dent); Morgan Paull (Brinker); William Campbell (Striker); Harry Middlebrooks (Dobie); X Brands (Chief).

Have Gun—Will Travel, "Deliver the Body" (1958). Director: Lamont Johnson; Story: Buckley Angell; Producer: Sam Rolfe; Music: Bernard Herrmann.

Cast—Richard Boone (Paladin); R.G. Armstrong (Mayor S.J. Lovett); James Franciscus (Tom Nelson); Robert Gist (Ben Tyler); Len Lesser (Boldt); Madlyn Rhue (Jean Nelson).

Have Gun—Will Travel, "The Hanging of Roy Carter" (1958). Director: Andrew V. McLaglen; Story: Gene Roddenberry; Producer: Sam Rolfe; Music: Bernard Herrmann. *Cast*—Richard Boone (Paladin); John Larch (Chaplain Robert April); Robert Armstrong (Sidney Carter); Scott Marlowe (Roy Carter); Paul Birch (Warden Bullock); Francis McDonald (Jesse); Barry Russo (Keno Smith); Michael Hinn (Marshal).

Have Gun—Will Travel, "The Last Judgment" (1961). Director: Gerald Mayer; Story: Shimon Wincelberg; Producers: Frank Pierson and Howard Joslin; Music: Leonard Rosenman. *Cast*—Richard Boone (Paladin); Harold J. Stone (Judge Greenleaf); Donald Randolph (Dr. Simeon Loving); Leo Gordon (Moley); James Anderson (Homer); Robert Stevenson (Cutler); Tom Holland (Hinsdale).

Have Gun—Will Travel, "Memories of Monica" (1962). Director: Gary Nelson; Story: Don Ingalls; Producer: Don Ingalls. *Cast*—Richard Boone (Paladin); Judi Meredith (Monica Reagan); Bing Russell (Sheriff Reagan); Hal Needham (Dink Turner); Garry Walberg (Charlie); Larry Ward (Ben Turner); Edward Faulkner (Deputy Ed Buhl); Chuck Couch (Webb); Jerry Gatlin (Olin).

Have Gun—Will Travel, "The Taffeta Mayor" (1958). Director: Andrew V. McLaglen; Story: Albert Aley; Producer: Sam Rolfe; Music: Bernard Herrmann. *Cast*—Richard Boone (Paladin); Norma Crane (Lucy Kellaway); Edward Platt (Arnold Oaklin); Robert Karnes (Clay Morrow); Bobby Hall (Ben Trask); Jeanne Bates (Harriet Morrow); Tom Steele (Bailey).

Have Gun—Will Travel, "Winchester Quarantine" (1957). Director: Andrew V. McLaglen; Story: Herb Meadow; Producer: Julian Claman; Music: Bernard Herrmann. *Cast*—Richard Boone (Paladin); Anthony Caruso (Joseph Whitehorse); Carol Thurston (Martha Whitehorse); Leo Gordon (Clyde McNally); Don Keefer (Kelso); Robert Karnes (Joe Peavey); Vic Perrin (Rheinhart).

The High Chaparral, "The Journal of Death" (1970). Director: Leon Benson; Story: Frank Chase and Ramona Chase; Producers: David Dortort and James Schermer; Music: David Rose and Harry Sukman. *Cast*—Leif Erickson (John Cannon); Cameron Mitchell (Buck Cannon); Mark Slade (Blue Cannon); Henry Darrow (Manolito Montoya); Linda Cristal (Victoria Cannon); John Colicos (Matthew Kendall); Morgan Woodward (U.S. Marshal Ted Garnett); Bob Hoy (Joe Butler); Roberto Contreras (Pedro).

Laramie, "Badge of Glory" (1963). Director: Joseph Kane; Story: George F. Slavin; Producers: John C. Champion and Daniel B. Ullman; Music: Cyril J. Mockridge and Stanley Wilson. *Cast*—John Smith (Slim Sherman); Robert Fuller

(Jess Harper); Spring Byington (Daisy Cooper); Dennis Holmes (Mike Williams); Lin McCarthy (John Holby); Jean Allison (Amelia Holby); Russell Johnson (Bob Talmadge); George Wallace (Sheriff Mason); Sheldon Allman (Sam Mason); Laraine Stephens (Laurie Adams); Gregg Palmer (Chuck Logan); Tru Garrett (Harry); Henry Wills (Weston).

Laramie, ".45 Calibre" (1960). Director: Lesley Selander; Story: Lee Erwin and Donn Mullally; Producers: John C. Champion and Daniel B. Ullman; Music: David Buttolph. *Cast*—John Smith (Slim Sherman); Robert Fuller (Jess Harper); George Nader (Vern Clark); Anna-Lisa (Louisa Clark); Lee Van Cleef (Wes Torrey); Katherine Warren (Mrs. Byrd); John Pickard (Sloane); Charlie Briggs (Charley Wilkes).

Laramie, "Hour After Dawn" (1960). Director: Francis D. Lyon; Story: John Dunkel and Daniel B. Ullman; Music: Harry Sukman. *Cast*—John Smith (Slim Sherman); Robert Fuller (Jess Harper); Hoagy Carmichael (Jonesy); Gloria Talbott (Maud Pardee); Ben Johnson (Billy Pardee); Robert Osterloh (Sheriff Mort Corey); Irving Bacon (Tooey); Russell Thorson (Townsman); Bruce Bennett (Tom Creighton); Clarence Straight (Sam); George Eldredge (Doc Huber).

Laramie, "Justice in a Hurry" (1962). Director: Joseph Kane: Story: Herman Epstein; Producers: John C. Champion and Daniel B. Ullman; Music: Cyril J. Mockridge. *Cast*—John Smith (Slim Sherman); Robert Fuller (Jess Harper); Spring Byington (Daisy Cooper); Dennis Holmes (Mike Williams); Diana Millay (Julie Keleher); George Mitchell (The Judge); Robert J. Wilke (The Sheriff); George Wallace (Marv Jackson); Paul Birch (Sam Norris); Dabbs Greer (Elmo Regis); Kathleen Freeman (Edna Holtzhoff); Hugh Sanders (Ev Keleher); Nolan Leary (Minister).

Laramie, "Men of Defiance" (1960). Director: Lesley Selander; Story: John C. Champion; Producers: John C. Champion and Daniel B. Ullman; Music: Cyril J. Mockridge and Stanley Wilson. *Cast*—Robert Fuller (Jess Harper); Don Megowan (Clint Gentry); Edgar Buchanan (Doc); Bing Russell (Reb); Mort Mills (Marshal); John Anderson (Frank Bannister); Denny Miller (Toby); John Pickard (Stewart); Norman Leavitt (Smokey).

Laramie, "Night of the Quiet Men" (1959). Director: Lesley Selander; Story: John C. Champion, Lee Erwin and Donn Mullally; Producers: John C. Champion and Daniel B. Ullman; Music: David Buttolph. *Cast*—John Smith (Slim Sherman); Robert Fuller (Jess Harper); Lyle Bettger (John McCambridge); Carl Benton Reid (Cole Rogers); Read Morgan (Ames); Anthony Caruso (Kurt Lang); Robert Knapp (Brodie); Karl Swenson (Becker); Bartlett Robinson (Sheriff).

Laramie, "The Track of the Jackal" (1960). Director: Francis D. Lyon; Story: Paul Savage and Daniel B. Ullman; Producers: John C. Champion and Daniel

B. Ullman; Music: Cyril J. Mockridge and Stanley Wilson. *Cast*—John Smith (Slim Sherman); Robert Fuller (Jess Harper); Robert Wilke (Sumner Campbell); Stephen McNally (Luke Wiley); Jeanne Bates (Sarah Campbell); Dabbs Greer (Mr. Colby); Stacy Harris (Firth); Steven Terrell (Jimmy Foster); Steve Darrell (Jason McIntire).

Lawman, "The Gunman" (1959). Director: Stuart Heisler; Story: Clair Huffaker; Producers: William T. Orr and Jules Schermer; Music: Mack David and Jerry Livingston. *Cast*—John Russell (Marshal Dan Troop); Peter Brown (Deputy Johnny McKay); Richard Arlen (Kurt Monroe); Gordon Jones (Chalk Hennesey); Hal Baylor (Harlan Smith); Frank Sully (Jenks Edwards); Baynes Barron (Al Horn); Paul Brinegar (Stage line clerk); Howard Negley (Hank); Dorothy Partington (Lucy Benson).

Lawman, "The Showdown" (1960). Director: Robert Sparr; Story: William F. Leicester; Producers: William T. Orr and Jules Schermer; Music: Mack David and Jerry Livingston. *Cast*—John Russell (Marshal Dan Troop); Peter Brown (Deputy Johnny McKay); Peggy Castle (Lily Merrill); John Howard (Lance Creedy); James Coburn (Blake Carr); Roberta Haynes (Mattie Creedy); Jim Hayward (Hartwell).

The Lone Ranger, "Journey to San Carlos" (1957). Director: Earl Bellamy; Story: Charles Larson; Producer: Sherman A. Harris. *Cast*—Clayton Moore (The Lone Ranger); Jay Silverheels (Tonto); Myron Healey (Ben Murray); Joseph Sargent (Jed Walker); Melinda Byron (Sally Walker); Harry Strang (Col. Ray Wickstrom); Rick Vallin (Blue Feather).

Lonesome Dove (1989). Director: Simon Wincer; Story: Larry McMurtry and William Wittliff; Producers: Suzanne De Passe, Robert A. Halmi, Dyson Lovell, Michael Weisbarth and William Wittliff; Music: Basil Poledouris. *Cast*—Robert Duvall (Gus McCrae); Tommy Lee Jones (Woodrow Call); Danny Glover (Joshua Deets); Diane Lane (Lorena Wood); Robert Urich (Jake Spoon); Frederick Forrest (Blue Duck); D.B. Sweeney (Dish Boggett); Ricky Schroder (Newt Dobbs); Anjelica Huston (Clara Allen); Chris Cooper (July Johnson); Timothy Scott (Pea Eye Parker); Glenne Headley (Elmira Boot Johnson); Barry Corbin (Roscoe Brown); William Sanderson (Lippy Jones); Barry Tubb (Jasper Fant); George O'Herlihy (Dan Suggs); Steve Buscemi (Luke); Frederick Coffin (Big Zwey); Jorge Martinez de Hoyos (Po Campo); Leon Singer (Bolivar); Adam Faraizl (Joe Boot); Nina Siemaszko (Janey).

Maverick, "Day of Reckoning" (1958). Director: Leslie H. Martinson; Story: Carey Wilber; Producers: Roy Huggins and William T. Orr; Music: David Buttolph, Max Steiner and Paul Francis Webster. *Cast*—James Garner (Bret Maverick); Jean Willes (Lil); Mort Mills (Red Scanlon); Tod Griffin (Jack Wade); Willard Sage (George Buckner); Virginia Gregg (Amy Hardie); Russell Thorson

(Marshal Walt Hardie); Jon Lormer (Somers); Murvyn Vye (Gus Wilson); Morgan Shan (Slim).

The Rifleman, "The Apprentice Sheriff" (1958). Director: James Neilson; Story: Barney Slater: Producers: Arthur Gardner and Jules V. Levy; Music: Herschel Burke Gilbert. *Cast*—Chuck Connors (Lucas McCain); Johnny Crawford (Mark McCain); Robert Vaughn (Marshal Dan Willard); Edward Binns (Keely Thompson); Russell Collins (Charlie Willard); William Bryant (Sandy Dixon); Grant Richards (Reed Barns).

The Rifleman, "Blowout" (1959). Director: James Neilson; Story: Arthur Browne, Jr.; Producers: Arthur Gardner, Arnold Laven and Jules V. Levy; Music: Herschel Burke Gilbert. *Cast*—Chuck Connors (Lucas McCain); Johnny Crawford (Mark McCain); Hugh Sanders (Ben Waller); Howard Ledig (Jake Porter); John Milford (Ross Porter); John Dehner (Al Walker); George Brenlin (Kid Porter); Bill Quinn (Frank Sweeney).

The Rifleman, "The Clarence Bibs Story" (1961). Director: David Friedkin; Story: Calvin Clements, Sr.; Producers: Arthur Gardner, Arnold Laven and Jules V. Levy; Music: Herschel Burke Gilbert. *Cast*—Chuck Connors (Lucas McCain); Johnny Crawford (Mark McCain); Paul Fix (Marshal Micah Torrance); Buddy Hackett (Clarence Gibbs); Denver Pyle (George Tanner); Joan Taylor (Millie Scott); Lee Van Cleef (Wicks); John Milford (Reade); X Brands (Pretty Boy Longden).

The Rifleman, "Closer Than a Brother" (1961). Director: Joseph H. Lewis; Story: Cyril Hume; Producers: Arthur Gardner, Arnold Laven and Jules V. Levy; Music: Herschel Burke Gilbert. *Cast*—Chuck Connors (Lucas McCain); Johnny Crawford (Mark McCain); Paul Fix (Marshal Micah Torrance); Rex Ingram (Thaddeus); Barry Kroeger (Ansel Bain); Kelly Thordsen (Arthur M. Truelove); Bill Quinn (Frank Sweeney); Jack Wells (Mr. Carpenter).

The Rifleman, "Day of Reckoning" (1962). Director: Lawrence Dobkin; Story: Calvin Clements, Sr.; Producers: Arthur Gardner, Arnold Laven and Jules V. Levy; Music: Herschel Burke Gilbert. *Cast*—Chuck Connors (Lucas McCain); Johnny Crawford (Mark McCain); Paul Fix (Marshal Micah Torrance); Warren Oates (Willie Breen); L.Q. Jones (Charley Breen); Royal Dano (the Reverend Jamison); Billy E. Hughes (Aaron Jamison).

The Rifleman, "Death Trap" (1961). Director: Arnold Laven; Story: Arthur Browne, Jr.; Producers: Arthur Gardner, Arnold Laven and Jules V. Levy; Music: Herschel Burke Gilbert. *Cast*—Chuck Connors (Lucas McCain); Johnny Crawford (Mark McCain); Philip Carey (Dr. Simon Battle); James Drury (Spicer); Gigi Perreau (Vickie Battle); Hank Stohl (Britt); John Pickard (Stacey); Larry Perron (Sag); William Kendis (Stark); Steve Pendleton (Deputy Ben Johnson).

The Rifleman, "The Hangman" (1960). Director: Joseph H. Lewis; Story: Teddi Sherman and Ward Wood; Producers: Arthur Gardner, Arnold Laven and Jules V. Levy; Music: Herschel Burke Gilbert. *Cast*—Chuck Connors (Lucas McCain); Johnny Crawford (Mark McCain); Paul Fix (Marshal Micah Torrance); Whit Bissell (Volney Adams); Denver Pyle (Harold Tenner); Betty Lou Gerson (Ellie Aikens); Michael Fox (Joe Hannah); Richard Deacon (Col. Jebediah Sims).

The Rifleman, "The Indian" (1959). Director: Arnold Laven; Story: Cyril Hume; Producers: Arthur Gardner and Jules V. Levy; Music: Herschel Burke Gilbert. *Cast*—Chuck Connors (Lucas McCain); Johnny Crawford (Mark McCain); Paul Fix (Marshal Micah Torrance); Michael Ansara (Deputy U.S. Marshal Sam Buckhart); Herbert Rudley (Gorman); Lewis Charles (Slade); Mickey Simpson (Tub); Frank DeKova (Chief Hostay); Robert Chadwick (Eskimimzin); Eddie Little Sky (Apache Prisoner); Bill Quinn (Frank Sweeney).

The Rifleman, "The Long Gun from Tucson" (1961). Director: Joseph H. Lewis; Story: Calvin Clements, Sr.; Producers: Arthur Gardner, Arnold Laven and Jules V. Levy; Music: Herschel Burke Gilbert. *Cast*—Chuck Connors (Lucas McCain); Johnny Crawford (Mark McCain); Whit Bissell (Henry Waller); Peter Whitney (John Holliver); John Harmon (Eddie Halstead); Joe Higgins (Nils Swenson); Billy E. Hughes (Jeffrey Waller); Brian G. Hutton (Deecie).

The Rifleman, "Old Man Running" (1963). Director: Arthur H. Nadel; Story: A. Martin Zweiback; Producers: Arthur Gardner, Arnold Laven and Jules V. Levy; Music: Herschel Burke Gilbert. *Cast*—Chuck Connors (Lucas McCain); Johnny Crawford (Mark McCain); Paul Fix (Marshal Micah Torrance); John Anderson (Samuel Gibbs); Patricia Blair (Lou Mallory); Adam Williams (Mal Sherman); Rex Holman (Bob Sherman); Arthur Batanides (Littleboy Sherman); Joe Higgins (Nils Swenson).

The Rifleman, "The Retired Gun" (1959). Director: Arnold Laven; Story: Barney Slater; Producers: Arthur Gardner and Jules V. Levy; Music: Herschel Burke Gilbert. *Cast*—Chuck Connors (Lucas McCain); Johnny Crawford (Mark McCain); Paul Fix (Marshal Micah Torrance); Robert Webber (Wes Carney); Wallace Earl Laven (Clair Wheatley Carney); Jack Kruschen (Clyde Bailey); John Anderson (Owney Kincaid); Duke Snider (Jeff Wallace); Joseph Mell (Sam Moody); Herman Rudin (Morgan Bailey).

The Rifleman, "The Trade" (1959). Director: Joseph H. Lewis; Story: David Lang; Producers: Arthur Gardner and Jules V. Levy; Music: Herschel Burke Gilbert. *Cast*—Chuck Connors (Lucas McCain); Johnny Crawford (Mark McCain); Paul Fix (Marshal Micah Torrance); Paul Richards (Sam Morley); Chris Alcaide (Hamp Ferris); Dan Sheridan (Sheriff McVey); Michael Fox

(Trager); John Harmon (Eddie Halstead); Edgar Buchanan (Doc Burrage); Katherine Bard (Beth Landis).

The Texan, "The Ringer" (1959). Director: Erle C. Kenton; Story: George F. Slavin; Producers: Rory Calhoun, Victor M. Orsatti, and Jerry Stagg; Music: William Loose and John Seely. *Cast*—Rory Calhoun (Bill Longley); Regis Parton (Warren Masters); Grant Withers (Ed Martin); Adam Williams (Jebb Kilmer); Herb Vigran (Sandy Potts); Olive Sturgess (Mary Lou Martin); Vito Scotti (Juan Aruza); Ron Hayes (Rick Taber); Mel Welles (Matt Lane); Paul Brinegar (Ludwig); Maida Severn (Emma Martin).

The Virginian, "Siege" (1963). Director: Don McDougall; Novel: Owen Wister; Story: Donn Mullally; Producers: Winston Miller and Frank Price; Music: Percy Faith. *Cast*—Doug McClure (Trampas); Philip Carey (Duke Logan); Elinor Donahue (Carole Cole); Ron Hayes (Marshal Brett Cole); Joseph Campanella (Pedro Lopez); Nestor Paiva (Charley Sanchez); Myron Healey (Yance Cooper); Thomas Bellin (Sam Oliver); Ned Romero (Angelo).

Wagon Train, "The Colter Craven Story" (1960). Director: John Ford; Story: Tony Paulson; Producer: Howard Christie; Music: Stanley Wilson. *Cast*—Ward Bond (Major Seth Adams); Frank McGrath (Charlie Wooster); Terry Wilson (Bill Hawks); Carleton Young (Dr. Colter Craven); Anna Lee (Mrs. Allyris Craven); Paul Birch (Gen. Ulysses S. Grant); John Carradine (Park Cleatus); John Wayne, billed as Michael Morris (Gen. William Tecumseh Sherman); Chuck Hayward (Quentin Cleatus); Clff Lyons (Creel Weatherby); Dennis Rush (Jamie); Beulah Blaze (Jamie's mother); Willis Bouchey (Mr. Grant).

Wagon Train, "The Fort Pierce Story" (1963). Director: William Witney; Story: John McGreevey; Producers: Howard Christie and Frederick Shorr; Music: Cyril J. Mockridge and Arthur Morton. *Cast*—Robert Fuller (Cooper Smith); John McIntire (Christopher Hale); Frank McGrath (Charlie Wooster); Terry Wilson (Bill Hawks); Denny Miller (Duke Shannon); Ronald Reagan (Capt. Paul Winters); Ann Blyth (Nancy Winters); John Doucette (Col. Wayne Lothrop); Ron Hayes (Gil Fowler); Kathie Browne (Beth Fowler); Berkeley Harris (Sgt. Kincaid); Robert Wilke (Sgt. Wick).

Wagon Train, "The Jose Morales Story" (1960). Director: Virgil W. Vogel; Story: Gene L. Coon; Producer: Howard Christie; Music: Stanley Wilson. *Cast*—Ward Bond (Major Seth Adams); Lee Marvin (Jose Morales); Lon Chaney, Jr. (Louis Roque); Charles Herbert (Joseph Oliver); Terry Wilson (Bill Hawks); Frank McGrath (Charlie Wooster); Aline Towne (Patience Oliver); Clark Howat (Aaron Oliver); Steve Darrell (Dr. Stern); Alex Montoya (Paco); Jose Gonzales-Gonzales (Carlos); Gregg Palmer (Raleigh).

Walt Disney's Wonderful World of Color, "The Nine Lives of Elfego Baca" (1958). Director: Norman Foster; Story: Norman Foster; Producer: James C.

Pratt; Music: Franklyn Parks. *Cast*—Robert Loggia (Elfego Baca); Robert F. Simon (Deputy Marshal Ed Morgan); Lisa Montell (Anita Chavez); Nestor Paiva (Justice of the Peace); Leonard Strong (Zangana Martinez); Charles Maxwell (Dice Smith).

Wanted Dead or Alive, "The Legend" (1959). Director: Thomas Carr; Story: Tony Barrett; Producers: John Robinson and Frank Baur; Music: Herschel Burke Gilbert. *Cast*—Steve McQueen (Josh Randall); Victor Jory (Sam McGarrett); Michael Landon (Clay McGarrett); Kenneth Tobey (Vince Slater); Warren Oates (Billy Clegg); Nan Leslie (Beth McGarrett); Roy Barcroft (George Belden).

Zane Grey Theater, "Gift from a Gunman" (1957). Director: John English; Story: Russell S. Hughes and Charles A. Stearns; Producer: Hal Hudson; Music: Earle Dearth. *Cast*—Howard Keel (Will Gorman); John Dehner (Col. Overton); Jean Willes (March Overton); Michael Landon (Dan Overton); K.L. Smith (Jim Marshoot).

Zane Grey Theater, "License to Kill" (1959). Director: James Sheldon; Story: Kyle Mason and Antony Ellis; Producer: Hal Hudson; Music: Earle Dearth. *Cast*—Macdonald Carey (Sheriff Tom Baker); John Ericson (Lane Baker); Jacques Aubuchon (Mayor Danforth); Stacy Harris (Doc Currie); Richard Devon (Walker); Peter Whitney (Growler); George Cisar (White); Gene Roth (Wilkie); James Hyland (Torrence).

Zane Grey Theater, "A Thread of Respect" (1958). Director: John English; Story: Aaron Spelling; Producer: Hal Hudson; Music: Earle Dearth. *Cast*—Danny Thomas (Gino Pelletti); Nick Adams (George Pelletti); James Coburn (Jess Newton); Denver Pyle (Seth Robson); Tommy Cook (Link Harris); Chuck Courtney (Til Crow); James Beck (Nate Paris); Joseph Hamilton (Dave Radkin).

Zane Grey Theater, "A Threat of Violence" (1958). Director: Robert Gordon; Story: John McGreevey; Producer: Hal Hudson; Music: Earle Dearth. *Cast*—Cesar Romero (Carlos Gandara); Lyle Bettger (Sheriff Griff Evans); Chris Alcaide (Henry C. "Clay" Culhane); Jorja Curtright (Felicia Cheney); Harry Lauter (Hake Morris); Alex Gerry (James Ballinger); Bruce Cowling (Verg Cheney); Jess Kirkpatrick (William Newman); Jason Johnson (Dr. Harris).

Zane Grey Theater, "To Sit in Judgment" (1958). Director: John English; Story: Harry Julian Fink; Producer: Hal Hudson; Music: Earle Dearth. *Cast*—Robert Ryan (Sheriff Amos Parney); Betsy Jones-Moreland (Lucy Parney); Michael Pate (Deputy Charlie Spawn); Johnny Washbrook (Jamie MacPherson); Harry Dean Stanton (Robert MacPherson); Jean Inness (Mary MacPherson); Ben Erway (Doc Armstedter).

Bibliography

Bandy, M.L., & Stoehr, K. (2012). *Ride boldly ride: The evolution of the American Western.* Berkeley: University of California Press.

Basinger, J. (2007). *Anthony Mann.* (2nd ed.) Middletown, CT: Wesleyan University Press.

Bayles, M. (1989, February 6). Television: How the west was won. *Wall Street Journal,* p. 1, Leisure and Arts.

Bem, S.L. (1974). The measurement of psychological androgyny. *Journal of Consulting and Clinical Psychology, 42,* 155–162.

Butler, R.N. (1968). The life review: An interpretation of reminiscence to the aged. In B. Neugarten (Ed.), *Middle age and aging* (pp. 486–496). Chicago: University of Chicago Press.

Cawelti, J.G. (1999). *The six-gun mystique sequel.* Bowling Green, OH: Bowling Green University Popular Press.

Erikson, E.H. (1968). *Identity, youth, and crisis.* New York: Norton.

Erikson, E.H. (1982). *The life cycle completed: Review.* New York: Norton.

Finkel, E.J., & Campbell, W.K. (2000). Self-control and accommodation in close relationships: An interdependence analysis. *Journal of Personality and Social Psychology, 81,* 263–277.

Foster, G. (1994). The women in *High Noon*: A metanarrative of difference. *Film Criticism, 18/19,* 72–80.

Fowers, B.J. (1998). Psychology and the good marriage: Social theory as practice. *American Behavioral Scientist, 41,* 516–541.

French, P. (2005). *Westerns.* 4th ed. Manchester, UK: Carcanet.

Indick, W. (2008). *The psychology of the Western: How the American psyche plays out on screen.* Jefferson, NC: McFarland.

Jackson, J.J., Walton, K.E., Harms, P.D., Bogg, T., Wood, D., Lodi-Smith, J., Edmonds, G.W., & Roberts, B.W. Not all conscientiousness scales alike: A multimethod, multisample of age differences in the facets of conscientiousness. *Journal of Personality and Social Psychology, 96,* 446–459.

Kitses, J. (1998). Introduction: Post-modernism and the Western: In J. Kitses and G. Rickman (Eds.), *The Western reader* (pp. 15–31). New York: Limelight Editions.

Kitses, J. (2004). *Horizons West.* London: British Film Institute.

Kubler-Ross, E. (1969). *On death and dying.* New York: Macmillan.

Lenihan, J.H. (1980). *Showdown: Confronting modern America in the Western film.* Urbana: University of Illinois Press.

Lucas, B. (1998). Saloon girls and ranchers' daughters: The woman in the Western. In J. Kitses and G. Rickman (Eds.), *The Western reader* (pp. 301–320). New York: Limelight Editions.

Mansfield, S. (1996). *Never give in: The extraordinary character of Winston Churchill.* Nashville, TN: Cumberland House Publishing.

McCullough, M.E., Worthington, E.L., & Rachal, K.L. (1997). Interpersonal forgiving in close relationships. *Journal of Personality and Social Psychology, 73,* 321–336.

McGee, P. (2007). *From Shane to Kill Bill: Rethinking the Western.* Malden, MA: Blackwell Publishing.

McGregor, J. (2014, May 28). May Angelou on leadership, courage, and the creative process. *Washington Post.* Retrieved December 21, 2017, from http://www.washingtonpost.com.

Meuel, D. (2015). *The noir Western: Darkness on the range, 1943–1962.* Jefferson, NC: McFarland.

Nott, R. (2004). *The films of Randolph Scott.* Jefferson, NC: McFarland.

Peterson, C., & Seligman, M.E.P. (2004). *Character strengths and virtues: A handbook and classification.* Washington, D.C.: American Psychological Association.

Prince, R.M. (1984). Courage and masochism in psychotherapy. *Psychoanalytic Review, 71,* 47–61.

Putnam, E. (1997). Psychological courage. *Philosophy, Psychiatry, and Psychology, 4,* 1–11.

Rizkalla, L., Wertheim, E.H., & Hodgson, L.K. (2008). The roles of emotion management styles and disposition to forgive. *Journal of Research in Personality, 42,* 1594–1601.

Ryan, R.M., & Frederick, C. (1997). On energy, personality, and health: Subjective vitality as a dynamic reflection of well-being. *Journal of Personality, 65,* 529–565.

Rye, M.S., Loicacono, D.M., Folck, C.D., Olszewski, B.T., Heim, T.A., & Madia, B.P. (2001). Evaluation of the psychometric properties of two forgiveness scales. *Current Psychology, 20,* 260–277.

Shelp, E.E. (1984). Courage: A neglected virtue in the patient-physician relationship. *Social Science and Medicine, 18,* 351–360.

Springer, J.P. (2005). Beyond the river: Women and the role of the feminine in Howard Hawks' *Red River.* In P.C. Rollins and J.E. O'Connor (Eds.), *Hollywood's west: The American frontier in film, television and history* (pp. 115–125). Lexington: The University of Kentucky Press.

Vohs, K.D., Ciarococo, N., & Baumeister, R.F. (2003). *Interpersonal functioning requires self-regulatory resources.* Unpublished manuscript, University of Utah, Salt Lake City.

Way, N. (1985). "Can't you see the courage, the strength that I have?": Listening to urban adolescent girls speak about their relationships. *Psychology of Woman Quarterly, 19,* 107–128.

Way, N. (1998). *Everyday courage: The lives and stories of urban teenagers.* New York: New York University Press.

Worline, M.C., Wrzesniewski, A., & Rafaeli, A. (2002). Courage and work: Breaking routines to improve performance. In R. Lord, R. Klimoski & R. Kanfer (Eds.). *Emotions at work* (pp. 295–330). San Francisco: Jossey-Boss.

Yoggy, G.A. (1995) *Riding the video range: The rise and fall of the Western on television.* Jefferson, NC: McFarland.

Zoglin, R. (1989, February 6). Poetry on the prairie. *Time, 133,* 78.

Index

Numbers in *bold italics* indicate pages with illustrations

Ackerman, Bettye 89
Acosta, Rodolfo 52
Adams, Nick 98
Adiarte, Patrick 129
African-Americans 90–91
Akins, Claude 36
Alcaide, Chris 28
Alden, Norman 36
Allison, Jean 29
Allman, Sheldon 29, 132
Andersen, Herbert 61
Anderson, James 129
Anderson, John 25, 68, 93
Anderson, Judith 58
Andrews, Dana 127, *128*
Andrews, Tige 74
Angelou, Maya 164
Anna-Lisa 21
Ansara, Michael 84
"The Apprentice Sheriff" see *The Rifleman*
Archer, John 123
Aristotle 164
Arizona 116, 167
Arlen, Richard 102
Armstrong, R.G. 70, 77
Armstrong, Robert 73
Arness, James 30–32, 36, 74, 80, 89, 94, 106, 132
Arthur, Jean 66, *68*, 116
Ashley, Edward 23
Aubuchon, Jacques 97

Bacall, Lauren
Bacon, Irving 45
"Badge of Glory" see *Laramie*
The Badlanders 85, 167
Baker, Carroll 93
Bale, Christian 153
The Ballad of Gregorio Cortez 87–88, 167
Bandy, Mary Lea 20, 41–43, 146, 148
Bard, Katherine 26
Barrymore, John Drew 102
Barton, Dan 120
Basinger, Jeanne 34, 54–55, 57–58
Baumeister, B.F. 104
Baylor, Hal 102
Beaumont, Hugh 61
Beery, Noah, Jr. 23, 110, 122–123
Belafonte, Harry 91
Bell, James 54, 79
Bem, S.L. 111
Bend of the River 33–34, 47–49, 167–168
Bennett, Bruce 45
Best, James 26, 101
Betts, Jack 79
Bettger, Lyle 27
Betz, Carl 74
Bickford, Charles 63, 93
The Big Country 93, *94*, 168
The Big Valley: "The Murdered Party" 78–79, 180–181
Binns, Edward 96
Birch, Paul 73, 75
Bissell, Whit 55
Blake, Larry J. 136, 141
Blake, Robert 84
Blocker, Dan 79, 100, 130
"Blowout" see *The Rifleman*
Blyth, Ann 133
Boetticher, Budd 20, *124*

195

Index

Bogg, T. 104
Bolding, Bonnie 121
Bonanza: "The Crucible" 99–100, 181; "The Jury" 79, 181; "The Last Trophy" 23, 51, 181; "The Legacy" 100–101, 181; "Warbonnet" 120, 129–130, 181
Bond, Ward 37, 38
Boone, Richard 55, 73, 76, 82, 117, 122
Borgnine, Ernest 143, *144*
Bower, Tom 87
Boyd, Stephen 125, *126*
Brady, Scott 36
Brandon, Henry 39
Brands, X 93
The Bravados 125–126, *126*, 165, 168
Brennan, Walter 37, 51, 109
Brian, David 132
Bridges, Lloyd 135, 137
Briggs, Charley 22
Briggs, Matt 127
Broken Arrow 44, 81–82, 168
Broken Trail 88–89, 148
Bronco: "The Long Ride Back" 120, 181–182; "The Soft Answer" 95–96, 182
Bronson, Charles 5
Brynner, Yul 83
Buchanan Rides Alone 85, 168–169
Buck and the Preacher 91, 169
The Burning Hills 85, 169
Bush, Billy Green 108
Butler, Robert 117–118

Cagney, James 114
Calhoun, Rory 29
Callan, Michael 13
Campanella, Joseph 46
Campbell, W.K. 104
Carey, Harry, Jr. 38, *42*, 110
Carey, McDonald 97
Carey, Philip 24, 46
Carr, Paul 52
Carroll, John 123, *124*
Caruso, Anthony 82
Case, Allen 80
Cattle Empire 121–122, 169
Cattle Queen of Montana 116, 169
Cawelti, John 50–51, 115
Chandler, Jeff 44, 81
Chaney, Lon, Jr. 11, 136, 139
Charles, Lewis 84
Cheyenne: "Deadline" 34–35; "Decision" 74–75; "Home of the Brave" 84; "Incident at Indian Springs" 120–121
Cheyenne Autumn 82, 169
Chief Dan George 27, 129
Church, Thomas Haden 88
Churchill, Winston 164
Ciarococo, N. 104
"The Clarence Bibs Story" see *The Rifleman*
Clark, Davison 109
Clark, Susan 87

Clift, Montgomery 109
"Closer Than a Brother" see *The Rifleman*
Cobb, Julie 36
Cobb, Lee J. 47, *48*
Coburn, James 26, 98, 102
Cochran, Steve 58
Colbert, Robert 95
Coleman, Herbert *53*
Colicos, John 37
Collins, Joan 125
"The Colter Craven Story" see *Wagon Train*
Connors, Chuck 21, 24, 45, 55, 84, 94, 96
Conrad, Michael 31
Conroy, Frank 127, *128*
Conte, Richard 13
Cooper, Chris 160
Cooper, Gary 4–5, 13, *48*, 49, 56, 57, 135, *137*
Cooper, Scott 88
Corbin, Barry 88, 161
Coughlin, Kevin 89
Court, Hazel 23
Cowboy 113, 170
Cowling, Bruce 34
Coy, Walter 37
Crain, Jeanne 23
Crane, Norma 76
Crawford, Broderick 23
Crawford, Johnny 24, 84
Cristal, Linda 37, 130
Crowe, Russell 153
"The Crucible" see *Bonanza*
The Culpepper Cattle Company 108–109, 164, 170
Curtis, Ken 30, 32, 40, 80, 89, 118
Cypher, Jon 86

Dances with Wolves 82, 170
Dano, Royal 24, 52, *53*
Darrell, Steve 11
Darren, James 107
Davenport, Harry 127
Daves, Delmar *57*, *65*, 153
"Day of Reckoning" see *Maverick*
"Day of Reckoning" see *The Rifleman*
Deacon, Richard 55
"Deadline" see *Cheyenne*
Deadly Companions 58–60, 143, 170
"Death Trap" see *The Rifleman*
"Decision" see *Cheyenne*
Decision at Sundown 122–125, *124*, 170
Dee, Ruby 91
Dehner, John 23, 25, 27, 47, 129
Dekker, Albert 143, 147
del Lago, Alicia 125
"Deliver the Body" see *Have Gun—Will Travel*
Denning, Richard 74
DeRita, Joe 125
DeSantis, Joe 74

Index

Desilu Playhouse: "Silent Thunder" 92, 102–103
DeSoto, Rosana 88
Devil's Doorway 82, 170
DeWilde, Brandon 61, 66
Dierkes, John 5, 66
Donohue, Elinor 46
Dora, Leona 63
Dostoyevsky, Fyodor 60
Doucette, John 133
Douglas, Kirk 101
Dreyfuss, Richard 89
Dru, Joanne 110
Drury, James 24
Dubbins, Don 114
Duggan, Andrew 123
Duke, John 73
Durand, Kevin 154
Duryea, Dan 61
Duvall, Robert 88, 159–160
Dysart, Richard 149

Eastwood, Clint 26, 130, *131*, 142, *150*
Edmonds, G.W. 104
Egan, Richard 6, 129
Emhardt, Robert 64
Erickson, Leif 23, 37
Ericson, John 97
Erikson, Erik 1, 7, 105, 114, 116
Evans, Gene 125
Eythe, William 127

The Far Country 51, 53, 171
Faraizl, Adam 161
The Fastest Gun Alive 23, 47, 51, 171
Feng, Olivia 89
Finkel, E.J. 104
Firestone, Eddie 132
Fisher, Frances 130
Fisher, Shug 81, 106
A Fistful of Dynamite, aka *Duck, You Sucker* 142, 171
Fix, Paul 21, 25, 78, 85, 120
Flippen, J.C. 61
Folck, C.D. 92
Fonda, Henry 54–55, 81, 126, *128*
Fonda, Peter 154
Fong, Donald 88
Ford, Francis 127, *128*
Ford, Glenn 23, 63, *65*, 113
Ford, John *42*, 43
Forrest, Frederick 160
Fort Apache 142
"The Fort Pierce Story" see *Wagon Train*
".45 Calibre" see *Laramie*
Forty Guns 116, 171
Foster, Gwendolyn 141
Fowers, B.J. 50
Franciscus, James 77
Freed, Bert 23
Freeman, Kathleen 75

Freeman, Morgan 131
French, Philip 7
French, Valerie 124
French, Victor 89
From Hell to Texas 42, 70–72, 171
Frye, Forrest 155
Fuller, Robert 22, 29, 45, 68, 72, 134
The Furies 58, 116, 171–172

Gallant, Kathleen 125
Gammon, James 88
Garner, James 20, 44
Gates, Nancy 95
"Gentry's Law" see *Gunsmoke*
Gerry, Alex 28
Gerson, Betty Lou 55
Gierasch, Stefan 31
"Gift from a Gunman" see *Zane Grey Theatre*
Gish, Lillian 62
Gist, Robert 77
Glover, Danny 160
God Forgives, I Don't 147
"The Golden Land" see *Gunsmoke*
"Gone Straight" see *Gunsmoke*
"The Good People" see *Gunsmoke*
Gordon, Leo 82, 95–96
Grant, Kathryn 106
Gravers, Steve 80
Gray, Coleen 109
Greene, Lorne 100, 130
Griffith, James 114
Grimes, Gary 108
Gun for a Coward 21, 172
"Gunfighter R.I.P." see *Gunsmoke*
"The Gunman" see *Lawman*
Gunman's Walk 106–107, 172
Gunsmoke: "Gentry's Law" 105–106, 182; "The Golden Land" 89–90, 183; "Gone Straight" 74, 183; The Good People" 80–81, 183;"Gunfighter R.I.P." 31–32, 183; "Hackett" 30–31, 184; "I Have Promises to Keep" 118–119, 184; "Lobo" 132–133, 184"; "Lynch Town" 35–36, 184; "Passive Resistance" 94–95, 184; "The Squaw" 32–33, 184

"Hackett" see *Gunsmoke*
Hackett, Buddy 93
Hackman, Gene 130, *131*
Haggerty, Don 79, 121
Hall, Bobby 76
Hamilton, Joe H. 98
Hamilton, Richard 149
"The Hanging of Roy Carter" see *Have Gun—Will Travel*
The Hanging Tree 10, 56, *57*, 172
"The Hangman" see *The Rifleman* 55
Hardin, Ty 95, 120
Harley, Eileen 25
Harms, P.D. 104

Harris, Richard 131
Harris, Robert H. 100
Harris, Stacy 72, 78
Hartley, Mariette 18, *19*
Harvey, Don 21
Have Gun—Will Travel: "Deliver the Body" 77–78, 184–185; "The Hanging of Roy Carter" 73, 185; "The Last Judgment" 77, 185—"Memories of Monica" 55–56, 185; "The Taffeta Mayor" 76, 185; "Winchester Quarantine" 82–83, 185
Hawks, Howard 112
Hayes, Ron 46
Haynes, Roberta 102
Hayworth, Rita 13
Headly, Glenne 161
Healey, Myron 20
Heflin, Van 13, 63, *65*, 106
Heim, T.A. 92
Held, Karl 78
Hepburn, Audrey 62
Herbert, Charles 11
Heston, Charlton 93, *94*
The High Chapparal 37, 185
High Noon 5, 44, *137*, 148, 164, 172
High Plains Drifter 148, 172–173
Hindy, Joseph 89–90
Hodgson, L.K. 147
Holden, William 143, *144*
Holliman, Earl 30, 101–102
"Home of the Brave" see *Cheyenne*
Homeier, Skip 122
Hopper, Dennis 70
Horvath, Charles 54
"Hour After Dawn" see *Laramie*
Howard, John 83, 102
Howard, Ron 117
Howat, Clark 11
Hoyt, Clegg 79
Hubbard, John 122
Hunter, Jeffrey 21, 38, *42*, 90, 105
Hunter, Tab 13, 106
Huston, Angelica 159–160

"I Have Promises to Keep" see *Gunsmoke*
Iglesias, Eugene 113
"Incident at Indian Springs" see *Cheyenne*
"The Indian" see *The Rifleman*
Indick, William 1, 4, 41–42, 112, 115, 165
Ireland, John 109

Jackson, J.J. 104
Jaeckel, Richard 64
Jason, Peter 105
Jeris, Nancy 35
Johnson, Ben 45, 66, 143
Johnson, Brad 83
Johnson, Russell 30
Jones, Gordon 102
Jones, Henry 64
Jones, L.Q. 24

Jones, Tommie Lee 159–160
Jones-Moreland, Betsy 103
Jordan, Dorothy 37
Jordan, Richard 86
Jory, Victor 5
"The Jose Morales Story" see *Wagon Train*
"The Journal of Death" see *The High Chaparral*
"Journey to San Carlos" see *The Lone Ranger*
Jurado, Katy 135
"The Jury" see *Bonanza*
"Justice in a Hurry" see *Laramie*

Kammerling, Warren J. 35
Karnes, Robert 76, 82
Kashfi, Anna 113
Kearns, Geraldine 27
Keefer, Don 105
Keel, Howard 27
Keil, Richard 149, 151, 153
Keith, Brian 58–60
Keith, Robert 13, 52
Kelly, Grace 5, 135
Kelly, John 91
Kennedy, Arthur 34, 47
Kenyon, Sandy 132
King, Henry *126*
Kitses, Jim 1, 3, 18–19, 47, 49, 60, 113, 142, 147, 152–153
Kramer, Stanley *137*
Kroeger, Barry 21
Kruger, Otto 135
Kruschen, Jack 25
Kubler-Ross, Elizabeth 117

Lacy, Tom 118
Ladd, Alan 5, 66, *68*
Lampert, Zohra 51, *53*
Lancaster, Burt 62, 86
Landon, Michael 5, 27, 99, 129
Lane, Diane 160
Laramie: "Badge of Glory" 29–30, 185–186; ".45 Calibre, 186" 17, 21–22; "Hour After Dawn" 45, 186; "Justice in a Hurry" 75–76, 186; "The Men of Defiance" 68–69, 186; "Night of the Quiet Men" 27, 48, 186; "The Track of the Jackal" 72–73, 186–187
Larch, John 73
The Last Hunt 82, 152, 173
"The Last Judgment" see *Have Gun—Will Travel*
The Last Train from Gun Hill 101, 164, 173
"The Last Trophy" see *Bonanza*
Latham, Louise 106
Launer, S. John 45
Lawman: "The Gunman" 7, 102, 187; "The Showdown" 102, 187
Lawrence, Marc 127, *128*
"The Legacy" see *Bonanza*

Index

"The Legend" *see Wanted: Dead or Alive*
Leigh, Janet 57, **59**
Lemmon, Jack 113
Lenihan, John H. 3, 44
Lenz, Richard 117
Leone, Sergio 142–143
Lerman, Logan 153
Levine, Anna 130
Lewis, Forrest 54
Libby, Fred 90
"License to Kill" *see Zane Grey Theatre*
Litel, John 123, **124**
Little Big Man 82, 173
"Lobo" *see Gunsmoke*
Locke, Sandra 27
Lodi-Smith, J. 104
Loftin, Lennie 153
Loggia, Robert 85
Loicacono, D.M. 92
London, Julie **48**
The Lone Ranger: "Journey to San Carlos" 20, 47–48, 187
Lonesome Dove 159–163, 165, 187
Long, Richard 78
"The Long Gun from Tucson" *see The Rifleman*
"The Long Ride Back" *see Bronco*
Lord, Jack **48**
Lucas, Blake 1, 4, 115–116
Lummis, Dayton 101
"Lynch Town" *see Gunsmoke*
Lyden, Robert 38

MacLane, Barton 102
MacMurray, Fred 21, 105
Madia, B.P. 92
The Magnificent Seven 5, 83, 173
Majors, Lee 78
Malden, Karl 56
Mamakos, Peter 39
A Man Called Horse 82, 173–174
Man of the West 47–49, **48**
The Man Who Shot Liberty Valance 116, 164, 174
Mangold 153
Mann, Anthony 33, **48**, **59**, 51, 54, 58
Mann, Larry D. 78
Martel, Arlene 32
Martin, Dean 6, 36
Martin, Strother 58, 60
Marvin, Lee 11, 21, 99, 115
Maverick: "The Day of Reckoning" 20, 44, 47, 187–188
Maxwell, Charles 86
McCarthy, Lin 29
McClure, Doug 46, 62
McCrea, Joel 18, **19**, 118, 121
McCullough, M.E. 92
McGavin, Darren 31
McGee, Patrick 116, 138
McGregor, J. 164

McGuire, Michael 87
McIntire, John 133
McKinney, Bill 26, 117
McLaren, Wayne 89
McLiam, John 108
McNally, Stephen 72, 114
McPeak, Sandy 101
McQueen, Steve 5, 83
Meeker, Ralph 56, **59**
Megowan, Don 68
"Memories of Monica" *see Have Gun—Will Travel*
"The Men of Defiance" *see Laramie*
Meredith, Judi 55
Meuel, David 6, 64–66
Mexicans 6, 85–88
Meyer, Emile 5, 66
Miles, Vera 39, 116
Milford, John 93
Millay, Diana 75
Millican, James 137, **137**
Mills, Mort 68, 120
Mitchell, Cameron 6, 91, 129
Mitchell, Carlyle 121
Mitchell, George 75
Mitchell, Millard 56–57, **59**
Mitchell, Thomas 135
Monte Walsh 115, 174
Montell, Lisa 86
Moore, Clayton 20
Moreno, Antonio 39
Morgan, Henry 117, 126, 136
Morgan, Read 94
Moriarty, Michael 149, **150**
Morrow, Vic 51, 114
Mulkey, Chris 89
"The Murdered Party" *see The Big Valley*
Murphy, Audie 51, **53**, 61
Murray, Don 70
My Darling Clementine 81, 174

Nader, George 21
The Naked Spur 42, 47, 56–58, **59**, 164, 174
Native Americans 6, 81–85
Nelson, Ricky 37
Newell, William 136
"Night of the Quiet Men" *see Laramie*
Night Passage 61–62, 174–175
"The Nine Lives of Elfego Baca" *see Walt Disney's Wonderful World of Color*
North, Sheree 117
Nott, Robert 124–125
Nusser, James 133
Nuyen, France 31

Oates, Warren 24, 78, 143
O'Brian, Hugh 117
O'Connell, Arthur **48**
O'Hara, Maureen 58
O'Herlihy, Gavan 161
"Old Man Running" *see The Rifleman*

Olszewski, B.T. 92
Osterloh, Robert 45
O'Sullivan, Maureen 122
The Outlaw Josey Wales 26–27, 175
Overton, Frank 52
The Ox-Bow Incident 126–129, *128*, 175

Paget, Debra 81
Paiva, Nestor 46
Palance, Jack 5
Pale Rider 10, 148–153, *150*, 175
Palmer, Betsy 54–55
Palmer, Gregg 11, 30
Papas, Irene 114
Parton, Regis 28
"Passive Resistance" *see Gunsmoke*
Payne, John 106
Peck, Gregory 93, *94*, 125, *126*
Peckinpah, Sam *19*, 60, 142–143, *144*
Penn, Christopher 149
Penny, Sidney 149, *150*
Perkins, Anthony 54
Perrin, Vic 82
Perry, Ivan 109
Peterson, Christopher 5, 9–11, 17, 19, 50, 70–72, 92–93, 104, 120
Piazza, Ben 56
Pickard, John 22, 68
Pine, Philip 101
Pine, Robert 105
The Plainsman 116, 175
Platt, Edward 13, 76
Poitier, Sidney 91
Posse from Hell 50, 51–54, *53*, 175–176
Prince, R.M. 50
Putnam, E. 10
Pyle, Denver 55, 93, 98

Qualen, John 34, 38, 43
Quinn, Anthony 127, *128*

Rachal, K.L. 92
Rafaeli, A. 50
Ramsey, Ward 51
Randolph, Donald 77
Ray, Michael 54
Raymond, Paula 83
Reagan, Ronald 133
Red River 16, 41, 109–114, 176
Redford, Robert 84
Reed, Carl Benton 27
Reed, Walter 21
Reese, Tom 32
Reid, Carl Benton 94
Reprisal! 82, 175
"The Retired Gun" *see The Rifleman*
Rich, Dick 127
Richards, Paul 26
Ride Lonesome 26, 175
Ride the High Country 10, 18, *19*, 105, 114, 118, 142–143, 147, 164, 175

The Rifleman: "The Apprentice Sheriff" 96–97, 188; "Blowout" 25, 188; "The Clarence Bibs Story" 93, 188; "Closer Than a Brother" 21, 188; "Day of Reckoning" 24, 49, 188; "Death Trap" 24, 188; "The Hangman" 55, 189; "The Indian" 84–85, 189; "The Long Gun from Tucson" 44–45, 189; "Old Man Running" 26, 93, 189; "The Retired Gun" 25, 189; "The Trade" 26, 189–190
"The Ringer" *see The Texan*
Rio Bravo 6, 176–177
Rizkalla, L. 147
Road, Mike 95
Roberts, B.W. 104
Roberts, Dallas 154
Roberts, Mark 35
Roberts, Pernell 26, 79, 99
Robinson, Bartlett 27
Romero, Caesar 28
Ross, Katherine 84
Rubinek, Saul 131
Rudin, Herman 25
Rudley, Herbert 84, 125
Run of the Arrow 82, 177
Russell, Bing 55, 68, 122
Russell, Gail 21
Russell, John 7, 36, 102, 150
Russo, James 88
Ruysdael, Basil 81
Ryan, Robert 56, 58, *59*, 103, 143
Ryder, Alfred 94
Rye M.S. 92

Sage, Willard 20, 47
Salmi, Albert 62, 125, *126*
Sánchez, Jaime 143, 146
Sanders, Hugh 25, 75
Sargeant Rutledge 90–91, 177
Saxon, John 32, 52
Scacchi, Greta 88
Schell, Maria 56, *57*
Schroeder, Ricky 160
Schwimmer, Rusty 88
Scott, George C. 56
Scott, Ken 70, 125
Scott, Linda Gaye 130
Scott, Pippa 37
Scott, Randolph 18, *19*, 21, 26, 118, 122, *124*, 125
Scott, Timothy 87, 160
The Searchers 36–44, *42*, 47–48, 51, 93, 113, 142, 177
Seligman, Martin 5, 9–11, 17, 19, 50, 70–72, 92–93, 104, 120
Selles, Scott 89
Serna, Pepe 87
7 Men from Now 18, 21, 177
Shane 5, 66–68, *68*, 116, 148, 151–153, 177
Shannon, Richard 121
Shaughnessy, Mickey 107

Shelp, E.E. 50
The Shootist 116–117, 177
"The Showdown" *see Lawman*
"Siege" *see The Virginian*
Siemaszko, Nina 161
"Silent Thunder" *see Desilu Playhouse*
Silva, Henry 122, 125, *126*
Silvera, Frank 86
Silverheels, Jay 20
Simcox, Tom 80
Simmons, Jean 93
Simon, Robert F. 85
Simpson, Mickey 84
Smith, John 21, 27, 45, 72, 75
Smith, Milam 25
Snider, Duke 25
Snodgrass, Carrie 149, *150*
"The Soft Answer" *see Bronco*
Springer, J.P. 111
"The Squaw" *see Gunsmoke*
Stagecoach 44, 178
Stanton, Harry Dean 103
Stanwyck, Barbara 58, 116
Starr, Ron 18, *19*, 118
Steele, Karen 123, *124*
Stevens, George *68*
Stevens, Paul 89
Stevens, Rory 101
Stewart, Elaine 61
Stewart, James 33–34, 44, 47, 51, 56, 58, *59*, 61, 81, 116
Stewart, Marianne 74
Stockwell, Dean 21
Stoehr, Kevin 20, 41–43, 146, 148
Stone, Harold J. 77
Stone, Milburn 31, 80
The Strawberry Roan 85, 178
Stricklyn, Ray 95
Strode, Woody 90
Sturgis, Olive 29
Sweeney, D.J. 160
Swofford, Ken 35, 118, 132

"The Taffeta Mayor" *see Have Gun—Will Travel*
The Tall T 122, 178
Teal, Ray 74, 100, 107, 124
Tell Them Willie Boy Is Here 82–84, 178
Tension at Table Rock 6, 10, 48, 129, 165, 178–179
Terrell Steven 72
The Texan: "The Ringer" 28–29, 190
They Came to Cordura 6, 9, 12–17, 165, 179
Thomas, Danny 98
"Thread of Respect" *see Zane Grey Theatre*
"A Threat of Violence" *see Zane Grey Theatre*
3:10 to Yuma (1957) 63–66, *65*, 157–158, 179

3:10 to Yuma (2007) 148, 154–158, 179
Thurston, Carol 82
Time Magazine
The Tin Star 54–55, 179
"To Sit in Judgment" *see Zane Grey Theatre*
Toomey, Regis 83
Towne, Aline 11
"The Track of the Jackal" *see Laramie*
"The Trade" *see The Rifleman*
Tribute to a Bad Man 112–114, 179
Truax, John 35
Trueman, Paula 27
Tsiang, H.T. 31
Tubbs, Barry 162
Tucker, Forrest 129
Tudyk, Alan 154

Unforgiven 130–132, *131*, 179
The Unforgiven 62–63, 180
Urich, Robert 160

Valdez Is Coming 86–87, 180
Van Cleef, Lee 21, 26, 53, 93, 125, *126*, 135
Varsi, Diane 71
Vaughan, Bill 58
Vaughan, Robert 6, 96
The Virginian: "Siege" 45–47, 190
Vogel, Mitch 36
Vohs, K.D. 104

Wagon Train: "The Colter Craven Story" 37, 190; "The Fort Pierce Story" 133–135, 190; "The Jose Morales Story" 6, 11–12, 190
Wahlberg, Gary 55
Walker, Clint 34, 74, 83, 121
Wallace, George 30, 75
Walsh, Monte 115
Walt Disney's Wonderful World of Color: "The Nine Lives of Elfego Baca" 85–86, 190–191
Walton, K.E. 104
Wanted Dead or Alive: "The Legend" 5, 191
"Warbonnet" *see Bonanza*
Ward, Larry 55
Washbrook, John 103
Watson, Bobs 79
Way, N. 50
Wayne, David 36, 118
Wayne, John 36–37, *42*, 93, 109, 116, 141
Weaver, Dennis 74, 95
Webber, Robert 25
Wellman, William *128*
Wertheim, E.H. 147
West, Jennifer 30
Whipper, Leigh 127
White Feather 82, 180
Whitney, Peter 44
The Wild Bunch 143–148, *144*, 180
Wilke, Robert 61, 72, 75, 134–135

Willes, Jean 20, 27
Williams, Adam 29
Wills, Chill 58, 71
Wilson, Terry 11
"Winchester Quarantine" *see Have Gun— Will Travel*
Wiseman, Joseph 62
Withers, Grant 29
Witney, Peter 97
women 6, 115–116
Wooley, Sheb 135, 139
Wood, D. 104
Wood, Lana 38
Woodward, Morgan 30, 37, 80, 132
Woolvett, Jaimz 130–131
Worden, Hank 39
Worline, M.C. 50

Worthington, E.L. 92
Wrzesniewski, A. 50
Wyler, William *94*

Yeo, Gwendolyn 88–89
Yoggy, Gary 159
York, Dick 13
Young, Carleton 37

Zane Grey Theatre: "Gift from a Gunman" 27–28, 49, 191; "License to Kill" 97, 191; "A Thread of Respect" 97–99, 191; "A Threat of Violence" 28, 47, 191; "To Sit in Judgment" 103, 191
Zeller, Ben 87
Zoglin, Richard 159

www.ingramcontent.com/pod-product-compliance
Lightning Source LLC
Chambersburg PA
CBHW032059300426
44116CB00007B/806